Part I

From Modern to Postmodern Literatures

From a feminist viewpoint the question is not whether a literary work has been written by a woman and reflects her experience of life, or how it compares to other works by women, but rather how it lends itself to be read from a feminist position.

—Nelly Furman, "The Politics of Language: Beyond the Gender Principle?"

Contents

Men Writing the Feminine

Men Writing the Feminine

Literature, Theory, and the Question of Genders

Edited by

Thaïs E. Morgan

STATE UNIVERSITY OF NEW YORK PRESS

Published by
State University of New York Press, Albany

© 1994 State University of New York

Printed in the United States of America

For information, address State University of New York Press,
State University Plaza, Albany, N.Y., 12246

Production by Laura Starrett
Marketing by Nancy Farrell

Library of Congress Cataloging in Publication Data

Men writing the feminine : literature, theory, and the question of
    genders / edited by Thaïs E. Morgan.
        p.   cm.
    Includes bibliographical references and index.
    ISBN 0-7914-1993-2 : $49.50.—ISBN 0-7914-1994-0 (pbk.) : $16.95
    1. Authorship—Sex differences.   2. Point of view (Literature)
3. Literature, Modern—Men authors—History and criticism.   4. Women
in literature.   5. Sex differences (Psychology)   6. Identification
(Psychology)   I. Morgan, Thaïs E.
PN171.S45M46   1994
809'.93352042—dc20   93-43224
                                                                    CIP

10   9   8   7   6   5   4   3   2   1

Literature, Theory, and the Question of Genders

Thaïs E. Morgan

I write woman: woman must write woman.
And man, man; it's up to him to say where his
masculinity and femininity are at.

—Hélène Cixous, "The Laugh
of the Medusa"

And, as I am a man,
Instead of jutting crag, I found
A woman . . .

—William Wordsworth, "The Thorn"

What does it mean to say that a male author writes the feminine? Is he writing as (identifying with) a woman? Or writing like (mimicking, and perhaps mocking) a woman? Or writing through a woman (an Other that confirms his own identity as the Same)? The present collection of twelve essays explores these crucial questions about men's role in the construction of femininity in relation to masculinity in literature and in critical theory. The interaction of writing and gender is complex and fraught with cultural significance when the author projects a voice from the imagined perspective of the opposite sex. *Men Writing the Feminine* focuses on novels and poems from three national traditions—British, French, and American—spanning modern (beginning with the 1600s), modernist (after 1900), and postmodern eras, in which male authors write the feminine by speaking in the voices and describing the innermost thoughts and feelings of women. At the same time, the essays in *Men Writing the Feminine* intervene in current debates about gender by drawing upon postmodern theories in order to analyze how the feminine is represented and (re)created in literature. Are sex and gender separable in writing, or do both sex and gender have the epistemological status of fiction? What cultural effects does each literary instance of men writing the feminine produce? Ultimately, the essays in this collection raise questions about how literary critics and theorists position themselves in relation to today's politics of gender.

Men's Femininities

Part One of *Men Writing the Feminine* begins with four essays on how the feminine is constructed by men in canonical works of poetry and fiction. The first epigraph above, which comes from the work of the French feminist Hélène Cixous, serves to remind us of the long-fought battle between the sexes for the power of language, especially the power to define "woman" in relation to "man."[1] As feminist scholarship in both humanities and social sciences since the mid-1970s has emphasized, "sex," or the physiology of a male or a female body, is not the same as "gender," or the series of cultural distinctions made between persons displaying behavior categorized as either "masculine" or "feminine."[2] In a now famous article, "The Traffic in Women," the anthropologist Gayle Rubin argues that gender assignment governs the economic as well as the symbolic dimensions of life for both women and men: "The same social system which oppresses women in its relations of exchange oppresses everyone in its insistence upon a rigid division" between femininity and masculinity, or gender identities and appropriate roles in the division of labor.[3] It is to the effects of this system of "sexual difference" that Cixous's statement refers: Only men live and experience as men, only women live and experience as women; therefore, only women can speak as/for women and only men can speak as/for men.

If separate worlds obtain for men and women, though, then why and how do men write the feminine? Like many feminists over the last two decades, Cixous is ambivalent about men's relation to feminism as a politico-cultural movement of, by, and for women. (On this topic, see especially Conversation One, page 189.) Having reaffirmed the division between the sexes ("woman must write woman. And man, man"), Cixous nevertheless implies that gender is negotiable and may be aligned with either of the two sexes ("it's up to him to say where his masculinity and femininity are at"). If men can write the feminine (and women the masculine[4]), what happens to the notion of sex as an absolute determinant of the writer's gender identity? Each of the four essays in Part One answers this question differently.

In fact, men have been writing the feminine ever since men began writing: think of Plato's Diotima and Ovid's Sappho, for instance.[5] But which of the many constructs of femininity informs each male-authored text? What Toril Moi has called "sexual/textual politics" can be seen in action when men write the feminine in poems and novels throughout the Western tradition.[6] The first four essays here inquire into the sexual politics of literary texts, but they also reconsider the assumption, widespread in feminist literary criticism and theory, that men always reaffirm their masculinity—their superior placement in the "sex/gender system" or "patriarchy"—when they write the feminine.[7] The challenge here is understanding the precarious balance between men's appropriation of the category of femininity in order to strengthen their own authority and men's attempt to critique masculinity through adopting a feminine (and, in some cases, potentially feminist) position in the system of sexual difference.

In the first essay, "The Mourner in the Flesh: George Herbert's Commemoration of Magdalen Herbert in *Memoriae Matris Sacrum*," Deborah Rubin interrogates the several stages in this male poet's strategic adoption of a feminine persona. Rubin asks us to think about the cultural work of gender involved in the process of mourning a mother by (re)writing motherhood itself. The gender politics of William Wordsworth's influential poetics is examined by Susan Wolfson in the next essay, "*Lyrical Ballads* and the Language of (Men) Feeling: Writing Women's Voices." Significantly, both Herbert and Wordsworth contest the dominant ideals of masculinity in their respective eras by speaking in what were (and still are) considered to be markedly feminine poetic voices. In doing so, however, they reconfirm the definition of "woman" as ineluctably different from "man." Consequently, Herbert and Wordworth's poetry both preserves and crosses fixed boundaries between masculinity and femininity.[8]

In a reversal of the positions typically held by the male and the female writer in the literary tradition according to Sandra Gilbert and Susan Gubar in *The Madwoman in the Attic*, Carol Siegel, in "Border Disturbances: D. H. Lawrence's Fiction and the Feminism of *Wuthering Heights*," finds the male novelist writing the feminine after the model of a strong female precursor.[9] By adopting Emily Brontë's voice, Lawrence tries to revise the traditional symbolism that aligns men and masculinity with culture over and against women and femininity's alignment with nature. But the feminine literary presence in Lawrence's work also exacerbates his anxiety over the male writer's loss of authority to the woman writer. The topic of authorship, cultural power, and gender is presented from a different angle in the concluding essay of Part One, Peter Murphy's " 'To Write What Cannot Be Written': The Woman Writer and Male Authority in John Hawkes's *Virginie: Her Two Lives*." This postmodern male novelist attempts to deconstruct masculinity by imagining a female writer who constantly eludes the traditional sex/gender system, as epitomized by a Sadeian pedagogy for women. But to what degree is the novelist himself implicated in the fictional schoolmaster's voyeuristic pleasures as he teaches the young heroine how to think and write "as a woman"? And what is the reader's part in upholding sexual difference as s/he watches—and possibly enjoys—these scenes of instruction in how to perform the feminine?[10]

The Gendering Gaze

Men's practice of writing the feminine raises several important questions about desire and power: Is a male author engaging in voyeurism when he writes in a feminine voice about (what he thinks are) the intimate thoughts and feelings of women? Sigmund Freud defines *voyeurism* as an act of sadistic looking in which the subject exerts power over someone else by regarding him or (often) her as a sexual object.[11] Looking never comprises just one action but always instigates a sequence of gazes. Thus, the subject of the gaze derives pleasure not only from looking at someone else as a sexual object but also from imagining himself as a sexual object for the gaze of a third party. Developing Jacques Lacan's theory of "intersubjectivity," which stipulates the psychological interdependence of desire for and power over others, Jerry Aline Flieger has suggested that literature involves a triangle of gazes between author, character, and reader.[12] This triangle, as Flieger shows, parallels the narrative structure or "masterplot" that organizes a wide range of literary texts. In psychoanalytic terms, the triangular structure that recurs in literature reinscribes the oedipal triangle of a powerful father (representative of ideal masculinity), a sexually desirable mother (representative of ideal femininity), and the typical subject (presumptively male), who is perforce acculturated into the dominant system of sexual difference.[13] The theory of the gaze, therefore, has important implications for men writing the feminine and also for the reader of such texts. As a result of "the reader's identification with the writer's desire," which itself is " 'misrecognized' as that of the novel's protagonist [or the poem's persona]," we ourselves are always implicated in the complex vectors of desire and power, gender identification and gender crossing, which are mobilized when male authors write the feminine.[14]

Part Two, "The Gendering Gaze," consists of four essays that consider the ambiguous positionings of male authors who write the feminine in terms of gender identity, orientation of sexual desire, and cultural power. Béatrice Durand opens this topic with her essay on "Diderot and the Nun: Portrait of the Artist as a Transvestite." Diderot's cross-voicing and cross-dressing as a young girl who is seduced by other women at a convent in *La Religieuse* (*The Nun*) is a well-known example of literary pornography. Less often noticed, maintains Durand, is the way in which Diderot's performance of the feminine provides the point of departure for his influential work on aesthetics as a philosopher of the Enlightenment. Diderot's writing the feminine thus raises provocative questions about the connection between aesthetics and voyeurism, or between legitimate and illegitimate modes of looking.

In contrast, in " 'This Kind': Pornographic Discourses, Lesbian Bodies, and Paul Verlaine's *Les Amies*," Barbara Milech argues that Verlaine's ventriloquism in the sonnet sequence *The Women-Friends* serves as a strategic means of expressing his own homosexuality. Central to the genre of pornography, the voyeuristic gaze that asserts the male looker's absolute power over a female sexual object organizes

Verlaine's poems, too. Thus, Milech concludes, his celebration of feminine desire is suspect: Reinscribing the superiority of masculine over feminine subjectivity, Verlaine's texts implicitly reject the validity of female-female desire by offering lesbians as a spectacle for the male gaze.[15]

Yet another literary situation in which the gaze defines gender is discussed by Christopher Benfey in "The Woman in the Mirror: Randall Jarrell and John Berryman." As John Berger has pointed out concerning the representation of women in European oil painting, "woman" consistently appears as the object of desire for male (and heterosexual) artists and art viewers.[16] One of the major motifs through which this construction of the feminine has been transmitted in art is the woman holding, or standing in front of, a mirror. What happens to gender identity—and to cultural authority—when a man poses before and looks at himself in a mirror, as Jarrell does in several poems? Motherhood, too, has been traditionally assigned to the feminine domain: What, then, are the psychological and political effects of Berryman's writing in the voice of a woman giving birth in *Homage to Mistress Bradstreet*? Is the male poet trying to understand the feminine as different and other, or to appropriate motherhood for masculinity (the poem as *his* baby)? Finally, we might ask about the role of the reader in the triangulation of gazes set up in Jarrell's and Berryman's poems: Who is looking at whom, and why?

Part Two closes with Frann Michel's analysis of the power of the gaze, the mobility of gender identities, and the struggle over literary authority in "William Faulkner as a Lesbian Author." As in Lawrence and Hawkes, so in Faulkner, the male novelist projects a feminine voice while retaining an authority that is still aligned with masculinity and its full range of cultural privilege. Also, like Diderot and Verlaine, Faulkner both invites and fends off the feminine in his writing. Indeed, gender-crossing for the male author may entail both misogyny and homophobia.[17] (On these issues, see Conversation Two, page 192.)

Overall, the eight essays in Parts One and Two sound a note of cautious optimism about men writing the gender of the opposite sex. Recently, Jane Gallop, a feminist psychoanalytic theorist, has raised some crucial questions about the sexual/textual politics at stake in the works of influential male writers who attempt "critical thinking connected to the body."[18] Agreeing with Hélène Cixous that "men too must be capable of crossing the divide" of sexual difference, Gallop nevertheless asks us to examine "the ways in which it is both easier and harder for men" than for women to do so: "Harder because men have their masculine identity to gain by being estranged from their bodies and dominating the bodies of others [that is, women]. Easier because men are more able to venture into the realm of the body without being trapped there [as women seem to be]."[19]

Postmodern Theories: Beyond Gender?

Men Writing the Feminine is an effort to extend and nuance the conversation betwen women and men about theories of sexual difference, feminism, and gender identity which arose during the 1980s. Part Three of this book, "Postmodern Theories: Beyond Gender?," consists of two essays, a position paper, and a pair of conversations: All emphasize the need for further critical thinking about the ways in which gender has been theorized, in particular by psychoanalysis, deconstruction, and, most recently, postmodernism. (On postmodern theories of gender, see Conversation Two, page 192.)

A major theoretical issue throughout *Men Writing the Feminine* is the tension between the sexed body of the author (male) and the double gender-marking of his discourse: performatively feminine but politically masculine. In a well-known essay, "Signature/Event/Context," Jacques Derrida draws a series of distinctions between the person of the author (for example, a body with a penis) and the discourse signed with that author's name (for example, "Charles Dickens").[20] "The absence of the sender, the addresser, from the marks he abandons, which are cut off from him and continue to produce effects beyond his presence and beyond the present actuality of his meaning . . . belongs to the structure of all writing."[21] Derrida's unravelling of the intimate bond between "the man and his work," which is assumed in much literary criticism, has several important implications for men writing the feminine.

First, the "iterability" of an author's signature, which must be detached from the man writing in order for the text written to circulate among readers and to survive his death, ambiguates the literary biographical question: "Who is speaking?" Iterability, or the deconstructive theory of the scission between signifier and signified, language and referent, textual meaning and authorial presence, also applies to the poetics of "voice," or individual style. Can sexual difference in the author's body be directly represented by voice in the language of the text? Yes and no. A text written "in a woman's voice" may be authored by a woman, but it might just as well be authored by a man (or, conceivably, by both together or alternately). When viewed as a conventionalized use of language, then, the feminine is an iterable, imitable gender-"mark" and, hence, not necessarily mimetic of, or equivalent to, the sex of the author's body. The paradoxically repeatable essence of femininity renders it central to the practice of what feminists, including Elaine Showalter and Marjorie Garber, have recently analyzed as literary and critical cross-dressing.[22] From a psychoanalytic point of view as well, "womanliness can be . . . worn as a mask," so that no stable boundary can be established between being-a-woman and acting-like-a-woman: "They are the same thing."[23]

A second aspect of Derrida's deconstruction of authorship that bears upon *Men Writing the Feminine* involves the "trace," or the idea that for any absolute value to function, it must silently include at least some elements of its very opposite. This necessary but "dangerous supplement" in every term leads to a situation of contradiction ("*aporia*") and to its eventual undoing as an absolute "ground" for truth.[24] When placed in the context of gender studies, Derrida's theory of the trace provides a useful way for understanding how hegemonic masculinity, or "patriarchy," works in relation to the supplementary category of femininity. Presupposing heterosexuality as a norm, the dominant category of masculinity throughout most of Western cultural history has defined itself as an absolute, superior category in opposition to the devalorized category of femininity. Although by definition comprising a set of traits innate in women, femininity is, in practice, also attributed to men who do not conform to the dominant code for masculinity; hence, the marginal category of "effeminacy," which is a point of much anxiety among the male poets and novelists whose works are analyzed in this volume. In terms of deconstruction, therefore, effeminacy—specifically, the male author's fear of becoming feminine himself through the act of writing the feminine—is an exemplary case of the trace: Masculinity "always already" bears strong elements of the very femininity from which it seeks to distinguish itself.

The logic of the trace in the politics of gender can be seen in each of the literary texts discussed in Parts One and Two of *Men Writing the Feminine* as well as in the contemporary theories of gender debated in Part Three. For example, Wordsworth (see the second epigraph, above) discovers the feminine—in his poetics, "the spontaneous overflow of powerful feeeling"—where he expected to find the hard bedrock of his masculinity as a writer. From a psychoanalytic perspective, the way in which the iterability of writing severs language from physical presence provokes a continuous state of castration anxiety in the male writer. In this sense, his signature at the bottom of a literary or theoretical text written in the feminine becomes a displacement of the phallus—that symbol of cultural power which constantly circulates between men and women without ever being securely possessed by anyone—and thus a form of fetishism.[25] At the very same time, men's activity of writing the feminine may serve to multiply male pleasure and power through narcissism and voyeurism. Certainly, several essays in this volume suggest that adopting a feminine persona enables the male author to feel, think, and say things that are otherwise forbidden to him as a masculine- and heterosexual-identified member of the patriarchy.

The initial pair of essays in Part Three of *Men Writing the Feminine* confronts these and other questions of gender by examining postmodern theories in relation to literature. In "Objects of Postmodern 'Masters': Subject-in-Simulation/Woman-in-Effect," Martina Sciolino deconstructs what the feminist Alice Jardine has dubbed "gynesis," or the practice of writing the feminine among poststructuralist male theorists, including Derrida, Lacan, and Gilles Deleuze.[26] As they "attempt to create a new *space* or *spacing within themselves*" in response to the crisis of the subject and the crumbling of master narratives in the West after the 1960s, leading male theorists seem to have appropriated the feminine once again for their own purposes.[27] Like the heroes of postmodern novels by Thomas Pynchon and John Barth, theoretical gynesis depends on a fantasized bigendered male body. Thus, Sciolino argues, such postmodern writing of the feminine ends up establishing a zone for the free play of gender, desire, and power for men only.

Another viewpoint on contemporary debates about gender is offered by

Charles Bernheimer in "Against Aversion: Closing the Gaps in Theory." Like Sciolino, Bernheimer is interested in the sexual politics implicit in deconstruction, which he rethinks through psychoanalysis. This line of inquiry leads him to wonder about the kind(s) of gendered subjects produced by psychoanalytic theory and literary criticism as discourses that assume, and thereby promote, ideals of masculinity and femininity for men and women, respectively. Above all, Bernheimer asks his readers to reconsider the important role that the male body of the writer himself plays in the production of literary theory and criticism. What does a man writing the feminine by engaging in feminist discourse finally mean?

As we in the 1990s continue to ponder the material and cultural effects of the ways in which genders have been represented in literature and in theory, we need to remind ourselves of the recent history of this discussion. One milestone is *Men in Feminism,* a 1987 collection of position papers written by female and male literary critics and theorists.[28] (For discussion of this work, see Conversation One, page 189.) Included here, Jonathan Culler's paper, "Five Propositions on the Future of Men in Feminism," delivered on a panel at the Modern Language Association meeting in 1988, is an important document in the ongoing controversy about men's and women's relations to feminism. In order to encourage further discussion, *Men Writing the Feminine* ends with two conversations between myself and Robert Con Davis on the range of issues raised in the present volume. While Conversation One focuses on connections between "Women's, Gay & Lesbian, and Gender Studies," Conversation Two looks at various "Postmodern Theories of Gender," considering their political implications as well as areas for research and debate. The selected bibliography that follows the conversations provides a short list of recent books of interest to those working on literature, theory, and gender.

When men write the feminine, or what they imagine to be women's voices and bodies, their discourse becomes what Mikhail Bakhtin has termed "dialogical": "It serves two speakers at the same time and expresses simultaneously two different intentions."[29] Of central importance to the project of *Men Writing the Feminine* is dialogue between women and men in an effort to understand representations of gender in the past and their possible revision for the future. We invite our readers to join us in this venture.

Notes

1. Hélène Cixous, "The Laugh of the Medusa," trans. Keith and Paula Cohen. 1975; reprinted in *The Signs Reader: Women, Gender, and Scholarship,* eds. Elizabeth Abel and Emily K. Abel (Chicago: University of Chicago Press, 1983), 279–97.

2. See, for example, Nelly Furman, "The Politics of Language Beyond the Gender Principle?," in *Making a Difference: Feminist Literary Criticism,* eds. Gayle Greene and Coppelia Kahn (New York: Methuen, 1985), 59–79; and Cynthia Fuchs Epstein, *Deceptive Distinctions: Sex, Gender, and the Social Order* (New Haven: Yale University Press, 1988).

3. Gayle Rubin, "The Traffic in Women: Notes on the 'Political Economy' of Sex," in *Toward an Anthropology of Women,* ed. Rayna R. Reiter (New York: Monthly Review Press, 1975), 180.

4. For a theoretical discussion of women writing the masculine, see Eve Kosofsky Sedgwick, "Across Gender, Across Sexuality: Willa Cather and Others," in *Displacing Homophobia: Gay Male Perspectives in Literature and Culture,* eds. Ronald R. Butters, et al. (Durham: Duke University Press, 1989), 53–72.

5. On the centrality of men writing the feminine to the French literary tradition, see Joan de Jean, *Fictions of Sappho, 1546–1937* (Chicago: University of Chicago Press, 1989).

6. Toril Moi, *Sexual/Textual Politics: Feminist Literary Theory* (New York: Methuen, 1985).

7. The term "sex/gender system" is still widely used in American feminist theory in the social sciences, as, for example, Epstein's book, *Deceptive Distinctions,* shows.

8. On the importance of boundaries in sexual politics, specifically from the perspective of the male writer "embattled with the patriarchal terms of [his] gendered construction," see *Out of Bounds: Male Writers and Gender(ed) Criticism,* eds. Laura Claridge and Elizabeth Langland (Amherst: University of Massachusetts Press, 1990). As the introduction states, this volume "concentrate[s] on language, voice, and form": if literature represents "the experience of individuals," then it is "formal innovation" that enables male writers to engage with "the feminine" (12, 17).

9. Sandra Gilbert and Susan Gubar, *The Madwoman in the Attic: The Woman Writer and the Nineteenth-Century Literary Imagination* (New Haven: Yale University Press, 1979).

10. On gender as a performance rather than a natural state, see Judith Butler, *Gender Trouble: Feminism and the Subversion of Identity* (New York: Routledge, 1990): "gender proves to be performative—that is, constituting the identity it is purporting to be. In this sense, gender is always a doing" (25).

11. See, for instance, Sigmund Freud, "Instincts and Their Vicissitudes" in *The Standard Edition of the Works of Sigmund Freud,* vol. 14, esp. 125–40.

12. Jacques Lecan, "Seminar on 'The Purloined Letter,' " trans. Jeffrey Mehlman, *Yale French Studies* 48 (1976): 39–72. Jerry Aline Flieger, "The Purloined Punchline: Joke as Textual Paradigm," reprinted in *Contemporary Literary Criticism: Modernism through Post-Structuralism,* ed. Robert Con Davis (New York: Longman, 1986), 277–94.

13. For a feminist critique of the psychoanalytic theory of triangulation and the gaze, see Kaja Silverman, *The Subject of Semiotics* (New York: Oxford University Press, 1983), esp. chapters 4, 5.

14. Flieger, "The Purloined Punchline," 283.

15. On the representation of lesbians as surrogates for male-male desire in nineteenth-century literature and art, see Thaïs E. Morgan, "Male Lesbian Bodies: The Construction of Alternative Masculinities in Courbet, Baudelaire, and Swinburne," *Genders* 15 (Winter 1992), 37–57.

16. See John Berger, *Ways of Seeing* (New York: Penguin, 1978), 36–64.

17. On the double force of misogyny and homophobia in nineteenth-century

literature written by men, see Eve Kosofsky Sedgwick, *Between Men: English Literature and Male Homosocial Desire* (New York: Columbia University Press, 1985).

18.   Jane Gallop, "Thinking Through the Body," in *Thinking Through the Body* (New York: Columbia University Press, 1988), 1–9.

19.   Ibid., 7.

20.   Jacques Derrida, "Signature/Event/Context" in *Margins of Philosophy* (Chicago: University of Chicago Press), 309–30. For another important critique of the relationship of author and works, see: Michel Foucault, "What Is an Author?" in *Textual Strategies: Perspectives in Post-Structuralist Criticism,* ed. and trans., Joseph Harari (Ithaca: Cornell University Press, 1979), 141–60.

21.   Ibid., 313.

22.   Elaine Showalter, "Critical Cross-Dressing: Male Feminists and the Woman of the Year" in *Men in Feminism,* eds. Alice Jardine and Paul Smith (New York: Methuen, 1987), 116–32. Marjorie Garber, *Vested Interests: Cross-Dressing and Cultural Anxiety* (New York: Routledge, 1991). See also Sandra Gilbert and Susan Gubar, "Cross-Dressing and Re-Dressing: Transvestism as Metaphor" in *No Man's Land,* vol. 2: *Sexchanges* (New Haven: Yale University Press, 1989), 324–76.

23.   Joan Rivière, "Womanliness as Masquerade," rpt. in *Formations of Fantasy,* ed. Victor Burgin et al. (London: Methuen, 1986), 38.

24.   Derrida focuses on the "trace" and the "supplement" in relation to *"différance"* in the section on "Writing and Telecommunication" in "Signature/Event/Context," 311–21.
     Derrida discusses the "dangerous supplement" in connection with Jean-Jacques Rousseau in pt. 2, ch. 2, *Of Grammatology* (Baltimore: Johns Hopkins University Press, 1976), 144–64.

25.   On fetishism in Lacanian theory, see Jane Gallop, *The Daughter's Seduction: Feminism and Psychoanalysis* (Ithaca: Cornell University Press, 1982): "The phallus, unlike the penis, is lacking to any subject, male or female" (95).

26.   Alice A. Jardine, *Gynesis: Configurations of Modernity* (Ithaca: Cornell University Press, 1985), 25, her emphasis. A much discussed example of gynesis, or men writing the feminine in postmodern theory, is Derrida, *Spurs/Eperons,* trans. Barbara Harlow (Chicago: University of Chicago Press, 1979).

27.   Jardine, *Gynesis,* 25.

28.   *Men in Feminism,* eds. Alice Jardine and Paul Smith (New York: Methuen, 1987). In 1988, the Modern Language Association convention program featured a panel on "The Future of Men with Feminism, the Future of Feminism with Men" (chaired by Thaïs E. Morgan), which consisted of position papers by Alice Jardine, Leslie Rabine, Robert Scholes, and Jonathan Culler. Culler's paper is printed in Part II of this volume.

29.   Mikhail M. Bakhtin, "Discourse in the Novel," in *The Dialogic Imagination,* ed. and trans., Michael Holquist and Caryl Emerson (Austin: University of Texas Press, 1981), 324.

SECTION ONE: MEN'S FEMININITIES

The Mourner in the Flesh: George Herbert's Commemoration of Magdalen Herbert in *Memoriae Matris Sacrum*

Deborah Rubin

> *There was a Birth, certainly,*
> *We had evidence and no doubt. I had seen birth*
> *and death,*
> *But had thought they were different; this Birth*
> *was*
> *Hard and bitter agony for us, like Death,*
> *our death.*

—T. S. Eliot, "Journey of the Magi"

I

A month after the death of Magdalen Newport Herbert Danvers on June 8, 1627, a memorial volume containing works by her close friend John Donne and her seventh child, George Herbert, was entered in the Stationers' Register.[1] Donne's sermon and George's sequence of Latin and Greek poems, both composed on the occasion of Magdalen's death, are tributes to this Renaissance Englishwoman, distinguished for her intelligence, literary gifts, piety, musicality, family and estate management, and hospitality. The occasion of their publication on July 7 is a conventional one, their stated purpose to remember and praise the dead woman. Donne takes as the double structure of his sermon "To instruct the Living, and then To commemorate the Dead," (63) while George, in "*Memoriae Matris Sacrum 2*," calls upon the Cornelian and Sempronian matrons of Rome and virtuous women everywhere to join him in praising this mother.

The urgent need to praise and remember has its origin in the work of mourning, as recent psychoanalytic and literary studies have demonstrated.[2] Where praise takes the form of idealized portraiture, it may compensate for exaggerated feelings of anger against the deceased[3]; where it is less extreme, it is part of the normal process of grieving that allows the bereaved to eventually resume life without the beloved. Because of its roots in the subconscious, this process is particularly irrational, repetitive, and subjective. Texts that appear to be written in traditional genres for public occasions (funeral sermon, Latin and Greek elegiac verse) function as well on an intensely personal level.[4] This is, of course, true of many public genres, whose rhetorical and prosodic qualities satisfy emotional as well as social and esthetic purposes. The phenomenon is intensified, here, however, by the extremity of emotion associated with death.

The conflict between an apparently objective, public form and the subjective uses to which it is put is of special interest to the project of recovery of Renaissance women that has engaged some scholars and theorists in recent years. I was initially tempted to read these two works for biographical information on Magdalen Herbert, a woman who has been silenced by the loss of almost all of her extensive correspondence and other written records. Along with Edward Herbert's autobiography and Izaac Walton's biographies of John Donne and George Herbert, which also touch upon Magdalen Herbert, they form an extraordinary constellation of texts at whose center lies a mute subject.[5] I soon gave over this project, however, because it became clear that I was reading not descriptions of Magdalen Herbert but projections of George Herbert and John Donne onto her person.

These projections take various forms, including the disintegrating corpse—a reduction of individual to Christian symbol or psychic anarchy—and the *imago*—the external image stripped of personality. They appear also in reverse, as introjections, where the imagined body of the beloved enters that of the mourner, in the form of a fetus or a disease. In all of these variations, we are struck by the distortion of the imagined female body, the merging of mourner and dead beloved, and the ventriloquistic illusion of a man and a poet speaking through the body of a woman.[6] Where there is some attempt to represent the dead woman as she was while living, an obsessive focus on the agony and sacrifice of the mourner still displaces the deceased within the poem. What remains in voice and image is not the historical Magdalen Herbert but traces of her influence on the men who knew her, and of their struggle to refashion her to meet their needs.

Since the context is literary representation rather than actual experience, and since there are few historical traces of Magdalen's life, the reader/observer has no neutral ground from which to compare the actual woman to the projected one. He or she is obliged to occupy the same perspective as the author and to enter into his fantasy of the subject. The reader may struggle against this enforced vantage point, seeking to peel off the projection and recover the woman beneath it, but she is not there. What we have are words, ink, pages.

II

A recurring theme in George Herbert's acts of commemoration and grief is the self-sacrifice of the mourner. In a variation on the Orphic plot, calling back the lost beloved involves the destruction of the bereaved. "*Memoriae Matris Sacrum* 1," in many respects a more balanced and traditional elegy than the later poems, is nevertheless notable for its focus on the mourners rather than the deceased. A frame without a portrait, it calls upon the reader to witness not the dead woman or even a tribute to her, but a struggle to approach the task. The subject is not Magdalen Herbert but George; the agony is not her death but his anxiety over insufficient grief:

> *Ah Mother, where's the fountain to lament you?*
> *What drops can measure up my grief?*
> *Neighboring Thames seems dry, to all my tears;*
> *I, dryer than your virtues' chorus.*
> *If, burning, I were poured in the dark river*
> *I'd never be fit ink for praise.*
> *Grateful, I write this, lest to me alone*
> *You're "Mater"; grief gives birth to meter.*[7]

George's preoccupation with measurement, by which in *The Temple* he seeks to understand Christ's agony and thus his own unworthiness ("The Agonie," "Good Friday"), is here employed to understand his relation to his mother: the amount of her worth, the value others place on her, the adequacy of his own grief. The task of mourning that he sets himself is immense—unbearable—from the start, and extends beyond the production of enough tears. As burning pitch is reduced to lampblack and then moistened to form ink, so he imagines himself burning and then melting to write her praises with his body.[8] By means of synecdoche, not the hand but the entire body writes, merging with a river of tears to form a river of words. As lines 5–8 establish, George's goal is the recreation of his mother; he himself is both alchemist and base metal for the task.

The metamorphosis in line 8 from "*Dolor*" to "*Metra*" sets forth in deceptively straightforward terms the enterprise of the sequence. Most simply, Herbert seeks to transmute inarticulate private grief into public verse, thereby lessening his pain and winning his mother a lasting memorial. "*Dolor*" gives birth to "*Metra*"; out of his travail comes poetry. His verse will stand in the place of the mother, speak for the mother, or be the mother reborn in the tradition of epitaph and elegy, where the dead speak from the tombstone and a poem confers eternal life. Magdalen Herbert is to be the subject of the poem; grief for and memory of her compel Herbert to write (against his will, as *"Memoriae Matris Sacrum* 19" claims); the poem is the product of his action.

But *"Mater," "Dolor,"* and *"Metra"* yield other relationships as well. If we follow the logic of the metaphor, sorrow is the mother of verse, verse the child of sorrow. The sequence of nouns in line 8—*Mater, Dolor, Metra*—recapitulates the triangle: the loss of Mother caused sorrow, which gave birth to verse. *"Metra,"* however, is also *"Mater,"* as the first and last words of the line punningly proclaim, or, more accurately, the latter has been transformed into verse. Thus it follows that the poet, mother to his verse, is mother to his mother, too. Not only has the poet created the poem; lines 5–6 suggest that his body is the poem, for it was written in ink extracted from his flaming flesh and bones. Since the poem is a substitute for Mother, we are forced to contemplate an extraordinary pair of equations. George is his mother's mother, but he is also Mother.

A similar conceit, of body changed to ink to write of grief, obtains in "Good Friday," where Herbert writes,

> *O my chief good,*
> *How shall I measure out thy blood?*
> *How shall I count what thee befell,*
> *   And each grief tell?*
>   *. . .*
> *Since bloud is fittest, Lord, to write*
> *Thy sorrows in, and bloudie fight;*
> *My heart hath store, write there, where in*
> *One box doth lie both ink and sinne.   (1–4; 21–24)*

In what is here a traditional gesture, Herbert offers his body as a means to write and to worship, and, in imitation of Christ, imagines a bloody sacrifice. In *"Memoriae Matris Sacrum* 1" such imitation has been transferred from God to a mother, raising questions of gender identification and religious decorum. In his devotional verse as well as in his memorial verse, Herbert writes less about the beloved than about the psychology of the lover, and for similar reasons. The drama of personal salvation is crucial for him in both genres: In *The Temple,* salvation requires the shaping of a "true Aaron" through the subduing of wrong impulses, and in *Memoriae Matris Sacrum,* salvation requires the shaping of a true mourner through similar means. *The Temple,* however, incorporates countervailing poems of praise where God is the object; in *Memoriae Matris Sacrum,* Magdalen Herbert is almost never in view.

A partial exception is *"Memoriae Matris Sacrum* 2," the longest poem in the sequence and the only one to describe the living Magdalen Herbert in appearance, character, and action. Significantly, Herbert attributes to Magdalen the very qualities for which he is known: musical ability, "sharp and fiery prayer," and linguistic virtuosity. Representing her as genitrix and teacher, Herbert stresses her influence and his indebtedness. The first is remarkable in Renaissance literature. I am not aware of another male poet in Renaissance England who acknowledges a woman as an "ancestor," or literary model, as the giver of social identity or of language, and I have argued elsewhere that George views Latin in these poems as a "mother tongue."[9] The second is more common and problematic; excessive indebtedness, here a part of what Pigman terms "unresolved mourning" (see note 9 and *passim*), results in a reflexive focus on the self rather than the other, and in a return to the theme of sacrifice.

That both indebtedness and sacrifice are conceived in terms of language is not surprising, given the values of mother and son. Writing in Latin, George acknowledges his mother's gift of the very letters with which he constructs his verse:

> You, indeed, Mother will be praised perpetually
> By a grieving son: the letters in which you educated me
> Owe this to you; they blot the pages of their own accord,
> Attaining the greatest fruit of my labors
> By praising my Mother, while the ignorant oppose this.[10]   (61–65)

"*Litterae,*" whether letters of the alphabet, words and language, or literature, were first given by his mother, who also commanded language in her own right. In lines 29–41 of "*Memoriae Matris Sacrum* 2," George praises her abilities as a speaker and writer who possesses a distinctive style, social and moral substance, and a distinguished readership. By emphasizing not only Magdalen's education and character but her innate intelligence and linguistic gifts, George claims an indebtedness that transcends a child's to a conscientious parent or teacher: he and Magdalen are bound physically and psychologically by aspects of a shared identity. Challenging the Renaissance association of chastity with silence in the character of a gentlewoman, George authorizes and publishes her voice, and acknowledges her as an ancestor and literary precursor. In praising Magdalen's skills, George not only allows her in memory unusual scope for the expression of her personality and authority as a Renaissance woman; he defines his poetic gifts in relation to hers.

The power of such an identification is apparent later in "*Memoriae Matris Sacrum* 2," where George enters into a confrontation with an imagined or real critic of his grief, who has challenged his right to mourn. His response is an angry assertion of his right to speech itself.

> *But you who are of the opinion that these saying are*
>   *unsuitable for a son,*
> *Taking away from a son the praise of a parent,*
> *Go away, blockhead, with your embarrassment.*
> *Therefore shall I myself alone be silent and foolish*
> *While the world clatters with jingling proclamations?*

> *To me alone is my mother's urn shut up,*
> *Plants faded, rosemary dried up?*
> *Shall I restore my tongue to my mother only to bite it?*
> *Go away, stupid. How devotedly shameless I am in*
>   *this!*[11]   *(53–60)*

Praise of his mother has for George a special meaning: not merely recognition and proclamation of her virtues but the giving back of borrowed words. Her first claim to words of praise originates in "the words with which you educated me," which, he argues, demand repayment in equivalent words of praise and gratitude. Indeed the original letters long to speak for themselves, blotting the pages "of their own accord" (63–65). It remains for George, however, to speak articulately, to shape the incoherent, passionate voice of his mother into intelligible speech.

An underlying motivation is to restore to the dead woman her own voice. The image George employs in the conclusion of *"Memoriae Matris Sacrum* 2" is a strange and intimate one. "Shall I restore a tongue to my mother only to bite it?" he exclaims, challenging the critic to stop him from praising her, and refusing to participate in what he claims is the wounding of her reputation. The characteristic omission of possessive adjectives in Latin renders the question particularly ambiguous: *"Matrine linguam refero"* may mean "Shall I restore *a* tongue to you?" or "Shall I restore *your* tongue to you?" or even "Shall I restore *my* tongue to you?" That the tongue should be hers is clear from the choice of verb: That which is restored returns to its original and rightful owner. That it must be restored suggests that it is no longer in her possession. Literally, she lacks a tongue because she is dead and can no longer speak; symbolically, she lacks language because she has given it to her son.

The economy of scarcity implied by such a transaction and its reversal is crucial to an understanding of *Memoriae Matris Sacrum*. While speech is free-floating, amorphous, recyclable, tongues are rooted in a single mouth, physical, irreplaceable. Without a tongue, language as George conceives of it is impossible. While Magdalen could be said to have given George speech by teaching him—assisting him in imitating the words she possessed—the implication here is that she gave him a tongue by silencing her own. What began as a poem about inheritance, gratitude, and its appropriate expression has become a formulation of extreme deprivation. In the process, the emphasis has shifted from Magdalen to her son.

The possibility of biting that tongue, raised by George in his rhetorical question, forces the reader to consider other reasons and occasions for such wounding of the organ of speech. Has his mother given him the tongue by biting it off? Will he return it to her by a reciprocal gesture of self-mutilation? This occasion for speech seems to require sacrifice, heroic love, the renunciation of one's own identity in favor of the beloved. Ovid's Philomela comes to mind, and the reader must confront the erotic implications of lingual exchanges, whether pleasurable or forced. Philomela's loss of tongue is associated with her rape, ostensibly because Tereus wishes to silence her. On a deeper psychoanalytic level, where the tongue is a phallic object and the mouth is identified with other orifices, it is also an act of castration. Chastity for women in the Renaissance is equated with silence; lack of a phallus and lack of a tongue are necessary correlatives for female virtue.[12]

The exchange between Magdalen and George hinted at by the gift and return of a tongue is less brutal than that in Ovid but equally as complex. Its fundamentally erotic character is apparent, along with a blurring of boundaries. If George can restore the tongue and yet bite it, as line 59 suggests, loss and gain are not absolute; in this sense, George and Magdalen Herbert seem to be one person, to share one tongue and one voice. One model for understanding such merging of identities is erotic; another is the model of the mother and the newborn child. Until birth the child has been a part of the mother's body; it has gained autonomy by ripping itself away from her, leaving an absence and a wound. Freud suggests that the child may represent a phallus, a symbolic completion of the mother's body, but it also represents a loss. In the final lines of the second poem, lingual exchange has some of the privative qualities of the latter conception. Language was Magdalen Herbert's gift to her son, and he pays it back on the "just day," to borrow Ben Jonson's phrase. Rather than act as an independent voice in place of hers, he sees himself as becoming, poetically, the medium for her speech.

This act of restoration, however, is costly to both mother and son. The sacrifice is painful for the latter, whether measured figuratively or in terms of the suffering inscribed within the poem. The price for the former is also high: a poem that begins as a memorial to Magdalen's life ends as a battlefield where George defends himself against imagined or real critics of his grief (52–65). One of the few available portraits of Magdalen Herbert is never concluded.

III

As *Memoriae Matris Sacrum* progresses, George Herbert's attempts to recapture his absent mother reveal even greater unease, and the representations are increasingly distorted. In the face of death, what remains of the beloved is a corpse, memory, and imagination. All of these, intensely present, are other than the living person; specter-like, they invade the page and the mind. In *"Memoriae Matris Sacrum 5,"* which I have discussed elsewhere,[13] the corpse is a depersonalized, potent presence:

> *Gardens, dear to my mistress, droop at last;*
> *You have adorned the coffin, but cannot endure.*
> *See how your beauty bristles with thorns,*
> *Calling back the gardener with sharp grief.*
> *Your flowers smell of earth and death: the mistress'*
> *corpse*
> *Breathes on the nearby plants; they, on the roses.*

> *Dark-headed violas bend to the earth,*
> *Showing by their weight whose mistress' house it*
> *is.[14]   (1–8)*

The disproportionate power of the dead woman, whose breath imparts a fatal contagion to surrounding nature, is striking. George's projection of grief and depression upon the drooping flowers and upon nature in general may be characterized as pathetic fallacy; however the assignment of a universally corrupting influence to the corpse is something else. One senses a deep pre-Christian fear of the dead, which, in psychoanalytic terms, would be explained as part of "unresolved mourning," where anger against the departed is rationalized by projecting threatening characteristics upon her. The implicit eroticism of this poem's echo of Catullus 3 ("*passer, deliciae meae puellae*"/ sparrow, beloved of my mistress), which I have discussed in "Let your death be my *Iliad*," further complicates the emotions in this poem. Anxiety over his erotic and angry responses impels George Herbert to supplant his mother's memory with her corpse, and then to appropriate and ventriloquize it.

As the sequence progresses from the biographical to the autobiographical, from poems whose subject is the praise of Magdalen Herbert to poems describing her son's own predicament, from poems about her character while alive to poems about her corpse and her existence after death, Magdalen's living portrait is obscured. Mediated from the first by social conventions of praise and mourning as well as by literary conventions and Herbert's personal sense of the uses of language, the sequence plunges into descriptions of subjective experience that are hallucinatory in their intensity and strangeness. Poems 5, 6, and 7 constitute the center of the Latin sequence and its nadir. Grief and the impulse to praise or remember give way to depression and confusion in these poems, where language seems inadequate to compensate for loss or to interpret it.

In "*Memoriae Matris Sacrum 7*" George confronts Magdalen's *imago,* her guardian spirit, an even harsher representation of the son's state of mind, made at the expense of the mother's individuality. The corpse-like spirit is animated but malevolent, an embodiment of deprivation and malice:

> *My mother's spirit's shade, bloodless and pale,*
> *Are joys now changed to mists and things like you?*
> *Must you, deceiving shade, in mother's stead,*
> *With breasts of air elude my gaping mouth?*
> *Woe, cloud, heavy with rain, not milk,*
> *Mocking my tears, (as water, colorless)!*
> *Why don't you flee? My Juno never was*
> *So slow a form, untouched by vernal dawn,*
> *So faint a mother, replacing fleeting ash.[15]   (1–8)*

Here, George has cast off a Christian conception of death as the afterlife and the purpose of human existence. It is replaced, not by a stoical trust in personal memory but by another symbolic system more obliterative of the individual. Dripping with moisture, the *imago* of Lady Danvers steps from the grave or the underworld. It bears little resemblance to the woman George knew.[16] His vision of the shade as a depriving mother, withholding her milk, or as a false semblance of a mother, "deceiving shade, in mother's stead," is the naked cry of a pagan child rather than a Christian poet. Startling in the intensity of greed, disappointment, rage, and fear it records, it is a departure from George's English poetry in important ways. Most obviously, such rage against the interlocutor is impossible in *The Temple,* where George is addressing God. Equally strong emotions flood the *Temple* poems, but the negative ones must be turned against George himself, in the form of shame, unworthiness, anger and regret. Even desire for God must be tempered, since salvation cannot be forced or claimed as a right, and grace comes undeserved. The residue of purer feelings—love and gratitude, pity for the agonies of Christ, worship of the Creator, longing to be perfected and to know God—can then be turned heavenward.

In addressing his mother, George feels a similar need to split off his negative emotions, but he does so by creating a good and bad mother. The *imago,* appearing as both the mother who has abandoned him by dying, and as the usurping false mother, receives all of the anger and cannibalistic greed from which George wishes to shield his idealized mother. As a safeguard, George assigns to this specter qualities and gestures that serve as an objective correlative for each emotion he expresses. The gaping mouth of the child meets with breasts of air; his tears are mocked with rain, which is neither milk nor tears; his eager pursuit of mother is reciprocated by a languid, faint form. The good mother is described in lines 10–33 of the poem, where Magdalen is identified with *"Themis alma"* and Astraea, and also earlier in the sequence in the more formally epideictic poems. Both the good and bad mothers are synthetic, constructs of George's emotions, witnesses only to his reaction to the historical woman.

"Memoriae Matris Sacrum 6," the third of the central group, goes even further in objectifying Magdalen Herbert and in defining her through her son's experience. Through a process of introjection, the *imago* now lies within the body of the poet; the cannibalizing infant has met with success. "Mother" now exists only as he feels her; she cannot be seen or heard at all. Bodily decay is the subject of *"Memoriae Matris Sacrum* 6" as well as "5," but in the later poem the body in question is the poet's own. In an ambivalent admission of his own illness, both physical and psychological, George reduces Magdalen to a virus, a foreign body, or to his creature, an embryo:

> *Galen, pressing me wretch, in vain,*
> *Why flood me with so many questions,*
> > *Dragging at my pulsing arteries*
> > *Of flesh and fluid mass?*
> *I'm sick in mind, which neither pillboxes*
> *Nor slow drugs can relieve.*

> *Should you sack India, or Indies too,*
>   *The outlaw spirit would extend beyond.*
> *You're impotent to heal, even if I die:*
> *Not then should I be led to my best parent:*
>   *Unless, like Mother, I depart in grace,*
>   *I'll be deprived by death of her still more.*
> *But come, see how you're wrong, ignorant,*
> *Examining a sound arm! If it's inflamed and burns,*
>   *It glows with writing's heat.*
>   *My mother lies inside the springing vein.*
> *If, swollen, I grow large and groan,*
> *Don't blame my limbs. The cause lies in the spirit,*
>   *Which labors with a parent's praises,*
>   *And medicine is unsafe for pregnancies.*
> *My condition now is unusual:*
> *My flesh cannot conform to other men's.*
>   *What you judge a fever is salutory*
>   *And, alone, it heals the spirit.*[17]

Addressed to Galen, a pagan ministering to the flesh, the poem illustrates George's obsession during this period with Magdalen's mortality to the exclusion of her identity. While lines 9–12 propound a Christian perspective on death and the afterlife, the poem as a whole focuses on the physical aspects of sickness and suffering and on their inverted moral significance. The extraordinary physician of the poem diagnoses by "blaming" the afflicted bodily parts (18), forcing George into a defensive posture from which he wards off painful examination, censure, and bad advice. Like the critics whom George attacks elsewhere in "*Memoriae Matris Sacrum* 2" and "12," Galen is a projection of his own guilt, enacting positions that George finds troubling so that he may denounce them.

Galen is characterized as over-literal, intrusive, and inept. He dissects his patient, reducing the person to "flesh and fluid mass" (4). He mistakes illness of the spirit for illness of the body, and attempts to cure by means of pointless interrogations, anatomical probings, and drugs. The possible outcomes of his treatment, health or death of the body, do not include the end George claims finally to seek, death in grace. In opposition, George casts himself as a Christian Platonist, championing the "outlaw spirit" (*animus exlex*), untouched by the outrages of the material world, burning with a holy fever. To complete the opposition and to challenge the authority of Galen, he defines himself as suffering in the mind.

The balance of the poem, however, explores the physical manifestations of his grief or mental illness. The underlying logic is contorted and dense, as George simultaneously focuses on and denies the body. On the simplest level, George is healthy in body but emotionally troubled by the death of Lady Danvers. His state of mind, however, leads to an obsessive interest in the physical, both as a natural aspect of the mourning process and as a result of his erotic attachment to his mother.[18] This focus inspires anxiety, and in *"Memoriae Matris Sacrum* 6," he displaces his interest in the physical to Galen in order to deny it. In criticizing Galen, however, he substantiates the latter's empirical observations and directs our attention back to the body. Rebuking the physician for "examining a sound arm," he admits in the same breath that it may not be sound at all but inflamed and burning with "writing's heat" (13–15). While authorship, not disease, has produced this disorder, his intellectual and emotional passion has found a physical seat. In a final elaboration of the conceit, George imagines himself laboring to deliver his mother through the language of praise.

He introduces this image three times in lines 14–22, each time more explicitly. In lines 14–15, he mentions only two of the three elements, writing and physical sacrifice. Here, he argues that writing his mother's praises leads to a kind of writer's cramp, or a bodily exaltation. Line 16, with its baldness of Latin phrasing and literalness of sense, pushes the image further. Now *"mater,"* not her praise, has possessed the poet's arm and penetrated to a throbbing life center. The image is powerful and disturbing in its combination of pathology, eroticism, and inversion of the natural order of things. The presence of a foreign organism encysted or pulsing within the body suggests initially a disease, then pregnancy, and finally sexual intercourse.

But however it is interpreted, the implied relationship between mother and son is unusual. If the mother within his arm is an unborn child, the inversion of the parent-child relationship and George's self-presentation as a mother is striking. If the *"saliente vena"* (pulsing arteries) suggest an aroused sexual organ, the position of female inside of male is notable. In lines 17–22, George strips the veil from his metaphor and elaborates upon it. While Renaissance male writers not uncommonly describe themselves as giving birth to poems, I know of no other poet who expatiates upon the image as George does, or who explicitly sets himself off from other men as he does in line 22.[19]

In the conceit of childbirth, George Herbert extirpates the historical Magdalen Herbert and positions himself at the center of all gazes.[20] At the same time, he contrives to present his body as agonized and deformed, deserving of sympathetic attention. Magdalen Herbert has become a secret sharer, an almost unspeakable double, existing only in opposition to his existence and glorified by his struggle to give her identity. In a sense, George has come full circle, returning to *"Memoriae Matris Sacrum* 1," in which writing and giving birth to the mother are also central. In *"Memoriae Matris Sacrum* 6," however, these activities have devolved into pure anguish and illness. In the earlier poems,—"there was a Birth, certainly,"—out of *Dolor* came *Metra* and *Mater,* but in the later poems there is only a swallowing up. After Magdalen Herbert's death, George is able to speak for himself and through her, to represent his own body and to evoke her dead or demonic body. He is unable to speak for her or to evoke the living woman.

Notes

1. "A Sermon of Commemoration of the Lady Danvers," and *Memoriae Matris Sacrum.* I take the sermon's text from *The Sermons of John Donne,* ed. Evelyn M. Simpson and George R. Potter, 10 vols. (Berkeley and Los Angeles: University of California Press, 1953–62), 8:61–93 and Herbert's poems from *The Works of George Herbert,* ed. F. E. Hutchinson (Oxford: Oxford University Press, 1941). In citing from these texts, I have substituted "v" for "u," "i" for "j," and "j" for "i" to conform with modern orthographical practices; I have also omitted some of Donne's italics and all of George Herbert's accents.

For English translations of *Memoriae Matris Sacrum,* one may consult volume two of *The Complete Works in Verse and Prose of George Herbert,* ed. Alexander B. Grosart (n. p.: Fuller Worthies' Library, 1874), 57–84 or the free verse translation of Mark McCloskey and Paul R. Murphy, *The Latin Poetry of George Herbert: A Bilingual Edition* (Athens, Ohio: Ohio University Press, 1965).

Three excellent articles on *Memoriae Matris Sacrum* are: E. Pearlman's "George Herbert's God," *English Literary Renaissance* 13 (1983): 88–112; Rhonda L. Blair's "George Herbert's Greek Poetry," *Philological Quarterly* 64:4 (1985): 573–84; and William Kerrigan's "Ritual Man: On the Outside of Herbert's Poetry," *Psychiatry* 48 (February, 1985): 68–82. For general overviews of George Herbert's Latin verse, see W. Hilton Kelliher, "The Latin Poetry of George Herbert," in *The Latin Poetry of English Poets,* ed. J. W. Binns (London: Routledge, 1974), 26–57; Herbert H. Huxley, "The Latin Poems of George Herbert (1593–1633)," in *Acta Conventus Neo-Latini Amstelodamensis: Proceedings of the Second International Congress of Neo-Latin Studies, Amsterdam 19–24 August 1973,* ed. P. Tuynman, G. C. Kuiper, and E. Kessler (Munich: Wilhelm Fink Verlag, 1979), 560–65; and Edmund Blunden, "George Herbert's Latin Poems," in *Essays and Studies by Members of the English Association* 19 (1934), 29–39; reprint London: Dawson, 1966.

2. With the exception of two public occasional poems, this is the only work George Herbert published during his lifetime, an index of the urgency of the situation.

A useful introduction to recent psychoanalytic theory on mourning and its application to Renaissance texts is G. W. Pigman III's *Grief and English Renaissance Elegy* (Cambridge: Cambridge University Press, 1985). Important discussions of the genres of mourning include George W. McClure's "The Art of Mourning: Autobiographical Writings on the Loss of a Son in Italian Humanist Thought (1400–1461)," *Renaissance Quarterly* 39:3 (1986): 440–75; Peter M. Sacks's *The English Elegy: Studies in the Genre from Spenser to Yeats* (Baltimore: Johns Hopkins University Press, 1985); Arnold Stein's *The House of Death: Messages from the English Renaissance* (Baltimore: Johns Hopkins University Press, 1986); O. B. Hardison's *The Enduring Monument: A Study of the Idea of Praise in Renaissance Literary Theory and Practice* (1962; reprint, Westport, Conn.: Greenwood, 1973); and Barbara Kiefer Lewalski's *Donne's Anniversaries and the Poetry of Praise: the Creation of a Symbolic Mode* (Princeton: Princeton University Press, 1973). Lewalski's book includes studies of Donne's sermons, including a discussion of Magdalen Herbert's funeral sermon, 201–05.

For socio-historical findings on death in the Renaissance, see Lawrence Stone, *The Family, Sex and Marriage in England 1500–1800* (London: Weidenfeld and Nicholson, 1977); and Philippe Aries, *Western Attitudes Towards Death: from the Middle Ages to the Present,* trans. Patricia M. Ranum (Baltimore: Johns Hopkins University Press, 1974).

John Bowlby's *Loss: Sadness and Depression* (New York: Basic Books, 1980), part of a three-volume study on attachment, separation, and loss, provides more clinical background.

3. See Pigman's introduction and 45–47. Pigman argues that literary elegy "represents a form of mourning" and that praise is a secondary characteristic, often a displacement of lament (5).

4. *Memoriae Matris Sacrum* is composed in a variety of classical meters, including elegiacs, but, in the broader sense, the entire sequence is elegiac in tone and occasion.

5. *The Life of Edward, First Lord Herbert of Cherbury,* begun c. 1643. I have used the edition of J. Shuttleworth (London: Oxford University Press, 1976). Izaak Walton, *The lives of Dr. John Donne, Sir Henry Wotton, Mr. Richard Hooker, Mr. George Herbert* (London: 1670). Walton's lives evolved throughout a long period of his life, as David Novarr demonstrates; the later editions are substantially revised.

6. I take the term "ventriloquism" from the work of Elizabeth Harvey, and particularly from page 117 of her article "Ventriloquizing Sappho: Ovid, Donne, and the Erotics of the Feminine Voice," *Criticism* 31:2 (1989): 115–138.

7.   Ah Mater, quo te deplorem fonte? Dolores
         quae guttae poterunt enumerare meos?
  Sicca meis lacrymis Thamesis vicina videtur,
         Virtutumque choro siccior ipse tuo.
  In flumen moerore nigrum si funderer ardens,
         Laudibus haud fierem sepia iusta tuis.
  Tantum istaec scribo gratus, ne tu mihi tantum
         Mater: & ista Dolor nunc tibi Metra parit.

8.   Thanks to Lauren Silberman for information on inkmaking.

9.   I use "ancestor" in the sense that Edward Herbert uses it in his autobiography. He classes fathers, grandfathers and great-grandfathers in this category, and lists only his brothers as the "children" of his parents. He is concerned entirely with the male line, and mentions women in each case as an afterthought (1, 8, and *passim* in the early pages).

I have discussed Latin as a "mother tongue" in two papers: "George Herbert's *Memoriae Matris Sacrum:* Grief and the 'Mother Tongue' " (Paper delivered at the Modern Language Association Convention, San Francisco; December 27, 1987); and " '*Semel scribo, perpetuo ut sileam*': The Choice of Latin for George Herbert's *Memoriae Matris Sacrum*" (Paper delivered at the Seventh International Congress of the International Association for Neo-Latin Studies, Toronto, August 12, 1988).

10.   Tu vero mater perpetim laudabere
    Nato delenti: literae hoc debent tibi
    Queis me educasti; sponte chartas illinunt
    Fructum laborum consecutae maximum
    Laudando Matrem, cum repugnant inscii.

11.   At tu qui inepte haec dicta censes filio,
    Nato parentis auferens Encomium,
    Abito, trunce, cum tuis pudoribus.
    Ergo ipse solum mutus atque excors ero

Strepente mundo tinnulis praeconiis?
Mihine matris urna clausa est unico,
Herbae exoletae, ros-marinus aridus?
Matrine linguam refero, solum ut mordeam?
Abito, barde. Quam pie istic sum impudens!

12.   Recent critical literature on Tudor/Stuart prescriptions of female silence and chastity is extensive and, by now, often cited. Three central texts are: Suzanne W. Hull, *Chaste, Silent and Obedient: English Books for Women, 1475–1640* (San Marino: Huntington Library, 1982); Margaret P. Hannay, ed., *Silent But for the Word: Tudor Women as Patrons, Translators, and Writers of Religious Works* (Kent, Ohio: Kent State University Press, 1985); and Constance Jordan, *Renaissance Feminism: Literary Texts and Political Models* (Ithaca: Cornell University Press, 1990).

Linda Woodbridge, in *Women and the English Renaissance: Literature and the Nature of Womankind, 1540–1620* (Urbana: University of Illinois Press, 1986) discusses the Renaissance formal controversy regarding the nature of women, which focused largely around issues of speech and chastity. Katherine Usher Henderson and Barbara F. McManus, in *Half Humankind: Contexts and Texts of the Controversy about Women in England, 1540–1640* (Urbana: University of Illinois Press, 1985) provide some of these texts, along with a long introduction. Elaine V. Beilin's *Redeeming Eve: Women Writers of the English Renaissance* (Princeton: Princeton University Press, 1987) addresses these issues in the context of individual women's lives and works. Two essays in *Rewriting the Renaissance: The Discourses of Sexual Difference in Early Modern Europe,* ed. Margaret W. Ferguson, Maureen Quilligan, and Nancy J. Vickers (Chicago: University of Chicago Press, 1986), address the matter of missing women in literature, silenced by their absence.

The (M)other Tongue: Essays in Feminist Psychoanalytic Interpretation, ed. Shirley Nelson Garner, Claire Kahane, and Madelon Sprengnether (Ithaca: Cornell University Press, 1985) examines related issues of tongue and phallus.

13.   " 'Let your death be my *Iliad*': Classical Allusion and Latin in George Herbert's *Memoriae Matris Sacrum.*" In *Reconsidering the Renaissance,* ed. Mario A. di Cesare. *Medieval & Renaissance Texts and Studies,* vol. 93. (Binghamton, New York, 1991).

14.   Horti, deliciae *Dominae,* marcescite tandem;
        Ornastis capulum, nec superesse licet.
Ecce decus vestrum spinis horrescit, acuta
        Cultricem revocans anxietate manum:
Terram & funus olent flores: Donimaeque cadaver
        Contiguas stirpes afflat, eaeque rosas.
In terram violae capite inclinantur opaco,
        Quaeque domus Dominae sit, gravitate docent.

All translations from *Memoriae Matris Sacrum* are my own. The Latin text is from Hutchinson's edition.

15.   Pallida materni Genii atque exanguis imago,
        In nebulas similesque tui res gaudia nunquid
        Mutata? & pro matre mihi phantasma dolosum
        Uberaque aerea hiscentem fallentia natum?
        Vae nubi pluvia gravidae, non lacte, measque

Ridenti lacrymas quibus unis concolor unda est.
Quin fuguias? mea non fuerat tam nubila Iuno,
Tam segnis facies aurorae nescia vernae,
Tam languens genitrix cineri supposta fugaci:

16.   In "Let your death be my *Iliad*," I discuss the ancestry of this *imago* in epic descents to the underworld but also in European folkloric accounts of revenants, the unquiet dead returned from the grave.

17.   Galene, frustra es, cur miserum premens
    Tot quaestionum fluctibus obruis,
      Arterias tractans micantes
        Corporea fluidaeque molis?
    Aegroto mentis: quam neque pixides
    Nec tarda possunt pharmaca consequi,
      Utrumque si praederis Indum,
        Ultra animus spatiatur exlex.
    Impos medendi, occidere si potes,
    Nec sic parentem ducar ad optimam:
      Ni sancte, uti mater, recedam,
        Morte magis viduabor illa.
    Quin cerne ut erres, incie, brachium
    Tentando sanum: si calet, aestuans,
      Ardore scribendi calescit,
        Mater inest saliente vena.
    Si totus infler, si tumeam crepax,
    Ne membra culpes, causa animo latet
      Qui parturit laudes parentis:
        Nec gravidis medicine tuta est.
    Irregularis nunc habitus mihi est:
    Non exigatur crasis ad alterum.
      Quod tu febrem censes, salubre est
        Atque animo medicatur unum.

18.   Biographical information suggests that his relation to his mother was an unusually close one, and other poems in this sequence point toward an unresolved oedipal attachment. The facts—that George's father died when he was three years old, a crucial age in terms of the resolution of oedipal conflicts, and that Magdalen Herbert married Sir John Danvers, a man in his twenties, when George was not quite sixteen—support this possibility.

19.   See, for instance, Sidney's first sonnet in "Astrophel and Stella": "Thus, great with child to speak, and helpless in my throes" (12).

20.   Susan Rubin Suleiman's essay, "Writing and Motherhood," in *The (M)other Tongue* (352–77) illuminates both the erasure of Magdalen Herbert and George's supplanting of her position as mother. She argues that traditional, and even revisionist, psychoanalytic theory considers the mother/child relationship exclusively from the child's point of view, and that writers are always conceived of as children, not parents (read "mothers"):

psychoanalytic theory invariably places the artist, man or woman, in the position of the child. Just as motherhood is ultimately the child's drama, so is artistic creation. In both cases the mother is the essential but silent Other, the mirror in whom the child searches for his own reflection, the body he seeks to appropriate. . . . A writer, says Roland Barthes, is "someone who plays with the body of his [her?] mother."   (356–57)

Lyrical Ballads and the Language of (Men) Feeling: Wordsworth Writing Women's Voices

Susan J. Wolfson

I: The Gender of Feeling

> *It was my wish . . . to show the manner in*
> *which such men cleave to the same ideas . . . to*
> *take care that words, which in their minds are*
> *impregnated with passion, should likewise*
> *convey passion to Readers who are not*
> *accustomed to sympathize with men feeling in*
> *that manner.*
>   —William Wordsworth, Note to "The
>   Thorn," *Lyrical Ballads,* 1800

In 1712, Pope sported in *The Rape of the Lock* with an epidemic of the vapors in which "Men prove with child, as powerful fancy works" (4.53). By the century's end, Wordsworth was proving in a more sober study how even "men . . . utterly destitute of fancy" (*LB* 288) may impregnate their very words, conceiving them as implicitly feminine vessels for a burgeoning passion. The crossover into feminine gender turns out to be not just the peculiar aberration of men like the superstitious speaker of "The Thorn"; it is an integral part of Wordsworth's own way with words in the poetics of "feeling." Of the poems he assembled for *Lyrical Ballads,* several are expressed in the voices of displaced, vagrant, distraught, abandoned, forsaken, and mad women, especially mothers. And several more feminize men of feeling. We hear of one man's affection, "if tears / Shed . . . / And hauntings from the infirmity of love, / Are aught of what makes up a mother's heart, / This old Man . . . / Was half a mother" to his grandsons ("The Brothers" 234–39), and of another's: "oftentimes / Old Michael, while [his son] was a babe in arms, / Had done him female service, not alone / For dalliance and delight, as is the use / Of Fathers, but with patient mind enforc'd / To acts of tenderness; and he had rock'd / His cradle with a woman's gentle hand" ("Michael" 162–68).

These last two sentimental cases occupy a poetic program whose overt concerns are more general than gendered: Wordsworth's Preface of 1800 speaks of "the essential passions of the heart," of "illustrat[ing] the manner in which *our* feelings and ideas are associated in a state of excitement," and of a poetry in which "the feeling . . . developed gives importance to the action" (*LB* 245, 247, 248, my italics). Yet if Michael's "exceeding . . . love" for Luke and the poet's own fervid love for nature in "Tintern Abbey" bear no stigma of unmanliness, Wordsworth sometimes felt, as he did later about "Tintern Abbey," that he had shown "passionate expression uttered incautiously" (*Letters, MY* 2:188). A reflex of caution appears in the concern of the 1800 Preface to define masculine feeling, perhaps because of the several new poems in this edition involving men of feeling: "The Brothers," " 'Tis said, that some have died for love," "She dwelt among th'untrodden ways," "A slumber did my spirit seal," "Strange fits of passion," "The Two April Mornings," "Michael." Describing "the fluxes and refluxes of the mind when agitated by the great and simple affections of our nature," Wordsworth not only specifies a "maternal passion" but also presents men of feeling in situations less idiosyncratic and less extreme in emotional flux and reflux. Theirs are "less impassioned feelings" (1802; *LB* 248n), not pathological but ideal and exemplary, showing "the strength of fraternal, or . . . more philosophically, of moral attachment" (248).

If they *are* passionate, such feeling is legitimized by extraordinary natural impressions, an urgency of parental affection, or the vulnerability of old age. Otherwise, there is a deprecation. The balladeer of "The Last of the Flock," noting "a healthy man, a man full grown / Weep in the public roads" (3–4), makes a point of saying how unusual and unsettling such a sight is, and he reports the weeper's own shame: "he saw me, and he turned aside, / As if he wished himself to hide. . . . 'Shame on me, Sir!' " (11–12, 17). Leonard of "The Brothers" is overcome "by feverish passion" (56) and when he weeps on learning of his brother's death, the village Priest (who does not recognize him) seems slightly put off by the spectacle: "If you weep, Sir, / To hear a stranger talking about strangers, / Heaven bless you when you are among your kindred!" (239–41). When, at the close of their conversation, Leonard again feels "tears rushing in," he, like the shepherd of "The Last of the Flock," turns away, later admitting a "weakness of his heart" at that moment (422, 446). Similar judgment issues from the narrator of "Michael": "Luke had a manly heart; but at these words / He sobb'd aloud" (367–68)—*but* implying the anomaly of this "spontaneous overflow of powerful feelings" (*LB* 246) to norms of manliness. Even as some of Wordsworth's poems present men capably feminized and ennobled in manliness by feeling, the qualifications that accrue across the field of *Lyrical Ballads* intimate a concern that a possession by feeling may effeminize men, eroding the social figure of manliness that depends on clear gender difference.

Noting such differentials, Anne Mellor and others have argued that Wordsworth "embraced the patriarchal construction of the female as nature—and its attendant association of femininity with passivity, emotionality, irrationality and corporeality."[1] And there have been a number of arguments that Romanticism empowered male expression with resources of sensibility previously deprecated as feminine. Alan Richardson cites the prototype of Steele's boyhood sympathy with his mother's grief—"There was a Dignity in her Grief . . . which . . . seized my very Soul, and has made Pity the Weakness of my heart ever since. . . . I imbibed Commiseration, Remorse and an unmanly Gentleness of Mind"—and sees in this site of "compassionate sensibility" a stirring of the Romantic poetics in which the masculine ego "covet[s] conventionally 'feminine' qualities to the point of striving to incorporate them."[2] Yet while he reads their able appropriation of "the feminine for male subjectivity" (21–22), the prefigurative passage he quotes from Steele shows the genesis of something inverse: a male subjectivity being eroded of its sense of manliness. The erosive effect of this incorporation is missed in accounts of Romantic poetry that equate it with "distinctive masculinist postures and premises," within which Wordsworth, for one, is said to gain "poetic identity" by "quest[ing] for masculine self-possession" and never questioning "how [such] identity sustains sexual and political hierarchies." "The aggressive male," so this story goes, "is inscribed in each of the lyrics and tales that has determined Wordsworth's status in our literary canon and his influence in our cultural history."[3]

I want to bring closer attention to fluxes and ruptures in Wordsworth's poetics of gender, showing how its inscriptions of masculinity inhabit texts that question, confuse, and destabilize the necessary differentials and hierarchies—and suggesting, by the presence of these complications in the poet whom some critics see as the epitome of appropriative and aggressive masculinity, the need for a more nuanced account of Romanticism and gender. Wordsworth's patriarchal constructions, I argue, contain an uneasy sense that "femininity" is not just female, but may claim men of feeling. In more than a few texts in *Lyrical Ballads,* as we shall see, the overflow of men's feelings is infused with strains of psychological aberrance and extravagance that threaten to subvert the rational capacities and self-possession with which Enlightenment discourse equates with manly character. There are, moreover, extravagances of women's feelings. Wordsworth's programmatic concern with "feeling" refracts in *Lyrical Ballads* into a fascination with its transgressive female voicing—the capacity of their voices to impregnate, even feminize, the bodies and words of men. If imagining female voices of feeling opens an exciting resource for a male poet of feeling, Wordsworth's texts report a disturbing apprehension: that a man writing the feminine may be discovering and engendering more complex involvements of gender than he first imagined.

II: The Gender of "The Poet"

In great poets there is an exquisite sensibility
both of soul and sense that sympathizes like
gossamer sea-moss with every movement of the
element in which it floats. . . . Wordsworth
shows less of this finer feminine fibre of
organization than one or two of his
contemporaries, notably Coleridge or Shelley;
. . . he was a masculine thinker.
                         —James Russell Lowell (1894)

Wordsworth's differentiations of "maternal passion" from "fraternal . . . attachment" and of Mad Mother from impassioned Poet are sensitized by a long-standing tradition of polarizing reason and passion as masculine and feminine, respectively.[4] What are the consequences for a poet who is a man of feeling? "Mr. Wordsworth, in . . . the Lyrical Ballads, gave considerable testimony of strong feeling and poetic powers, although like a histerical schoolgirl he had a knack of feeling about subjects with which feeling had no proper concern," sneered *Le Beau Monde* (2:138). The simile is continuous with Thomas Gisborne's *Inquiry into the Duties of the Female Sex,* to take a representative instance from earlier conduct literature, which defined the "native worth of the female character" by "the dispositions and feelings of the heart" and its "sympathising sensibility" (22–23). Wordsworth's Preface can't quite deflect such gendering. When the 1802 text presents "the Poet" as having a "more lively sensibility, more enthusiasm and tenderness . . . than are supposed to be common among mankind" (255), the intent is to ally him with ethics of social sympathy; but the differentiation from common mankind bears a potential differentiation into the feminine. And in the statement that this poet's purpose is to give "immediate pleasure" (257), readers could be reminded of ideals of female conduct: as Hannah More asserted in her immensely popular *Strictures on . . . Female Education* (1799), women have a "natural desire to please" (2:144).

No wonder, then, that notwithstanding Mackenzie's *The Man of Feeling* (1771) and the cult of sensibility it nurtured, men of feeling risked judgment as *un*manly, even effeminate and "histeric." Fordyce's *Sermons to Young Women* (6th edition, 1769), pauses in the midst of praising the influence of female conversation on the manners of men to explain that this does not mean that "men . . . will become feminine," only "that their sentiments and deportment will contract a grace" (1:23). Writing in 1796 for *The Watchman* (a journal for "Men of Letters" [5]), Coleridge genders his denigration of "Sensibility," calling it the delicate exercise of a "fine lady's nerves" as she reads and "weep[s] over the refined sorrows" of fictional characters and deeming it an agent of "effeminate and cowardly selfishness" (139). He regarded *Lyrical Ballads* as tuned to something other than a fine lady's nerves, of course, but his caution underscores the liabilities that may accrue to a poetics of feeling. He makes a point of calling "Tintern Abbey" a "manly reflection" (*BL* 1:79) and stresses the necessity of men writing in a "correct and manly" vein (2:64). He does his part in his own sonnet of sensibility itself, "To The Rev. W. L. Bowles," written in the same decade as *Lyrical Ballads.* Praise for the soothing "soft strains" of Bowles' poetry stresses its "manliest melancholy"—the aura masculinized by an emphatic superlative. The concern about gender and sensibility was critical not just for masculine poetics, it also mattered to women intent to reform female manners and enhance female moral authority. Wollstonecraft's *Vindication* derided the culture of sensibility as a debasement for men and women alike; although More had little praise for this tract, it is telling that she found common ground in her own long chapter in *Strictures* "On the Danger of an Ill-directed Sensibility," which also cautions young women to shun "feeling . . . indulged to the exclusion of reason" (2:128).

The poetics of *Lyrical Ballads,* advocating feeling over mere reason, were susceptible to this feminine stigma. Epic was the manly genre, not only presenting examples of manly conduct but its very production equated with manly powers of conception. Poets of lesser forms were not so securely gendered, and in the 1790s defenses seemed advisable. When William Taylor introduced his translations of Bürger in *The Monthly Magazine,* he pointed to the "manly" style and a host of related attributes, describing a poet "every where distinguished for manly senti- ment and force of style . . . extraordinary powers of language . . . hurrying vigour" (118). Wordsworth uses a similar rhetoric in the Preface to *Lyrical Ballads.* "Poets in general" are gendered as "a body of men" and "the Poet" is aligned with historically male professions: the "Man of Science, the Chemist and Mathematician . . . the Anatomist, the Botanist, of Mineralogist" (258–60). His Poet is, famously, "a man speaking to men," and he gives "pleasure" to his audience not as the female subordinate but "as a Man"; his task should not "be considered as a degradation" (255, 257–58). His style is "manly" (263), disdaining all things "idle and extravagant" (249)—the chief qualities of those "frantic novels" and "sickly and stupid" melodramas popular among women and idle men of sensibility. The Wordsworthian Poet writes "for men," as one who "thinks and feels in the spirit of the passions of men" and "express[es] himself as other men express themselves" (261).

Conscious of the teary eponym of *The Man of Feeling,* Wordsworth arms this Poet of feeling against suspicion of female weakness. Rejecting "unmanly despair" (257) and wedding feeling to potency, he insists that "all good poetry" is the work of "powerful feelings" (246) corresponding to and influenced by "powers" in the external world (249). These feelings are "forcibly communicated" in order "to excite rational sympathy"—sympathy, that is, with a masculine infusion (245). Adding to the Preface in 1802, he endows this feminine poetic with a transhistori- cal lineage and the universal authority of "natural" origination: "The earliest Poets of all nations generally wrote from passion excited by real events; they wrote naturally, and as men: feeling powerfully as they did, their language was daring" (314). Here, passion is no excess of sentiment, but a response to the epic dimension of the "real" in which the act of writing "as men" is aligned with the pace of history and infused with the force of nature itself. Feeling is harnessed to power, a source of inspiration fully in accord with masculine codes of heroic enterprise, and language itself is "daring."

It is a sign of ideological instability, however, that this rhetoric has such a strange fit with what several of the poems display. One disruption is the transgressive power of female passion and its influence, to the point of possession, over its male audience. Harry Gill is doomed to a chattering repetition of a woman's shivering complaint, and his balladeer's chattering verse seems similarly afflicted. And if Betty Foy, the Idiot Boy's mother, displays narrative incapacity—"oh saints! what is become of him?" (232)—the poet who speaks of her is almost too in tune: "Oh gentle muses! let me tell / But half of what to him befel" (349–50). Similarly, Martha Ray's mysteriously haunted cry—"Oh woe is me! oh misery!"—persists as a refrain of a ballad whose speaker verges on inarticulation—"I cannot tell; I wish I could"—despite his emphatically gendered protest, "as I am a man" (196), that there's a tale worth telling. This blurring of gender distinction under the influence of passion also resonates intertextually in *Lyrical Ballads,* wherein the trances of a Female Vagrant, the fervors of a Mad Mother, and the passion of a self-reflecting Poet all echo each other.

The song that begins, "Strange fits of passion," as this peculiarly tensed set of opening words may suggest, shows what is at stake for the figure of masculinity. Cast entirely within a monologic male subjectivity, the ballad concerns an imaginative errancy: its poet's nighttime ride to his beloved's cottage, towards which the moon, as if in rival approach, appeared to descend. As it "dropp'd" below the cottage roof, he recalls, he was seized by a fear of her death. The patent irrationality of this sensation is conceded by the heightened self-consciousness and the circumspect tone of the opening stanza:

> *Strange fits of passion I have known,*
> *And I will dare to tell,*
> *But in the lover's ear alone,*
> *What once to me befel. (1–4)*

Here is a man speaking to men, but with unease—invoking an idiom of heroic exploit for a domestic trauma, or perhaps ironizing the trauma with a mock heroic. It is not the idiom per se that makes his "language . . . daring" (Preface) but its admission of delusions that call into question the ethos of the heroic—namely, manly self-possession. Roland Barthes elucidates the risk: "In any man who utters the other's absence *something feminine* is declared," he proposes; the "man who waits and who suffers from his waiting is miraculously feminized. . . . feminized . . . because he is in love" (14).

Wordsworth gives his balladeer a rhetoric sensitive to this liability, half-disowning the passion it reports: this is a "strange" rather than familiar event; a "fit" rather than a habitual disorder; something that "befel," as if by external rather than internal agency. The poet offers himself as the site of a generic psychopathology, an affliction of all lovers, and he stresses this status by capitalizing "Lover" in his last stanza as he reads himself with knowing irony: "What fond and wayward thoughts will slide / Into a Lover's head—" (25–26). He would make light of it all, treating his anxiety as the fond, wayward tendency of any Lover. Mocking the ominously fatalistic tone of his initial "what once . . . befel," he now muses, "what . . . thoughts will slide," a kind of head-shaking about a comic predictability. Even his summary description of the moon as a "planet" ("When down behind the cottage roof / At once the planet droop'd" [23–24]) seems lightly coded with irony: deriving from the Greek word for "wanderer," "planet" winks at the psychic wandering with which the moon's motion has been invested.

Yet the invitation is nervously proffered. For all this poet's wit about the shaping fantasies of which the lunatic, the lover, and the poet are compact, his ballad does not defuse the obsession it glosses, and glosses over—namely, the passion of the rider who "bent [his] way" (7), "fix'd [his] eye" (9), and pressed forward, "hoof after hoof," in a motion that "never stopp'd" (21–22). This narrative itself is so mechanically, almost hypnotically, rehearsed as to leave uncertain even whether the poet, in retelling his fit, is also reexperiencing it—another strange fit of passion, this one self-induced by narration. The whole rehearsal converges on a revoicing of the first event of wayward thought, renewing its urgency: "O mercy!" to myself I cried, / "If Lucy should be dead!" (27–28). The plural "fits" and the past progressive "I have known" spell the psychic corollary to these motions, exposing a recurrent seething of the brain.[5]

This Lover's pathology finds its strongest verbal parallel in *Lyrical Ballads* not in the voice of another man but in Martha Ray ("The Thorn"): "to herself she cries." The effect for Wordsworth's reader is to see the Lover's potentially unmanly fit as a variation on the more tenacious forms of madness traced elsewhere in these pages: "that deranged state, in which from the increased sensibility the sufferer's attention is abruptly drawn off by every trifle, and in the same instant plucked back again by the one despotic thought, and bringing home with it, by the blending, *fusing* power of Imagination and Passion, the alien object to which it had been so abruptly diverted, no longer an alien but an ally and an inmate." This is Coleridge admiring the "expressive" pathos of the Mad Mother (*BL* 2:150), but his terms just as aptly—and tellingly for the question of gender in passion—interpret the state of increased sensibility from which the male lover's strange fits of passion issue.

Just as tellingly, these affinities compete in "Strange fits" with emphatic defenses. If Wordsworth shows a balladeer not quite convincing in his ironic self-reading, he also writes another strain for him consisting of *un*ironic intimations of accurate, creditable prophecy. We hear this at the very outset, where a simple reportorial past holds out a suggestion of radical historical closure: "When she I lov'd, was strong and gay / And like a rose in June" (5–6). Even the trite simile, "like a rose in June," is of uncertain import: does "in June" imply the later fate of such early flowers? How encoded is this narrative? The question matters, for on it depends the difference between the pathology of an hysterically rehearsed passion and the artistry of manipulating a reader's assent to a peculiar, but ultimately sensible discourse. It also bears on the account of the ride: is the poet's acceleration from "and" to "and" a sign of his hypnotic (re)possession or his design to lead his reader to, and thereby credit, a Lover's superstitious conclusion? Wordsworth experimented with amplifying this latter hint of credit—pointedly, by using and discrediting a woman's voice. In a subsequently canceled final stanza, he had the balladeer report Lucy's gentle mockery of his passionate association of ideas in a state of excitement, and then ominously imply her error:

> *I told her this: her laughter light*
> *Is ringing in my ears:*
> *And when I think upon that night*
> *My eyes are dim with tears.   (Poetical Works 2:29)*

The irony of this stanza, different from the balladeer's ironic self-regard, is tragic. In the short run, it is he who seems foolish: what he confesses in the lover's ear alone was at first a female mockery in *his* ears. But in the long run, it is he who rings the last word, if not the last laugh: his poem is implicitly her epitaph. Gendering the voice of common sense as feminine, Wordsworth then radically deauthorizes it with the confirmation of the Lover's anxiety. The version of the ballad he published subsumes this plot, canceling the woman's voice and representing her only as the silent object of male erotic discourse. Even so, the flux of revision reveals the informing issue: how to define a rational base to a poet's fit of passion.

III: The Passions of Forsaken Women

The affinity of this fit of passion to the passions of the several forsaken women of *Lyrical Ballads* destabilizes traditional hierarchies and discriminations of gender. "The Female Vagrant" poses another transgressive text. Its title bodes gender-specificity, but in its Wordsworthian intertext, its verses turn out to dramatize not so much a *female* malady as a displacement into female experience of a distress that attenuates gender difference. Its story of a "wanderer" whose "poor heart" has "lost all its fortitude" (262–64) and is burdened by a "perpetual weight" on the "spirit" (267–70) evokes the dark passages of Wordsworth's autobiographical writing in the 1790s, "Tintern Abbey" and *The Prelude*. "The Female Vagrant," as Paul Sheats remarks, is Wordsworth's "first history of an individual mind" (87).

　　Feminizing this history is critical, for if, as even "The Last of the Flock" suggests, vagrancy in other than old men (e.g. the Old Cumberland Beggar) risks negative judgment, a "female" vagrant gives Wordsworth a voice of loss and displacement without courting questions about unmanly failing. There is a further advantage in this gendering: female distress evokes a code of chivalry and its hierarchy of capable male power and female dependency. This gendering of emotional plight and social dislocation, again with a chivalric cast, inflects "The Complaint of a forsaken Indian Woman." A complaint is a genre that men as well as women may voice, but Wordsworth's gendering is insistent—not only in his title but also in the headnote that describes a tribal policy of abandoning those too weak to continue migratory treks: although "it is unnecessary to add that the females are equally, or still more, exposed to the same fate" (*LB* 108), he indulged the addition. In the poem itself, moreover, we find that the forsaken woman is a new mother (31–33). Aside from the odd locution of the headnote, the gendering of her plight is nowhere stated, but Wordsworth implies its force in the way he makes her repeated efforts to dissociate herself from her body—"Before I see another day, / Oh let my body die away!"—coincide with a tribal view of women's bodies as interchangeable: "My child! they gave thee to another, / A woman who was not thy mother. . . . from my arms my babe they took" (31–33). Her grief focuses less on being "forsaken" herself than on imagining her motherless child as "poor" and "forsaken" (65).

Wordsworth enhances the poignancy of her situation by showing its exclusion of any chivalric ethic, which, he implies through the woman's lament, ought to claim a universal ground in human consciousness:

> *When from my arms my babe they took*
> *On me how strangely did he look!*
> *Through his whole body something ran,*
> *A most strange something did I see;*
> *—As if he strove to be a man,*
> *That he might pull the sledge for me.*
> *And then he stretched his arms, how wild*
> *Oh mercy! like a little child.   (32–40)*

For English readers, this fantasy idealizes what is palpably absent: a social system of beneficent male power and female dependency. Wordsworth heightens the scandal of this absence as the mother hallucinates, through desire, the alternative ethic of masculine rescue of female distress—one in which the boy born of her body rescues her from her body. So forceful is the visionary "as if" that casts the babe as a man that his actual helplessness recedes into mere simile, "like a little child."

The concentration of both social system and personal despair on the plight of a woman's body defines the passion of this poem, as well as many others in the volume. Such embodiments urge us to rethink Robert Langbaum's argument that in "The Complaint" and in "The Affliction of Margaret" the speakers are "are simply spoke*smen* for an emotion" (72, my italics). His casual re- or ungendering of these female speakers calls attention to what is not simple, even in apparently monologic lyrics such as these, for Wordsworth has gendered their social contexts in ways that impose on a reader's, if not the speaker's, attention. This gendering is crucial to the interest of passion in "The Mad Mother," whose eponym is also forsaken, but raving rather than complaining, and still in possession of her baby boy. Despite this companion, her madness is more radically isolating than even the Indian Woman's, and as such produces a poetic sensationalism that marginalizes issues of social justice: the embodiment of madness in motherhood, as Words-worth's Preface makes clear, is what charges this poem with interest. His balladeer names his subject as female nine times in his first stanza before submerging the pathos of her social plight in the alarming voice of her passion. This passion is impressive not just for the madness it produces in her, but for its grievance of male culpability. Within this turmoil, in fact, there is a potential male target, her son—at once the sole counter-influence of his mother's madness and the stimulus for its perpetuation. He is utterly possessed by her:

> *"Sweet babe! they say that I am mad,*
> *But nay, my heart is far too glad;*
> *And I am happy when I sing*
> *Full many a sad and doleful thing:*
> *Then, lovely baby, do not fear!*
> *I pray thee have no fear of me . . .   (11–15)*

Her assertion of gladness against the social judgment, "mad," might evince happy self-possession, were not the claim so contradicted by the theme of her song and the danger she poses to the well-being of her boy. She means her cooing lullaby to countermand his fear, but her negative exhortations expose it:

> *Oh! love me, love me, little boy!*
> *Thou art thy mother's only joy;*
> *And do not dread the waves below,*
> *When o'er the sea-rock's edge we go.   (41–44)*

This boy is imperiled not only by his mother's passion but also by his gender: she addresses him with erotic dependency ("Oh love me, love me . . . Thou art [my] only joy"), a passion whose voice blurs frequently into grievance against the absent father in ways that threaten their "little boy of flesh and blood" (28) with the burden of recrimination. Even as her passion calms with his suckling, his very presence at her breast evokes the renegade: "Thy father cares not for my breast, / 'Tis thine, sweet baby" (61–62). The chiasmus of this substitution (father-breast-baby) collapses into delusional superimposition: "What wicked looks are those I see / Alas! alas! that look so wild, / It never, never came from me" (86–88).

The threat latent in this mother's passion, retribution against a world of cruel fathers, is realized through the agency of a woman's voice in *Goody Blake, and Harry Gill,* a poem whose title-figures give a gender to social privation and social cruelty, respectively. The insinuation of an effective curse—the unnatural supernaturalism that seems to sponsor retribution for the woman—stages radical consequences for the self-possession of male identity and its links to male society. The ballad is framed as both a sensational and a cautionary tale. Subtitled "A True Story," described in the 1798 Advertisement as "founded on a well-authenticated fact" in the public domain, represented in the Preface as "a *fact*" (*LB* 8, 267), it was based on an account in Erasmus Darwin's *Zoönomia; or, the Laws of Organic Life* (2:359), a study of delusional illness. But both he and Wordsworth mediate the facts through equivocal moral perspectives. Darwin notes the obsessive and gratuitous cruelty of a young farmer's intent to "convict" the "thief": "He lay many cold hours under a haystack . . . then springing from his concealment, he seized his prey with violent threats." Yet he also demonizes the thief, representing her as "an old woman, like a witch in a play," with access to supernatural power: "she kneeled upon her bottle of sticks, and raising her arms to heaven beneath the bright moon then at the full, spoke to the farmer already shivering with cold, 'Heaven grant, that thou never mayest know again the blessing to be warm.' He complained of cold all the next day." Wordsworth's balladeer shapes these events shape into a moral tale: he converts the terms of temperature, "cold" and "warm," from psychosomatics into a language of social compassion; he sympathetically describes Goody as "poor" and "old"; and he grants her speech the moral authority of a prayer to the "God that is the judge of all."[6]

Yet this frame of sympathy and its hints of divine corroboration fade as soon as Goody speaks. After her prayer, her social plight drops out of the poem, and the focus shifts to Harry. While Wordsworth may mean to show him caught in the trap of his own imagination (like other men listening to extravagant female voices[7]), he still invests Goody's words with something of the alien, supernatural power of Darwin's "witch," especially in their apparent effect in instantaneously producing her bodily affliction in Harry:

> She pray'd, her wither'd hand uprearing,
> While Harry held her by the arm,
> "God! who art never out of hearing,
> "O may he never more be warm!"
> The cold, cold moon above her head,
> Thus on her knees did Goody pray,
> Young Harry heard what she had said,
> And icy-cold he turned away.   (97–104)

The contradictory bearings of "wither'd" epitomize Wordsworth's equivocation, evoking both the pathos of bodily deprivation and the iconography of the witch. At least two male reviewers were provoked by the poem's shift from its initial sympathy for a frail female body to a pagan rite supervised by the cold moon and concentrated on the unsettling power of a female voice. Southey wondered whether the ballad was "promot[ing] the popular superstition of witchcraft" (200), and Dr. Burney, although conceding that "distress from poverty and want is admirably described," still protested, "are we to imagine that Harry was bewitched by Goody Blake?" (206–07). He was even moved to make a kind of backhanded case for Harry's rights: "If all the poor are to help, and supply their wants from the possessions of their neighbours, what imaginary wants and real anarchy would it not create?"

The threat to social integrity by the theft of male property that Burney intuited has a more immediate impact in the ballad itself: a man is supernaturally possessed by a woman's pain. Here, Wordsworth even goes Darwin one better, elaborating the psychopathology to make it seem that Goody's revenge takes possession not just of Harry's body but his very voice:

> *No word to any man he utters,*
> *A bed or up, to young or old;*
> *But ever to himself he mutters,*
> *"Poor Harry Gill is very cold."*   *(121–24)*

Here is yet another man left in passion speaking only "to himself." It is a fate that in the world of *Lyrical Ballads* at once exiles him from male rhetorical culture and aligns him with socially marginalized females: as Adela Pinch nicely argues, we witness the "painful disintegration of the masculine subject into a chattering old woman" (842). The implication for masculine poetics of Harry's lapse from the circuit of men speaking to men is symbolically registered in the voice Wordsworth writes for his balladeer. He begins and ends with an onomatopoeia of Harry's accursed chattering:

> *Oh! what's the matter what's the matter?*
> *What is't that ails young Harry Gill?*
> *That evermore his teeth they chatter,*
> *Chatter, chatter, chatter still;*
>
> . . .
>
> *ever to himself he mutters*
>
> . . .
>
> *His teeth they chatter, chatter still.*   *(1–4; 123, 126)*

Goody's voice not only affects Harry's body and voice, it ultimately claims the poem's body and voice: her prayer to a God who is "never out of hearing" (99) at once supplies the answer to the ballad's opening question and is ever heard in its rhythms and rhymes. At the close, Harry even echoes her speech act, "pray," to exhort the male rural community: "Now think, ye farmers all, I pray, / Of Goody Blake and Harry Gill" (102–3). Patrocinio Schweickart has suggested that the "woman in the text" has a capacity to convert "the text into a woman, and the circulation of this text/woman becomes the central ritual that establishes the bond between the author and his male readers" (41). If so, *Goody Blake, and Harry Gill* establishes this bond with a difference. In Wordsworth's staging, the men who hear and hear of Goody Blake do not so much confirm masculine priority in the exchange of her story, but find themselves, instead, figuratively feminized by the eerie capacity of this "text/woman" to take possession of their voices and imagination.

IV: "As I Am a Man": "The Thorn"

Uncontrolled vocal excesses (laughing, crying, ranting) or disorders in which speech is possessed by other voices, is incoherent, inarticulate, or blocked altogether, are frequently read as symptoms of hysteria. Both the etymology of "hysteria" (named by Hippocrates as a disease of the womb) and its Englishing into "the mother" report the original gendering of the malady and account for its emergence as a synecdoche of sexual difference.[8] "For centuries," reports Mark Micale, "hysteria has served as a dramatic medical metaphor for everything that men found mysterious or unmanageable in the opposite sex. The wildly shifting physical symptomology of the sickness was thought to mirror the volatile and unpredictable nature of women. The exaggerated emotionality of the hysterical woman was understood as a pathological intensification of natural feminine sensiblity" (320). This feminizing was clearly a defense, however, for well before Good's *Study of Medicine* admitted in 1822 that "men may labour under the hysteric passion as well as women" (3:401), literary tradition and popular discourse had recognized as much. Hysteria was not only a wandering mother within the female body but also erratic behavior in men, particularly in crises of self-definition and the sustaining hierarchies.[9] Thus, Shakespeare has King Lear, sensing an erosion of both his paternal and royal authority, cry out, "O! how this mother swells up toward my heart; / *Hysterica passio!* down, thou climbing sorrow! / Thy element's below" (2.4.54–56). His anguished realization is that passion may invade masculine identity with what should be subordinate and female: emotion, weakness, incapacity.[10] Wordsworth's Harry Gill, echoing the dispossessed son in the same play ("Poor Tom's a-cold" [3.4.144, and so on]), finds his speech and body usurped by the condition of the woman whom he had abused. That some readers interpreted this as bewitchment further blurs distinction of gender, for in diagnostic discourse from the Middle Ages to the seventeenth century, the symptoms were not only not sex-differentiated but the language of report was the same as that for hysteria.[11]

Not just an isolated spectacle, hysteria is also a dangerous contagion. "As she laughed I was aware of becoming involved in her laughter and being part of it. . . . I was drawn in by short gasps, inhaled at each momentary recovery, lost finally in the dark caverns of her throat, bruised by the ripple of unseen muscles," writes Eliot in "Hysteria." In English letters, there are numerous cases of "hysteria" being used not just to name female ailments but to name and stigmatize male behavior. Coleridge praises men who are able, in the midst of political crisis, to "feel with reason, and to reason with feeling" over those "men, whose delicate religion is frightened into hysterics by . . . transient babble.[12] It is significant to the nervous tracks of feeling in *Lyrical Ballads* that poets especially were suspected of this delicacy. The "wayward Queen" in *The Rape of the Lock* who is the "Parent of Vapours and of female wit" also has power to "give th'hysteric or poetic fit" (4.58–60), the "or" implying equivalence. No wonder that in 1817, Coleridge would welcome the opportunity to distinguish the "legitimate language of poetic fervor self-impassioned" from "the madness prepense of Pseudo-poesy, or the startling *hysteric* of weakness over-exerting itself, which bursts on the unprepared reader in sundry odes and apostrophes" to be found in popular anthologies and magazines (*BL* 2:84–85).

Testing the line between legitimate fervor and pseudo-poetic hysterics, Wordsworth, more than once in *Lyrical Ballads,* represents male imaginations captive to the spectacle, and sometimes specter, of female hysteria. "The Thorn" is his most probing study, spoken by a narrator whose fascination with the voice of female suffering exposes a perilous transgressiveness: within his report, a woman named "Martha Ray" figures not only as a distraught mother but also as a generator of disturbance in his own imagination. Uneasily naming her as the source of his passion, he enacts classic female hysterics: blocked speech—"I cannot tell; I wish I could" (89; cf. 105–6, 111, 155–56, 214, 243), and possession by other voices—his fixated repetition of her cry, "Oh woe is me! Oh misery!" (65; cf. 76, 201, 209, 253). Even his notorious garrulity, as Coleridge's sneer at frightened babble indicates, suggests hysteria. Passion, remarks Barthes, is always drawn into "that region of hysteria where language is both *too much* and too little" (99, his italics). Wordsworth's lengthy note to the poem (*LB* 288–89) brings in further feminizing tropes for such men of feeling. He tells us that "words . . . in their minds are impregnated with passion," as if turned into vessels analogous to a female body and bearing a similar reproductive power, able to "convey passion to Readers." Byron was more direct, snidely comparing this species of male impregnation to the hysterical pregnancy of Joanna Southcott, who claimed to have conceived a second messiah.[13] That she was able to convince a considerable public is not beside the point: the syntax of impregnation in Wordsworth's Note blurs the origin of passion, suggesting his awareness of how its turns are potentially and potently transgressive, moving from speaker to listener, teller to hearer, poet to reader.[14] In the hisitory hinted at by the balladeer, passion is originally Martha Ray's; in the ballad's text, it is all that can be heard in her voice; in the Note, it is the term defining both the speaker's imagination and what he communicates to his audience. It is also what the poet hopes to convey to his readers and what, over the course of the Note, is disseminated as the definition of poetry itself: "Poetry is passion," a kind of expression wherein words are "not only symbols of the passion, but . . . are of themselves part of the passion."

Wordsworth's sense of how words bear passion both semantically and physically is the reciprocal of Foucault's analysis of the passionate body as a place where "the soul and the body are in a perpetual metaphorical relation in which qualities have no need to be communicated because they are already common to both" (88)—and, as Wordsworth's poetics suggest, holding a logic incommunicable to others, its expressive spell notwithstanding. His Note posits this as common knowledge: "every man must know that an attempt is rarely made to communicate impassioned feelings without something of an accompanying consciousness of the inadequateness of our own powers, or the deficiencies of language." Such density of feeling, Foucault goes on to argue, may convey passion into madness, an excess that ruptures the unity of body and soul (88–89). In "The Thorn," Wordsworth presents a balladeer haunted by this threat, especially its symptom of incommunicability, and who resorts to defenses supplied by gender difference: it is Martha Ray who is deranged, not he; she speaks "to herself," he to others. But the Note tells another story: Wordsworth's remark that a "Speaker will cling to the same words, or words of the same character" in "a craving in the mind" to "communicate its feelings" gets demonstrated in "The Thorn" both by a man's narration and by the woman's cries on which he fixates. He is talky and she is spare, but the urgencies are similar. Indeed, the most radical effect of this ballad may be to expose the instability of gender as a term for securing difference.

Because her cry exists only in his report, Stephen Parrish made the ground-breaking argument that "The Thorn" is not "about a woman" or "maternal passion" but is, in the present tense of its dramatic monologue, "about a man (and a tree)" (99–101). Yet even within this monology, we might ask why a woman is seen in (the) place of a tree—in effect, gendering "the spot" that marks the narrator's trauma, by calling up (or, as Parrish proposes, inventing) a specter of female causality. This gendering, in fact, was part of Wordsworth's inspiration. Having seen "on a stormy day, a thorn which I had often passed in calm and bright weather without noticing it," he recalls, "I said to myself, 'Cannot I by some invention do as much to make this Thorn permanently an impressive object as the storm has made it to my eyes at this moment?' " (*PW* 2:511). The invention is a double gendering: a balladeer who protests his integrity "as a man" that he has seen a "wretched," "poor," "unhappy" woman (63, 68, 81, 101) at a spot near "the mountain-path." He gradually introduces "her name" and "her tale," but well before, he is busy gendering "the spot": it has a little hill covered by a "mossy network . . . As if by hand of lady fair, / The work had woven been" (40–42)—a fantasy of the feminine soon converted into a matter of fact:

> . . . *oft there sits, between the heap*
> *That's like an infant's grave in size,*
> *And that same pond of which I spoke,*
> *A woman in a scarlet cloak,*
> *And to herself she cries,*
> *"Oh misery! oh misery!"*   *(60–65)*

This seems objective reportage, a voice of historical certainty. Urged on by an insistent questioner ("why sits she beside the thorn . . . wherefore does she cry . . . wherefore? wherefore? . . . wherefore to the mountain-top? . . . what's the thorn?

and what's the pond? . . . what's the hill of moss to her?" [VIII, X, XX]), the speaker soon issues a tale about a woman made mad by a false lover, illicit pregnancy, and perhaps infanticide.

Wordsworth's poetics, however, query this story and expose its suspect manipulation of gender. In the discursive structure of "The Thorn," the balladeer's report of female pathology and his encounter with its misery precedes, as if to pre-read, his disclosure of another event, one bearing on his manly self-esteem:

> *When to this country first I came,*
> *Ere I had heard of Martha's name,*
> *I climbed the mountain's height:*
> *A storm came on, and I could see*
> *No object higher than my knee.*

> XVIII
> *'Twas mist and rain, and storm and rain,*
> *No screen, no fence could I discover,*
> *And then the wind! in faith, it was*
> *A wind full ten times over.*
> *I looked around, I thought I saw*
> *A jutting crag, and off I ran,*
> *Head-foremost, through the driving rain,*
> *The shelter of the crag to gain,*
> *And, as I am a man,*
> *Instead of jutting crag, I found*
> *A woman seated on the ground.*

> XIX
> *I did not speak—I saw her face,*
> *Her face it was enough for me;*
> *I turned about and heard her cry,*
> *"O misery! O misery!"*
> *And there she sits . . .   (183–203)*

By introducing this episode only after he has told of Martha Ray's fixation on the spot, the balladeer implies his accidental witnessing of her obsessive behavior—a stance he bolsters with a rhetoric of logical process ("For . . ."; 180–81) and legal oath ("I will be sworn is true"). Yet, as Parrish argues, Wordsworth's poetics pose a different logic of cause and effect, one that questions whether this encounter has any "existence outside the narrator's imagination": "When a credulous old seaman catches sight in a storm of a suggestively-shaped tree hung with moss and later crams his head with village gossip, then his imagination can turn the tree into a woman, the brightly-colored moss into her scarlet cloak, and the creaking of the branches into her plaintive cry" (100–1; 105). What is intriguing about this *post hoc ergo propter hoc* is its correlation to the rhetorical inversion, *hysteron proteron,* a logical feint whose etymology is wound up with that of the feminine-gendered psychosomatic disorder, *hysteria.*[15] If this linkage seems too canny, or uncanny, we don't need lexical history to read the anxiety about manhood agitating the balladeer's recollection of his panic on the mountain. His protest, "as I am a man" (the first and only event of this masculine noun in the entire poem), spells a need to affirm what may have been uncertain during the storm. Elaine Showalter has noted how signs of male hysteria in the Greeat War, described as "shell shock," were related to crises wrought by "social expectations of the masculine role in war." Wordsworth's balladeer, defined minimally but significantly by the masculine role of sea captain, confronts a similar, if more private, crisis: it is one that, like the battlefield, presses codes of masculinity into hysterical conflict: "Placed in intolerable circumstances of stress, and expected to react with unnatural 'courage,' " Showalter argues, "thousands of soldiers reacted instead with the symptoms of hysteria" (171). "Shell shock" was a diagnosis valuable precisely for its "power to provide a masculine-sounding substitute for the effeminate associations of 'hysteria' and to disguise the troubling parallels between male war neurosis and . . . female nervous disorders" (172).

Wordsworth anticipates and plays out a local phase of this cultural drama in the gendering that subtends the narrative of "The Thorn." Having his balladeer confess to an hysterical episode of blocked speech ("I did not speak"), he shows him producing, after the fact, a female voice and presence as the cause—"I saw her . . . and heard her cry." At the same time, he exposes the balladeer's plot of difference—"I" and "her"—to a network of affinities. If the balladeer represents the woman as a figure of radical interiority—ever crying "to herself" (64, 75) in syllables that verge on referential opacity and pure expressiveness—Wordsworth's text implies that the balladeer, too, may be babbling only to himself, replaying an internal dialogue of question and reply against the threat of inarticulation: "I cannot tell; I wish I could."[16] Though cast as Martha Ray's pathology, the dialogue of the mind with itself is, in the intertext of *Lyrical Ballads,* also a male affliction, including the speakers of "The Thorn" and "Strange fits" ("to myself I cried") as well as Harry Gill, who is left muttering "to himself." In such interiority, all voices are one. "The Thorn" concludes with the woman's voice inside the balladeer's:

> And this I know, full many a time,
> When she was on the mountain high,
> By day, and in the silent night,
> When all the stars shone clear and bright,
> That I have heard her cry,
> "Oh misery! oh misery!
> "O woe is me! oh misery!"   (247–53)

Now claiming to have heard her not once but "full many a time," the balladeer's imagination seems not only inspired by but possessed by this spectral woman's voice: her repetition has become his. "The Mad Mother" represents a similar confluence but with an intriguing difference: whereas the text of "The Thorn" always marks Martha Ray's cries in quotation marks, the record of the Mad

Mother's voice does not close quotation at the end of the ballad, yielding a sense of its poet's inability to distance himself from the spell of the song that he rehearses. He may have so absorbed her voice and sensibility into his own that he can no longer contain and punctuate it as other.[17]

In these poetics of confusion, Wordsworth's casting the "feminine" as "other" recoils with resonance in the masculine self. All these male speakers voice a passion whose source they mean to mark as female but whose repetition has such impressive power as to obscure a distinctly female origin. Wordsworth is aware of this tendency in "the Poet" who conceives these speakers: not only does he have a "disposition to be affected more than other men by absent things as if they were present; an ability of conjuring," he also has the capacity to "bring his feelings near to those of the persons whose feelings he describes, nay, for short spaces of time perhaps, to let himself slip into an entire delusion, and even confound and identify his own feelings with theirs" (1802 Preface; *LB* 256). There are two ways to manage such slips. One is to reimpose distinction and difference: thus, Wordsworth's remarks both in 1798 and 1800 that "The Thorn" is "not supposed to be spoken in the author's own person" but in "the character" of a "narrator," which "will sufficiently shew itself in the course of the story" (8; cf. 288). The other is to concede certain binds of imagination and discursive tendency and plead for general excuse: thus his concern that his "language may frequently have suffered from those arbitrary connections of feelings and ideas with particular words, from which no man can altogether protect himself" (268).

Wordsworth's dilemma compels him to seek the authority of literary tradition for one such linguistic habit: repetition. This is the "Song of Deborah" (Judges 5), to which he refers briefly in his Note. Anyone who takes his cue and does consult "the whole of that tumultuous and wonderful Poem" will discover an interesting text of women's passions and women's voices. Sung by the prophet-judge, Deborah, and the victorious Israeli general, Barak, the "Song" recounts a national liberation: Barak, encouraged by Deborah's prophecy of enemy chariots balked by a timely flood, gathers an army against the Canaanites, slaying all but the leader Sisera, who flees, seeking refuge in the tent of Jael, the wife of a Hebrew ally. She feeds him milk and honey, then drives a tent nail through his head. It is significant that the three passages cited by Wordsworth in his Note as examples of repetition are also instances of strong female passion. The first, "Awake, awake, Deborah! awake, awake, utter a song!" (5), exhorts a celebration of the victory she had foretold. The second, on the murder of Sisera, declares Jael's supremacy and his fall: "At her feet he bowed, he fell, he lay down: at her feet he bowed, he fell: where he bowed, there he fell down dead" (27). And the third, half in sympathy, half gloatingly, renders the anguished voice of his mother: "Why is his chariot *so* long in coming? why tarry the wheels of his chariots?" (28). Together, these passages unearth a Wordsworthian interest in female passion as something other than private and pathological: "a mother in Israel" speaks as prophet and historian; the heroic action of another woman secures national liberation; and the song that honors them both tests a sympathy that transcends distinctions of ally and foe. If these implications remain buried in "The Thorn" itself, their latency in the Note suggests their import: the voices of female passion summoned as a resource for male balladeers also harbor a potential for disrupting this purchase, disclosing the feminine as a source of cultural authority and political action.[18]

V: The Gender of Naming

*Of all the men I ever knew, Wordsworth has
the least femininity in his mind. He is all man.*
—Coleridge (1828)

Lyrical Ballads concludes in a masculine domain. The last poem in the 1800 edition is "Michael": it is told by a man speaking to men and boys (23–27), and it concerns a "Son and a Father" (99) ("This Son . . . more dear" to the father than "his Help-mate" [149–50]), their "patrimonial fields" (234), their "Forefathers" (378), a bond to a "Brother's Son" (221), and a structure that serves as an "emblem of the life [their] Fathers lived" (420). Just before this summary fable of masculine culture is a subset called *Poems on the Naming of Places,* evoking an Adamic privilege of naming. But the promise is only ambiguously realized, thwarted by ironies that the very act of naming solicits. For all the concern with names, none of the poems is named (two bear inscriptions that refer half privately to women with a share in the place-names). Some of the most disruptive ironies, moreover, are cast in the agency of women's voices.

Two poems of this group, the one that begins "There is an Eminence" and "To Joanna," pose such peculiar contests between the poet's act of naming and the staging of a woman's reading of the poet that the gender of authority itself becomes an issue. In the former, a woman names a place for a man, the poet in fact. This may seem a liberal reciprocity of privilege, but the nervous risk is evident in the poem's design to contain her authority even as it displays her rationale. For one, the poet seems to usurp her name by beginning with his own description of the place in terms that personify with patent tendency: "There is an Eminence" (1), a "Cliff, so high . . . and so distant in its height" (5–6) that "the meteors make of it a favorite haunt" and "the star of Jove, so beautiful and large / In the mid heav'ns, is never half so fair / As when he shines above it" (9–12). The masculine companioned star of Jove clarifies what is already evident: this Eminence is a sovereign, remote masculine place—aloof, impressive, inaccessible. The clarity is crucial, for the effect is to depreciate the authority of female place-naming by thoroughly anticipating it. The poet's description of the Eminence is so knowingly loaded with self-reference that the woman's authority in having "said, this lonesome Peak shall bear my Name" seems secondary to that of the poem itself. Her name may be the poem's "point," but it seems redundant, anticlimactic.

Moreover, in the process of usurping, or making redundant, her name, the poem schemes to challenge and to supersede her authority. Not only does its text refuse to record her place-name, but its poet comes gradually, almost plaintively, to contest it:

> 'Tis in truth
> The loneliest place we have among the clouds.
> And She who dwells with me, whom I have lov'd
> With such communion, that no place on earth
> Can ever be a solitude to me,
> Hath said, this lonesome Peak shall bear my Name.   (12–17)

The poet's array of plural pronouns ("our hills," "Our Orchard-seat," "this Cliff . . . Above us," "our hearts") to mark a shared life, shared perspectives, and shared affections, states his grievance. It is only in the sentence about her naming that singulars appear—"And She who dwells with me, whom I have lov'd"—and even this syntax spells the claim of social affection, a poetic design against her singularizing name.

Yet in this contest of authority, larger balances of irony prove difficult to assess. Is the woman's place-naming exposed as error by the man's claim? Or does Wordsworth display the masculine poet in the perspective of irony, showing an egotism resisting female insight? Or does he show the poet himself disturbed by the disparity? As David Simpson remarks, the poem's "double vision" seems "projected to the point of schizophrenia" (214)—and pointedly, its interpretive crux is its quiet antagonism between the authority of the woman's voice and the protest that the poet addresses to his reader in her absence. The contest is more overt and the ironies more ambiguous in "'To Joanna," though the poem is framed as an affectionate letter. Its core event is an eruption of Joanna's voice that not only embarrassed the poet but seemed to receive uncanny amplification from nature.

Some emphatic preliminary frames suggest the unsettling effect, for they too palpably impose containments. First, the rhetoric of a letter necessarily reduces Joanna to absence and silence. The letter beings, moreover, by addressing her in a way that implies that her sympathies are other than the "kind" binding the poet and his circle; under the cover of affection, it quietly solicits his other audience, the reader, to view of her as alien.[19] This design is reinforced by a second preliminary, a report of the Vicar's greeting: "How fares Joanna, that wild-hearted Maid! / And when will she return to us?" (23–24). Within the community, the poet implies, Joanna is a problematic other, seeming to need government by "us"—Grasmere, but more specifically, by its two patriarchs, the Vicar of "grave looks" and the engraving poet himself, who "like a Runic Priest" is busy "chisel[ing] out / Some uncouth name upon the native rock" (28–30)—which turns out to be "Joanna's" (83), the origin of the place-name "Joanna's Rock."

That the story of this naming waits for thirty-eight lines suggests the importance of this prelude of men talking and writing. For what their voices preface, we discover, is an account of female vocal power, Joanna's wild-hearted laughter at the poet and its raucous echo throughout the hills. The occasion was the poet's rapture, one day while walking with her, at the beauty of the season: "I . . . stopp'd short," he recalls,

> *And trac'd the lofty barrier with my eye*
> *From base to summit; such delight I found*
> *To note in shrub and tree, in stone and flower,*
> *That intermixture of delicious hues,*
> *Along so vast a surface, all at once,*
> *In one impression, by connecting force*
> *Of their own beauty, imaged in the heart.*   *(43–50)*

The appetite of the eye—tracing, finding, noting—is answered by the force of beauty—connecting, impressing, imaging in his heart. But the enrapt gazer soon realizes that he, too, is being observed, and in retrospect stages its scene:

> *When I had gaz'd perhaps two minutes' space,*
> *Joanna, looking in my eyes, beheld*
> *That ravishment of mine, and laugh'd aloud.*   *(51–53)*

The ambiguous grammar of "that ravishment of mine" holds a number of possibilities of agent and object, ravisher and ravished: the poet is ravishing the landscape; his eyes are being ravished by it ("mine" refers to "eyes"); or his entire self is in a state of ravishment. This fluidity, as well as his objectification in Joanna's gaze, shifts the erotics of seeing into the embarrassment of being seen. Ravished by nature, he is ravished all over again by Joanna's look and laugh.

Both ravishments reverse the traditional female objectification by male gaze and action. In a cunning fragment on modern male enamoration, "Ravishment," Barthes ponders its "singular reversal" of "the ancient myth," in which a man captures and rapes a woman: whereas before, "the ravisher is active, he wants to seize his prey, he is the subject of the rape (of which the object is a Woman, as we know, invariably passive); in the modern myth (that of love-as-passion), the contrary is the case: the ravisher wants nothing, does nothing; he is motionless. . . . the lover—the one who has been ravished—is always implicitly feminized" (188–89).[20] The implicit feminization of Wordsworth's ravished poet is aided by the usual gendering of the gaze in *Lyrical Ballads,* where it is the female who is the object and the male who is the agent. As Joanna's text, the poet is like the Sister in "Tintern Abbey," whose companion "read[s]" the delight of her eyes (119–20) in an act of epistemic, if not erotic, ravishment. Wordsworth himself implies a feminizing in a later gloss on "To Joanna." Indeed, it seems to re-enact the original surrender to sensation: "I begin to relate the story [of the name]. . . . I begin—my mind partly forgets its purpose, being softened by the images of beauty in the description of the rock, and the delicious morning."[21] Not only was he ravished then, but he seems "softened" again by mere images of description in the poem's discursive "now" (13)—and still again in the halting present-tense syntax of his gloss.

This reverberation, in some ways, continues the aftershock of the original event, in which the ravishment by Joanna's laugh is protracted by an apparent natural, and female-infused, conspiracy, as all the mountains take up "the Lady's voice":

> The rock, like something starting from a sleep,
> Took up the Lady's voice, and laugh'd again:
> That ancient Woman seated on Helm-crag
> Was ready with her cavern; Hammar-Scar,
> And the tall Steep of Silver-How sent forth
> A noise of laughter; southern Loughrigg heard,
> And Fairfield answer'd with a mountain tone:
> Helvellyn far into the clear blue sky
> Carried the Lady's voice,—old Skiddaw blew
> His speaking trumpet;—back out of the clouds
> Of Glaramara southward came the voice;
> And Kirkstone toss'd it from his misty head.   (54–65)

In his gloss, Wordsworth tries to redeem the mockery of echoes by making himself, not Joanna, the agent of astonishment: "when I come to the 2 lines 'The Rock like something' *etc.,* I am caught in the trap of my own imagination. I entirely lose sight of my first purpose." But his poem tells another tale: it is Joanna's voice and not her companion's imaging "eye" that springs the trap, the domain of his gaze overwhelmed by the more powerful "connecting force" of the "one impression" engendered by her laugh. The world that he surveyed in delight is now heard in mocking alienation; even familiar place-names cannot humanize it. And Wordsworth's gloss, despite its tone of irony, perpetuates rather than manages the confusion: the chorus of amplifying laughter "describ[es] what for a moment I believed either actually took place at the time, or when I have been reflecting on what did take place I have had a temporary belief, in some fit of imagination, did really or might have taken place." To Coleridge's ear, Joanna's laugh carried an intertextual feminine reverberation—a passage in Drayton's "Poly-Olbion" about a symphony of female "song" broadcast throughout the land. He is not sure whether this amplification is a "noble imitation" on Wordsworth's part, or an unwitting "coincidence"—whether, that is, even in retrospect, the poet is in control of the echoes (*BL* 2:104).[22]

No wonder, then, that the remainder of "To Joanna" not only tames "the Lady's voice" but calls nature from the sway of feminine anarchy into a masculine domain of feminine property. The poet's first act is to resist this female-inspired chorus by substituting and wondering about a set of male options for interpreting the cacophony—whether:

> this were in simple truth
> A work accomplish'd by the brotherhood

> *Of ancient mountains, or my ear was touch'd*
> *With dreams and visionary impulses,*
> *Is not for me to tell . . .   (68–72)*

One way that Wordsworth tries to manage the confusion of what "actually took place . . . what did take place . . . or might have taken place" is to take the place itself as a subject for writing, and to control, therein, all feminine figures. As the colloquy shifts from Joanna and the hills to poet and Vicar, not only Joanna but the "ancient Woman" in the chorus that carried "the Lady's voice" are excluded from the terms of surmise: the hills are now consolidated as a "brotherhood." The poet then reduces Joanna to, and silences her within, an image of female fear seeking male protection—a small drama staged with the aura and ideology of a chivalric script:

> *And, while we both were listening, to my side*
> *The fair Joanna drew, as if she wish'd*
> *To shelter from some object of her fear.   (74–76)*

"The fair Joanna," an epithet from the days of England's ancient brotherhood, coincides with the "as if" that identifies a wish in the poet behind the one he attributes to her, to see her vulnerable and dependent. The rhetoric of conjecture is potentially self-ironizing, inviting us wonder whether Joanna drew herself to him for a reason other than the one he fancies, perhaps to assure him of her affection amidst his embarrassment. But the potential remains only that, and it is restrained by a Note appended to the poem that represents the "ancient Woman seated on Helm-crag" (the first to take up Joanna's voice) in a compatible image of "an Old Woman cowering" (*LB* 222).

The power of Joanna's laugh recedes even further in the poetic present, "eighteen moons" later, when she is absent and the poet is "alone . . . on a calm / And silent morning" (78–80). He "chanc'd" on a device to reclaim authority over her voice:

> *I chissel'd out in those rude characters*
> *Joanna's name upon the living stone.*
> *And I, and all who dwell by my fireside*
> *Have call'd the lovely rock, Joanna's Rock.   (82–85)*

His name, which disseminates from him to "all who dwell" in his domain, is, in effect, an epitaph on "living stone" that buries Joanna with "obsolete Idolatry." She becomes an "uncouth name" (27–30), requiring the poet's animation and elucidation. The poet's voice seems finally to win, claiming its victory at the very site of embarrassment: "W. . . . read us the poem of Joanna beside the Rothay by the roadside," Dorothy Wordsworth reports (22 Aug. 1800; *Journals* 35). Convinced that he speaks and engraves "in memory of affections old and true" (81)—or as the later gloss puts it, "a strain of deep tenderness"—Wordsworth invests poetic labor with containing the extravagance of female voices.

The priority of this labor persuades readers such as Parrish (echoing his argument that "The Thorn" is "not a poem about a woman") that "To Joanna" is "not a poem about Joanna, or a poem about the rock or about an incident there"; it is "a dramatic self-portrait, a poem about the contest between the poet's imagination and his sense of reality . . . a wild excitation in which his sense of reality is momentarily overwhelmed, then sinks once more under rational control, leaving a current of warm emotion as the poet looks tranquilly back through the filter of memory" (29). Like Wordsworth's own framings, Parrish's "portrait" draws attention to gender by his erasure of it. Both poet and critic exclude the force of feminine laughter and the masculine "sense of reality" it thereby overwhelms, and both resist recognizing how much the restoration of rational control and the emergence of tranquil memory involve subordinating and tranquilizing the feminine: first as helpless damsel, then as mere chiselling, then as name and text, and ultimately as addressee to be reproached. But the visibility of these strategies in the poem shows a "strain" in Wordsworth's imagination that runs deeper than the one of deep tenderness his gloss admits. Despite the poem's controlling frames, Joanna's laughter remains in the text as a female voice of fascinating, irruptive power. In the domain of passion, whether it is voiced by women or by men of feeling, Wordsworth uncovers more than a few questions of gender that expose the difficult containments to be managed by a man speaking to men.[23]

Notes

1.   "Teaching" 145; see also Margaret Homans, *Women Writers* 18–28, *et passim.*

2.   Steele, *The Tatler* 181; qtd. in Richardson 15, 23; I quote from Richardson 21, 16.

3.   My quotations, in order, are from Marlon Ross's essays, "Romantic Quest and Conquest" (28, 28, 49) and "Naturalizing Gender" (392). I use Ross as a representative voice not only because his essays are frequently cited as if their formulations were uncontestable but also because he presents these in a clear and forceful way.

4.   Although this polarization does not persist without oscillation, it constitutes what Wollstonecraft's *Vindication of the Rights of Woman* calls the "Prevailing Opinion" and thus focuses her "Animadversions" against the literature, especially *Paradise Lost,* that sustains and disseminates it.

5.   The fear "remains disturbingly present," remarks Heather Glen; it is "unexorcised by . . . self-disparagement" (48).

6.   For Wordsworth's interest in *Zoönomia,* see *Letters, EY* 199, 214–15. James Averill discusses the engagement with this study (153–59, 166–68), as does Mary Jacobus, who sees the ballad applying a "moral context" to Darwin's "flat reporting" in order to yield a "humanitarian lesson" (234–37).

7.   Thus Wordsworth describes his own "extravagating" on the "extravagance" of Joanna's laugh (*Poetical Works* 487). I return to this dynamic later in this essay.

8.   Alan Bewell resourcefully studies the legacy of this gendering in Wordsworth's fascination with female hysteria as "a medium of speculative argument, a means for forcefully delineating, as he notes in connection with *Lyrical Ballads,* the manner in which 'language and the human mind act and react on each other' " (360). He does not expand this suggestive study into figures of male hysteria, even though the texts he discusses often involve such manners of action in men: the Preface to *Lyrical Ballads* is one example; another is the poet's description of his mind in *The Prelude* as "beset / With images and haunted by itself" (1805 text, 6:179–80).

9.   In the early seventeenth century, the French physician Carolus Piso (Charles Lepois) declared that *"hysterica symptomata omnia fere viris cum mulieribus sunt communia"* (nearly all hysterical symptoms are common with men and women) (181). His case for hysteria as a disease of the passions, an affliction of mind rather than womb, was supported in the 1680s by Thomas Willis, who had studied his analyses. Willis thought women more susceptible to such disorders but recognized that "sometimes the same kind of Passions infest Men" (69). In the same decade, Thomas Sydenham was astonishing the medical community with the assertion that while hysteria is largely a "female" malady, men of "sedentary or studious life," who "grow pale over their books and papers, are similarly afflicted" (2:85). Ilza Veith, whose fine study alerted me to these documents, observes that medical analysis shifted its language to avoid the gender-inscription of "hysteria." Thus, male disorders were typically classed by Sydenham and others as "hypochondriasis" or *"suffocatio hypochondriaca,"* while "similar complaints in females were classed as hysteria" (144–45).

10.   For a valuable discussion of Shakespeare's representation of Lear's hysteria in relation to patriarchal social and family structure, see Coppélia Kahn's essay.

11.   For an illuminating account of the involution of hysteria and witchcraft in European and American social history, see Veith, chapter 4, and for a cogent overview of the significant of this "supernaturalizing" of hysteria, see Marc Micale, "Hysteria and Historiography" (234–37). Bewell observes (as does Veith) that "historically, hysteria played a major role in the demystification of witchcraft": "cases of demonic possession" were beginning to be understood as "symptoms of hysteria" (364).

12.   *Morning Post* (late 1799), *Essays* 1:43–44.

13.   In an unincorporated preface for *Don Juan,* Byron refers to the narrator of "The Thorn" as "the kind of Poet who, in the same manner that Joanna Southcote [he routinely misspells her name] found many thousand people to take her dropsy for God Almighty re-impregnated, has found some hundreds of persons to misbelieve in his insanities," producing "such trash as may support the reveries which he would reduce into a System of prosaic raving that is to supersede all that hitherto by the best and wisest of our fathers has been deemed poetry" (*Complete Poetical Works* 5:81–82).

14.   A precedent for such contamination is offered in a well known eighteenth-century treatise by the Scottish physician-physiologist Robert Whytt, who observed that hysteria could be induced by the strong impression of another's passion, even with literary mediation: "doleful or moving stories, horrible or unexpected sights," as well as "passions, frequently occasion the most sudden and violent nervous symptoms. The strong impressions made in such cases on the brain and nerves often throw the person into hysteric fits" (206–7).

15.   *Hysteron proteron* ("the later earlier," or "the latter first") refers both to discursive

patterns that reverse temporal order (popularly phrased in English rhetorics, such as Puttenham's, as "putting the cart before the horse") and, by extension, to the logical fallacy of taking as a premise (Martha Ray's presence at "the spot," for example) something that follows from what is to be proved (that the narrator "saw" and "heard" her there). Despite the common etymological base (in the Sanskrit *úttaras*) of this *hysteros* and *hystera* (the womb), the *Greek-English Lexicon* does not say why the womb is so called. For the etymologies, see 2:1905–6. Froma Zeitlin (Princeton University) suggests that *hystera* may draw on *hysteros* to name the second, or later, sex. John Belton (Rutgers University), noting that one meaning of *hysteron* is "afterbirth," proposes that this "later" stage of delivery may have been thought to have been the womb itself (*hystera*), a new one of which was supposed to grow back. Richard Rand offers a similar speculation (52).

16.   For my fuller reading of these poetics, see *The Questioning Presence* 53–60.

17.   When in 1815, this poem appears as "Her Eyes are Wild," the punctuation is clarified (*Poetical Works,* 2:110).

18.   The ideological challenge posed by this nonpathological female passion is suggested by the fact that Coleridge resists calling Deborah a "poet": "Nature is the Poet here" (*Lectures* 1:69); "I never think that she is a poet"; "the song . . . is the proper and characteristic effusion of a woman highly elevated by triumph, by the natural hatred of oppressors," he insists, adding, "we have no reason . . . to suppose that if she had not been agitated by passion, and animated by victory, she would have been able so to express herself; or that if she had been placed in different circumstances, she would have used such language of truth and passion" (2:494; cf. 1:310). Probing the analogies between the historical situation of the "Song of Deborah" and England in the 1790s, Karen Swann suggests Wordsworth's unacknowledged interest in the song as "the consolidation and liberation of a public voice": "In *Judges* 5 the mother Deborah rises not in madness, but in revolt and finally in prophecy. In that tumultuous and passionate poem, it is impossible to distinguish male from female voices, narrator from character: Deborah's voice mingles with Barak's, with that of the third speaker who wakes them both, and even, with the lament of Sisera's suffering mother, to sing the song of the liberation of the children of Israel by the woman, Jael."

19.   For the sake of this effect, Wordsworth departs from the basis in actual "incident" advertised for all the poems in this unit to indulge a fabrication: Joanna Hutchinson was neither city-bred (as the poem's opening sentence states), nor could she have been "distant from us . . . for two long years" (13), the Wordsworths themselves having arrived in Grasmere only a few months before; see de Selincourt and Darbishire, *Poetical Works* 2:487, and Harper 316.

20.   Thanks to Sonia Hofkosh (109) for bringing this essay to my attention. The ravished poet of "To Joanna" also evokes the symptom of female hysteria described by the physician Rondibilis in Rabelais's *Pantagruel:* "The entire feminine body is shaken, all the senses ravished, all the passions carried to a point of repletion, and all thought thrown into confusion" (477; Rabelais himself was a lecturer in medicine).

21.   Wordsworth's explication of "To Joanna" appears in the *"Peter Bell* notebook"; see *Poetical Works* 2:487 and Parrish 28–29.

22.   The passage cited is "The Thirtieth Song," 155–64:

Which COPLAND scarce had spoke, but quickly every hill
Upon her verge that stands, the neighbouring vallies fill;
HELVILLON from his height, it through the mountains threw.
From whom as soon again, the sound DUNBALRASE drew,
From whose stone-trophied head, it on the WENDROSS went,
Which, tow'rds the sea again, resounded it to DENT.
That BROADWATER, therewith within her banks astound,
In sailing to the sea told it to EGREMOUND,
Whose buildings, walks and streets, with echoes loud and long
Did mightily commend old COPLAND for her song!

Bate and Engell's *Biographia* (xxi) gives Coleridge's likely text as *The Works of the British Poets,* ed. Robert Anderson (13 vols., Edinburgh 1792–95; vol. 14, 1807).

23.   My thanks to Ronald Levao, William Keach, Peter Manning, Karen Swann, and Thaïs Morgan for careful advice on this essay.

Works Cited

[Allsop, Thomas]. *Letters, Conversations, and Recollections of Samuel Taylor Coleridge.* 2 vols. London: E. Moxon, 1836.

Averill, James H. *Wordsworth and the Poetry of Human Suffering.* Ithaca: Cornell University Press, 1980.

Barthes, Roland. *A Lover's Discourse: Fragments.* 1977; translated by Richard Howard. New York: Hill and Wang, 1978.

Le Beau Monde, or, Literary and Fashionable Magazine 2 (Oct. 1807). Review of *Poems, in Two Volumes:* 138–42.

Bewell, Alan J. "A 'Word Scarce Said': Hysteria and Witchcraft in Wordsworth's 'Experimental' Poetry of 1797–1798." *ELH* 53 (1986): 357–90.

Burney, Dr. Charles. Review of *Lyrical Ballads. Monthly Review,* 2d ser. 29 (June 1799): 202–10.

Byron, George Gordon, Lord. *Don Juan,* in vol. 5, *Lord Byron: The Complete Poetical Works.* Edited by Jerome J. McGann. 6 vols. Oxford: Clarendon Press, 1980–1990.

Coleridge, Samuel Taylor. *Biographia Literaria, Or Biographical Sketches of My Literary Life and Opinions.* 1817; 2 vols. Edited by James Engell and W. Jackson Bate. Princeton: Princeton University Press, 1983. Cited as *BL.*

———. *Essays on His Times in* The Morning Post *and* The Courier. 3 vols. Edited by David V. Erdman. Princeton: Princeton University Press, 1978.

———. *Lectures 1808–1819 On Literature.* 2 vols. Edited by R. A. Foakes. Princeton: Princeton University Press, 1987.

———. *The Poems of Samuel Taylor Coleridge.* Edited by Ernest Hartley Coleridge. London and New York: Oxford University Press, 1912.

———. *The Watchman.* Edited by Lewis Patton. Princeton: Princeton University Press, 1970.

Darwin, Erasmus. *Zoönomia, or the Laws of Organic Life.* 2 vols. London: J. Johnson, 1794–96.

Eliot, T. S. "Hysteria." *Prufrock and Other Observations.* 1917; *The Complete Poems and Plays: 1909–1950.* New York: Harcourt, Brace & World, 1952.

Foucault, Michel. *Madness & Civilization: A History of Insanity in the Age of Reason.* Translated by Richard Howard. 1965; New York: NAL, 1971.

Gisborne, Thomas. *An Inquiry into the Duties of the Female Sex.* 1796; 7th ed. London: T. Cadell and W. Davies, 1806.

Good, John Mason. *The Study of Medicine.* 1822.

Greek-English Lexicon. 2 vols. Compiled by Henry George Liddell and Robert Scott; revised by Henry Stuart Jones. Oxford: Clarendon Press, 1968.

Hofkosh, Sonia. "The Writer's Ravishment: Women and the Romantic Author—The Example of Byron." In Mellor, ed. *Romanticism and Feminism,* 93–114.

Homans, Margaret. *Women Writers and Poetic Identity: Dorothy Wordsworth, Emily Brontë, and Emily Dickinson.* Princeton: Princeton University Press, 1980.

Jacobus, Mary. *Tradition and Experiment in Wordsworth's* Lyrical Ballads, *(1798).* Oxford: Clarendon Press, 1976.

Judges. The Holy Bible, King James Version. New York: NAL, 1974.

Kahn, Coppélia. "The Absent Mother in *King Lear.*" In *Rewriting the Renaissance: The Discourses of Sexual Difference in Early Modern Europe.* Edited by Margaret W. Ferguson, Maureen Quilligan, and Nancy J. Vickers. Chicago and London: University of Chicago Press, 1986. 33–49.

Langbaum, Robert. *The Poetry of Experience: The Dramatic Monologue in Modern Literary Tradition.* 1957; New York: Norton, 1971.

Lowell, James Russell. "Wordsworth." *The Writings of James Russell Lowell.* 10 vols. Boston and New York: Houghton, Mifflin, 1894. 6:354–415.

Mackenzie, Henry. *The Man of Feeling.* 1771; edited by Brian Vickers. London: Oxford University Press, 1967.

Mellor, Anne K., ed. *Romanticism and Feminism.* Bloomington: Indiana University Press, 1988.

———. "Teaching Wordsworth and Women." In *Approaches to Teaching Wordsworth's Poetry.* Ed. Spencer Hall with Jonathan Ramsey. New York: MLA, 1986. 142–46.

Micale, Marc S. "Hysteria and Historiography: A Review of Past and Present Writings." *History of Science* 27 (Sept. and Dec. 1989): 223–61; 319–51.

Monthly Magazine 1 (March 1796).

More, Hannah. *Strictures on the Modern System of Female Education.* 1799; 2 vols. Reprinted. Vols. 7–8, *The Works of Hannah More.* 18 vols. London: T. Cadell and W. Davies, 1818.

Parrish, Stephen Maxfield. *The Art of the* Lyrical Ballads. Cambridge: Harvard University Press, 1973.

Pinch, Adela. "Female Chatter: Meter, Masochism, and the Lyrical Ballads." *ELH* 55 (1988): 835–52.

Piso, Carolus [Charles Lepois]. *Selectiorum observationum et conciliorum de praeteretis.* Pont-à-Mousson, 1618.

Pope, Alexander. *The Rape of the Lock.* 1712; Vol. 1, *The Poems of Alexander Pope.* 11 vols. Edited by John Butt et al. New Haven: Yale University Press, 1961–69. Vol. 1, edited by E. Audra and Aubrey Williams.

Rabelais, François. *Pantagruel.* 1532; in *The Portable Rabelais.* Translated by Samuel Putnam. New York: Viking Press, 1946.

Rand, Richard. "Hysteron Proteron, or 'Woman First.' " *Oxford Literary Review* 8 (1986): 51–56.

Richardson, Alan. "Romanticism and the Colonization of the Feminine." In Mellor, ed. *Romanticism and Feminism*, 13–25.

Ross, Marlon B. "Naturalizing Gender: Woman's Place in Wordsworth's Ideological Landscape." *ELH* 53 (1986): 391–410.

———. "Romantic Quest and Conquest: Troping Masculine Power in the Crisis of Poetic Identity." In Mellor, ed. *Romanticism and Feminism*, 26–51.

Schweickart, Patrocinio P. "Reading Ourselves: Toward a Feminist Theory of Reading." In *Gender and Reading: Essays on Readers, Texts, and Contexts*. Edited by Elizabeth A. Flynn and Patrocinio P. Schweickart. Baltimore: Johns Hopkins University Press, 1986. 31–62.

Shakespeare, William. *King Lear*. Edited by Kenneth Muir. London: Methuen, 1972.

Sheats, Paul D. *The Making of Wordsworth's Poetry, 1785–1798*. Cambridge: Harvard University Press, 1973.

Showalter, Elaine. *The Female Malady: Women, Madness, and English Culture, 1830–1980*. New York, Penguin, 1985.

Simpson, David. *Wordsworth's Historical Imagination: The Poetry of Displacement*. London and New York: Methuen, 1987.

Southey, Robert. Review of *Lyrical Ballads*. *Critical Review* 2d ser. 24 (October 1798): 197–204.

Sydenham, Thomas. "Epistolary Dissertation." Vol. 2, *The Works of Thomas Sydenham, M.D.* Translated by R. G. Latham. London: Sydenham Society, 1848.

Swann, Karen. " 'Martha's name,' or, the Strange Case of 'The Thorn.' " Forthcoming.

Veith, Ilza. Hysteria: The History of a Disease. 1965; rpt. Chicago: University of Chicago Press, 1970.

Whytt, Robert. *Observations on the Nature, Causes, and Cure of those Disorders which have been commonly called Nervous, Hypochondriac, or Hysteria: to which are prefixed some Remarks on the Sympathy of the Nerves*. 3d ed. Edinburgh: J. Balfour, 1767.

Willis, Thomas. *An Essay of the Pathology of the Brain and Nervous Stock in which convulsive Diseases are Treated of*. Translated by S. Pordage. London: Dring, Leigh, and Harper, 1684.

Wolfson, Susan. *The Questioning Presence: Wordsworth, Keats, and the Interrogative Mode in Romantic Poetry*. Ithaca: Cornell University Press, 1986.

Wollstonecraft, Mary. *A Vindication of the Rights of Woman*. 1792; edited by Carol H. Poston. New York: Norton, 1988.

Wordsworth, Dorothy. *Journals of Dorothy Wordsworth*. 2d ed. Edited by Mary Moorman. Oxford: Oxford University Press, 1971.

Wordsworth, William. *The Letters of William and Dorothy Wordsworth*. Edited by Ernest de Selincourt. *The Early Years, 1787–1805*. 2d ed. revised by Chester L. Shaver. Oxford: Clarendon Press, 1967; cited as *EY*. *The Middle Years, 1806–1820*. 2d ed. revised by Mary Moorman and Alan G. Hill. 2 vols. Oxford: Clarendon Press, 1969–70; cited as *MY*.

———. *Lyrical Ballads: Wordsworth & Coleridge. The text of the 1798 edition with the additional 1800 poems and the Prefaces*. Edited by R. L. Brett and A. R. Jones. 1965; London and New York: Methuen, 1986. My quotations follow this edition, cited as *LB*.

———. *The Poetical Works of William Wordsworth*. 2d ed. 5 vols. Edited by E. de Selincourt. Oxford: Clarendon Press, 1952. Cited as *PW*.

Border Disturbances: D. H. Lawrence's Fiction and the Feminism of *Wuthering Heights*

Carol Siegel

Over ten years ago Judith Fetterley pointed out that because most literary texts and critical methodologies presuppose a male reader, feminist criticism must involve an occasionally hostile interaction with texts and must concern itself with gendered reader response (xxiii). In current feminist criticism, such concern finds a variety of expressions, ranging from the critic reading her (feminine) self into the text, through identification with a female author, to her reading for the textually repressed "woman," the elusive feminine. However, in opening a dialogue about gender between ourselves and various texts, we sometimes seem in danger of ignoring—or worse, over-simplifying—the dialogue that has always existed between men's and women's fictions. Within the intertextual connections that traditionally define influence, the distinction between reader and writer dissolves and power relations come unfixed. In these connections, we can read the writer-as-reader and, thus, when influence crosses gender lines, we can recapture the richness of lost dialogues on gender. In the discussion that follows, I will be looking not only at a male author's attempts to write as a woman but also at the ways his reading of a female precursor informs those attempts.

Emily Brontë's influence on D. H. Lawrence is readily apparent and, indeed, has not been overlooked. Keith Sagar has pointed out the close correspondence between Brontë's and Lawrence's imagery, especially the symbolic use of darkness ("Originality" 149–51). Daniel Schneider has demonstrated the resemblance of Lawrence's first novel, *The White Peacock,* to *Wuthering Heights* in the details of both its romantic triangle plot and its dramatization of the dangers of repression, and has noted some reappearances of these similarities in Lawrence's later works (111–12). However, critical discussions of the intertextual connections between *Wuthering Heights* and Lawrence's fiction have not taken up the issue of gender. At the idea that Brontë is female and Lawrence male they reach a stop.

Yet *Wuthering Heights* and Lawrence's novels are most often read as gender-specific texts. Lawrence's often misogynistically framed insistence on gender difference has annoyed generations of feminists. Perhaps for this reason, when a representative of the masculine voice must be named, feminist critics turn to Lawrence with surprising frequency. In *The Second Sex,* Simone de Beauvoir gives him a prominent place in her discussion of writers who have created the myth that the ideal and only real woman is she "who unreservedly accepts being defined as Other" (209). If Lawrence does make woman Other, she returns the favor. Feminist critics, whether their focus is thematic, historical, psychological, or cultural, tend to see Lawrence as the masculine Other against whom the feminine can be defined. Annis Pratt believes that we can better understand woman's relationship to nature by comparing Lawrence's depiction of it to women writers' (481–83). Sandra Gilbert and Susan Gubar quote Lawrence to explain the foundation of "patriarchal poetics" (*Madwoman* 14). Mary Jacobus depicts the feminine understanding of fluid identity, free expression, and openness by contrasting it with what she believes is Lawrence's dichotomized world view, and his consequent desire to silence woman (30). Eve Sedgwick describes our present, "schizoid" homosocial culture as determined by "the triumph of Lawrence and 'Wilde' ": the polarization of male attitudes into Lawrencian homophobia or the feminine but misogynous homosexuality represented by the public concept of Oscar Wilde (215–17). Note that "Wilde" goes into quotes; Lawrence does not. Like other feminist critics, Sedgwick seems to see no reason to consider the standard opinion of Lawrence. Conversely, for the last twenty years, feminist critics have treated Emily Brontë as a spokeswoman for the repressed feminine. They have almost unanimously agreed that female experience in a misogynous culture is the major theme of *Wuthering Heights*. From Ellen Moers's *Literary Women* to Margaret Homans's *Bearing the Word,* Emily Brontë's heroine, Cathy Earnshaw, has been discussed as a "no-sayer" to patriarchal law, a savage advocate of Mother Nature, against man and the society he has made (Moers, 25, 163; Homans, 68–83).

The most serious challenge to this reading has been persuasively articulated by Harold Bloom. Unlike other critics who have compared Lawrence and Brontë in the discussions of influence, Bloom devotes respectful attention to the idea that *Wuthering Heights* is a feminist text. Ultimately, however, he describes both Cathy Earnshaw and her author as vitalists beyond concern with either the social or the natural world and, thus so "purely individual" in their concepts of wholeness as to be even "beyond gender" (9–11). Consequently, according to Bloom, Lawrence can, without difficulty, be considered Brontë's literary "heir," the inheritor of her "harsh vitalism" (1). By placing the relationship between *Wuthering Heights* and Lawrence's fiction outside gender, Bloom questions the concept of separate male and female literary traditions, that structures much feminist discourse. He also raises questions about the practice of gendering texts.

Of course, such questioning does not originate with Bloom. Some of the most intense debates in feminist theory of the 1980s center on the issue of gendering texts. Feminist critics have long recognized that "literature written by women" and "feminist literature" are not synonymous terms. An adequate self-definition for women cannot come directly from women's literary works because women are products of the same culture as men and, consequently, their understanding of the feminine develops in a similar way. Most women writers are to some extent male-defined because they inhabit a patriarchal culture. As much as the general female population, they need to question their own culturally determined concepts of woman.

Much feminist criticism focuses on the ways women writers attempt this questioning. Critics from Moers to Nancy Miller, who place women writers in a female literary tradition, have scrutinized texts written by women to find individual women's subversive voices—what Gilbert and Gubar call the palimpsest—beneath the authors' ostensible affirmations of patriarchal values.[1] The problem with this method, as psycho-linguistic feminist critics point out, is its aim of uncovering the real female beneath the socially imposed feminine, a goal that depends on the concept of men and women as opposites. Critics like Shoshana Felman and Mary Jacobus, who focus on the feminine voice rather than on the historical figure of the female author, object to this idea of "fixed gender" because they see "the production of sexual difference . . . as textual, like the production of meaning" (Jacobus, 4). Since gender is a construct to these writers, they look at works by both men and women to find the feminine manifesting itself as a disruptive force within the masculine order. Along these lines, one way of resolving the apparent contradiction between *Wuthering Heights*'s suggestion of specifically female rebellion and its indifference to the material world would be to say that Brontë expresses her feminism through a refusal to affirm gender difference.

Still, feminist approaches to literature characteristically involve a focus on gender difference. In fact, as Nina Baym remarks in apparent disgust, "all current [feminist] theory requires sexual difference as its ground" (46). Such annoyance with feminist literary theory seems somewhat unfair since all feminism, theory and practice, must begin not only with a recognition of a difference between the two sexes as we encounter them in the world, but also choose to treat men and women differently, to act in the best interests of one sex even if at the expense of the other. Because power is relative, all increases in woman's power decrease man's power over her. As Toril Moi puts it, "the feminist struggle must both try to undo the patriarchal strategy that makes 'femininity' intrinsic to biological femaleness, and at the same time insist on defending women precisely *as* women" (82).

Although "essentialism" is much decried by theorists like Moi, their own feminism and its expression in the choice to write as/for women necessarily involves the choice to treat women not as a category of humans upon whose natural androgyny gender has been arbitrarily imposed, but as beings fundamentally different from all other groups marginalized by the patriarchal structure. In "Dreaming Dissymmetry," her brilliant attack on "the hegemony of the discourse of indifference," Naomi Schor finds it significant that attitudes toward difference (and what could easily be described as female essence) separate male and female feminist theorists: "no feminist theoretician *who is not also a woman* has ever fully espoused the claims to a feminine specificity, an irreducible difference" (109, emphasis Schor's).

My attention to the dialogue between Brontë's and Lawrence's texts begins with the assumption that the gender of writers as figures in a historicized world has meaning. My intention is not to dismantle the model of literary territories, separated on gender lines, that structured such useful feminist literary criticism as Myra Jehlen's "Archimedes and the Paradox of Feminist Criticism" and, more recently, Gilbert and Gubar's *No Man's Land.* Rather, I will look at "confrontations on the border" between *Wuthering Heights* and Lawrence's fictions to reveal some of the ways this unusual literary relationship both marks and obscures a border between the genders in the process of making prominent the feminist voice of *Wuthering Heights* (Jehlen, 585).

The typical ungendering of the relationship between *Wuthering Heights* and Lawrence's work must always be done in opposition to Lawrence's reinscription of gender difference in his own direct references to Emily Brontë. In his introduction to M. G. Steegmann's translation of Grazia Deledda's *The Mother,* Lawrence refers to Emily Brontë as giving voice to a transhistorical, transcultural "sheer female instinctive passion" (*Phoenix* 265). To Lawrence such a voice compels male response; in fact, maleness can be measured by a man's ability to be moved by the female voice. In *John Thomas and Lady Jane* (an early version of *Lady Chatterley's Lover*), Clifford Chatterley's failure to be "stimulated" by *Wuthering Heights* is presented as indicative of his failure as a man, his retreat from his wife into his business affairs—which Lawrence describes as gynophobic—a direct result of his fear of her female power in their interactions (342–43).

Lawrence, who condemned liberalism as effete, would no doubt be aghast at the idea that his reading of *Wuthering Heights* and his attitude toward his female characters has affinities with liberal humanism's fundamental assumption of an identity that transcends social and cultural forces. More importantly, his philosophy breaks away from humanism at precisely the same point that feminism does. Lawrence sees gender difference as the most important human attribute and sees problems that arise from gender identity as the ones most deserving of attention. Like a feminist writer, or in what we might consider (because of his gender) an appropriation of the feminist position, he takes as his first priority the articulation of female experience both for and to women.

Lawrence not only habitually submitted his manuscripts to women he knew and dutifully made the editorial changes they suggested, but, as his novel, *Kangaroo* suggests, he also seemed most often to think of the reader of his published work as female.[2] *Kangaroo* is unique among Lawrence's fictions in the amount of material directly addressed the reader. Early on, we are made to know the narrator as someone who believes "himself entitled to all kinds of emotions and sensations which an ordinary man would have repudiated," and, who, thus, frequently finds it easier to talk to women than to men (8). The middle chapter, "Harriet and Lovat at Sea in Marriage," which summarizes the central conflict the characters face, takes the form of a lecture directed at "young married women"—complete with their (imagined) derisive interjections (172–78). At this point in the novel, Harriet's voice seems to merge with the imagined reader's just as Lovat's voice has merged periodically with the narrator's. Lovat learns about life through his wife's emotions and, by the end of the book, having attained some insight into life and his condition, speaks "very gently, like a woman" (343). This suggests that listening to a woman brings about speaking like a woman. Understanding passes quickly into identification: The male speaker who allows a female voice to enter his discourse soon both possesses and is possessed by it. An outcome that most masculinist writers would probably find nightmarish is presented as bringing Lovat psychic wholeness.

The parallel between Lawrence's relationships with the actual women who participated in his production of texts and his concept of his relationship to the reader is further clarified in the second section of *Mr Noon*. After Gilbert and Johanna have their first quarrel, Lawrence, as narrator, drops his archly urbane mask and continues the fight with the reader, beginning:

> And so, gentle reader—! But why the devil should I always *gentle-reader* you. . . . Time you became rampageous reader, ferocious reader, surly, rabid reader, hell-cat of a reader, a tartar, a termagant, a tanger.—And so, hell-cat of a reader, let me tell you, with a flea in your ear, that all the ring-dove sonata you'll get out of me you've got already, and for the rest you've got to hear the howl of tomcats like myself and she-cats like yourself, going it tooth and nail. (204–5)

Lawrence's interrelated fear of and dependence upon women are obvious, but, more interestingly, so is his determination to break through the literary decorum that separates the male voice from the female figure who receives it. She is important because her ideal attitude is the antithesis of passive receptivity. As the "fiery one" whose released anger can "consume the flabby masses of humanity, and make way for a splendider time," she is the supreme goddess of his fictional cosmos; her attention to his work makes possible his creation of the new heaven and earth (*Mr. Noon* 209). In other words, her voice deconstructs so that his can construct. In Lawrence's revisionary responses to *Wuthering Heights,* we see some of what he would construct.

Lawrence's construction of a "new" world begins, in *The White Peacock,* with the reconstruction of the major themes of *Wuthering Heights.* His voice is, thus, possessed by a specific female voice and is generally feminized by its concerns, since, for Brontë, female experience is the touchstone of meaning. In close parallel to *Wuthering Heights, The White Peacock*'s main narrative depicts a woman's vacillation between two suitors, one of whom represents nature and the other culture. Both Brontë and Lawrence draw a thick line between male and female, despite Cathy's famous cry, "I *am* Heathcliff." However, this delineation of difference is not a reinscription of conventional fictional representations of gender. Heathcliff is, as Cathy continues, "always, always in my mind," as a symbol of nature, freedom, and essential self, "as my own being" (74). While Cathy, and Lettie, the heroine of *The White Peacock*, are dialogic subjects divided between social and natural selves, both authors' male characters are pure symbolic representations of the contending forces "always, always" within woman. In a reversal of the usual order, masculinity/maleness are understood only as symbolic statements whose reference is woman.

In *The White Peacock*, Lawrence initiates the practice, carried over into much of his subsequent fiction, of creating a male character, like Heathcliff, who seems in some ways a nature spirit, but who is denied a male voice. In *The White Peacock*, Annable, the keeper, who appears to the others "like a devil of the woods," is this sort of figure. Annable tries, almost pathetically, to speak as a man against woman, whom he perceives as unnatural. But he is repeatedly forced by circumstances into traditionally feminine situations—and silence. His first wife courts him, gives him "a living," uses him sexually, and generally controls him until she tires of him (177). It is, ironically, only in the context of the feminine that Annable has any meaning at all, and that meaning is in contradiction to the very concept of a male subject. But, although Annable's marginal and dependent situation in the world recall Heathcliff's, these characters are most alike in functioning as expressions of the wild half of woman. Cicio in *The Lost Girl*, Count Psanek in *The Ladybird*, Henry in *The Fox*, Don Cipriano in *The Plumed Serpent*, and Parkin in *The First Lady Chatterley* also share Heathcliff's demonic power to represent nature. All are like Heathcliff in that their wildness, the essence of their own being, is not posited as specifically male, but is, instead, a displaced aspect of the woman.

In their identification with nature, these men are objectified. Because no women in either Lawrence's fiction or *Wuthering Heights* represent nature or are objectified in this way, both authors can be considered to approach the problem of gender through a kind of feminism of reversal of signs. Like Heathcliff and Hareton, Lawrence's men attain individual presence, are brought up out of the landscape, by being contemplated and used by women. In return they revitalize women by allowing them to hear the voice of nature—in Susan Griffin's words, "the roaring inside *her*"—that is muted for women by the socialization process that creates a second self, but that the men exist to represent.

Lawrence also takes on attitudes and tones implicit in *Wuthering Heights* by using a male as the figure for culture. Lawrence and Brontë conflate female socialization (with its inherent fragmentation of the self) and marriage. Cathy Earnshaw makes a fatal mistake in marrying. It is only through marriage that she will finish being "converted . . . into . . . the lady . . . the wife of a stranger; an exile, and an outcast, thenceforth, from what had been [her] world" (107). Edgar, as a representative of civilization and its laws, must, ultimately, insist upon his rights as her husband/master and try to make her bow down to the Law of the Fathers.[3] This law demands her death. In Brontë and in Lawrence's first novel, marriage appears as a social disease, in every sense of the term, which can only infect women. The males, parasitic in their dependence upon the women to give them meaning, have no immanent presence to be attacked. Their representation within marriage as the symbolic figure, husband, does not block their self-expression. Surface meaning, determined by their relation to woman's quest for an integrated self, is their all.

Brontëan or Lawrencian woman, in contrast, can be understood through the model of two concentric circles. Both writers envision the feminine as a socially constructed shell around the innate female. Marriage augments the shell so much that it destroys the living essence within it. Indeed, not a single woman in *Wuthering Heights* survives her husband. Lawrence's description of Lettie after three years of marriage evokes Brontë's depiction of the delirium that leads up to Cathy's death:

> Like so many women she seemed to live, for the most part contentedly, a small indoor existence . . . Only occasionally, hearing the winds of life outside, she clamoured to be out in the black, keen storm. She was driven to the door, she looked out and called into the tumult wildly, but feminine caution kept her from stepping over the threshold. (331)

In both passages, female freedom is equated with fresh air and marriage/feminine socialization with suffocating enclosure.

Both Brontë and Lawrence, in their revulsion against the feminine, create male monsters. Of all the writers presumed to have influenced Lawrence, Emily Brontë is the only one who apparently shares his admiration for pathologically antisocial characters. Lawrence's depictions of Annable, Cipriano, and Romero (in "The Princess") are all comparable to Brontë's Heathcliff, justified in his contempt for law and convention and majestic in his violence. Even Mellors's harshness toward his daughter is reminiscent of Heathcliff's offhanded cruelty to that pale, diminished version of Cathy, her daughter. In each case, the man's violence is ostensibly directed against the affectations that are called femininity. Lawrence's women protagonists are often completed by male halves who strike down the angel in the house as Heathcliff does Isabella. In both writers' worlds such violence seems necessary. When they are free from Heathcliff's abusive presence, Isabella and Catherine Linton accept the social roles they have been assigned in Edgar's world, behaving as if there was nothing in them beneath the veneer of ladylike sweetness, as if no power could come from them but the fairy/angel/mother magic that polishes the "rough diamond" to reveal male value (Brontë, 90). It is only in reaction to Heathcliff, as Françoise Basch has pointed out, that their lady selves are deconstructed and they discover primal, oppositional rage (92). Lawrence, perhaps most interestingly, translates this vision of gender relations into his own terms in *Women in Love,* where the end result of Birkin's continual battle with Ursula's sentimental pretensions and feminine posturing is her discovery of an incisive female voice that repeatedly and authoritatively undercuts his pronouncements. Because Birkin's voice is, to a large extent, aligned with Lawrence's, this is, as in *Kangaroo,* a seemingly undesirable outcome. But in Lawrence's fiction the absorption of the male into the female is presented as positively as Heathcliff's final merging with the ghostly Cathy, who has always possessed him and determined his utterance.

While Lawrence's later works abundantly show his eager acceptance of Brontë's influence, *The White Peacock* also comments obliquely on his acceptance of that influence. It is along this oblique line of connection that the complexities and contradictions in Lawrence's renunciation of male selfhood appear. By pointedly modeling the partially autobiographical narrator Cyril on Lockwood and by naming Cyril's sweetheart "Emily," Lawrence suggests the psychological significance of his adaptation of Emily Brontë's story. Lawrence's need to imagine a connection between himself and Brontë was first manifested in his idea that she was like his friend, Jessie Chambers. What Chambers saw as "a clumsy probing into [her] personality" was probably also Lawrence's awkward first attempt to understand the woman writer whose work charted his own emotional landscape of incestuous longings, ungovernable anger, rejection of conventional roles, and intense identification with wild nature (Chambers, 130).

His choice to identify himself with Lockwood, rather than with Lockwood's creator, points to a desire to be contained within Brontë's vision and, so, to have his meaning created through her expression of it. But this desire to enter into and become part of Brontë's fiction is problematized by the exigencies of his own production of texts. To fulfill his chosen mission of writing for women, he must write the female voice as well as being written by it. He begins by attempting to construct an Emily Brontë that comes from/through himself.

The Emily in Lawrence's novel very much resembles Miriam of *Sons and Lovers* and is clearly derived from Chambers in many ways, but she can also be seen to represent Lawrence's vision of a sensibility both passionate and timid, wildly rebellious yet controlled by Christian morality. If Lawrence's idea of Emily Brontë was formed by both *Wuthering Heights* and the 1850 "Biographical Notice" Charlotte Brontë attached to it, he would probably have believed not only that she had such a nature, but also that "an interpreter ought always to have stood between her and the world" (Charlotte Brontë, 8). Emily Brontë herself provides two such interpreters in *Wuthering Heights,* Lockwood and Nelly Dean. Lawrence expands the role of the former and, by making the narrator a significant actor in the drama, uses him as a vehicle for self-revelation. His revelations seem to be as much concerned with his relationship to women's literature as with his relationship with any individual woman. The narration emphasizes Lawrence's uneasiness about his role as an interpreter of the female voice. Lawrence does not make Cyril, his narrator, a character parallel to Lockwood; rather he uses Cyril to join Brontë in her story and comment on his literary relationship to her even as he re-creates her and (re)interprets her tale.

That Emily Saxton is meant to represent Emily Brontë is made clear by

Lawrence's inclusion of a famous incident from Brontë's life. By 1909, Lawrence had read both Elizabeth Gaskell's *The Life of Charlotte Brontë* and Charlotte Brontë's *Shirley* (Burwell, 208, 211). Gaskell's biography includes an account of Emily being bitten by an apparently mad dog and, because of "her nobly stern presence of mind, going right into the kitchen, and taking up one of Tabby's red-hot Italian irons to sear the bitten place, and telling no one, till the danger was wellnigh over, for fear of the terror that might beset their weaker minds" (274–75). The story also appears in *Shirley,* where Charlotte modifies the incident to make her heroine's behavior more conventionally feminine than her sister's. The changes she makes are consistent with Shirley's character and do not seem meant to minimize her sister's heroism. Lawrence's alteration of the anecdote is another matter. It virtually recasts Emily in the role of enemy to nature. There is no suggestion that the dog that bites Emily in *The White Peacock* is mad; he is simply wild. She is not trying to help him, but to kill him. This distortion of the actual behavior of Emily Brontë the person suggests that Emily Saxton is meant as Brontë in the authorial persona that most confused and disturbed Lawrence.

Having oppositionally defined maleness as a viruslike state, characterized by a lack of any essential self, and marriage as the medium that allows maleness, in its deadly social form, to close off the female self, Brontë could not possibly show Heathcliff and Cathy marrying and living happily ever after. Heterosexual union, in the novel, is only satisfactory when achieved outside the material body that inevitably connects us to the social body. Although Lawrence seems to have been fully receptive to the tone of the story of Cathy and Heathcliff's passion, he resisted Brontë's narrative resolution of it. Because of physicality's importance to Lawrence, he could not accept a consummation placed outside bodies and mortal life. He seems only able to understand such a resolution as a cowardly fear of the physical/natural world. Consequently, Emily Saxton is shown as perpetually shrinking from nature and physical experience.

Lawrence associates this shrinking with the feminine by changing the genders in his revision of one crucial scene of *Wuthering Heights.* In *Wuthering Heights,* Cathy is bitten by a bull dog, tended by the Lintons, and socialized/feminized in the process. In *The White Peacock,* Annable's son, Sam, is bitten by a bull dog and tended by Emily, who sets about taming him. She teaches him to read and one of the first sentences in his lesson is "shoot the fox"—foreshadowing the action that marks Henry's transformation from natural to social man in *The Fox* (231). To Lawrence, maleness, with its unself-consciousness and, indeed, apparent lack of inner content, allows one to draw close to and even identify oneself with nature. The male can be filled with nature. Conversely, the female who (wrongly) allows femininity to define her self must draw back from nature's violence and raw materiality. Literacy and fiction are the means by which Emily puts nature at a remove, and the means by which Lawrence creates a vision of Brontë's fiction-making as a specifically feminine complicity with cultural myths against nature.

In the midst of his acceptance of its influence, Lawrence shows distrust of

Brontë's fiction-making, using it to represent woman's fiction-making. As he presents it, the voice that comes from the feminine constitutes a real danger, but its threat is no greater than that posed by failure to hear and respond to the female voice so often covered by it. Lawrence continually links his narrator's attraction to and recoil from women to the need of all the male characters to understand the demands made by the female voice in order to prosper or even to survive. In *Wuthering Heights* the male characters paradoxically project onto the women meaning as both vital shelter and wild unknown, hence Lockwood's extreme terror when he dreams that a girl is trying to come into his room in the night and the penalty he pays for rejecting her. Unwilling to risk contact with the demanding but enigmatic and contradictory feminine he himself has literally dreamed up, or to respond to Cathy's transcendent female presence, Lockwood is left outside, his hearth cold. In *The White Peacock,* George's destruction comes about because he draws back from Lettie's confusing desperation and fails to interpret her veiled demands that he free her from marriage. George prefers his dream of Lettie as the Lady to confronting the reality of her social entrapment. Heathcliff, Lockwood, and George are all failures at holding the women who could save them. Because they shy away from understanding the women, the men cannot act decisively to free them from their unnatural and oppressive social lives. Consequently the men themselves are left meaningless and wither away. Cyril is equally unable to free Emily and, within his anxiety, which pervades their contacts, we can read Lawrence's anxiety about his own failure to bring into prominence what he saw as the female voice in Brontë, that which speaks the value of woman against her valuation by society.

That Lawrence was not satisfied with his first interpretation of *Wuthering Heights* is indicated in numerous details in his characterization of Emily Saxton. These details express an anxious realization that he is failing to speak as if from female experience and failing to evoke a female essence. In his first scene with Emily, Cyril tries to rouse her out of her habitual irritation into real rage by articulating her feelings for her—"It makes you wild," he says—but can only make her show "nervous passion" (18). Later Cyril is unable to teach Emily to dance. Like Brontë, according to Charlotte's account, Emily is "powerless in the tumult of her feelings" (117). But when Cyril's sister, Lettie, takes over, the two women dance well together. Just as Charlotte Brontë's introduction attempts to give a more genteel and feminine cast to her sister's self-expression, Lettie's lead tames Emily's passionate movements into feminine prettiness. Lettie's and Charlotte Brontë's gender enables them to bond with the less socialized woman and, so, shape and direct (interpret) her self-expression so that her female passion is represented within the limits of feminine decorum. Without some source of interpretive authority, Lawrence knows that he must leave women's literature to the women, just as Cyril must stand and watch Lettie lead Emily in the dance.

Characteristically, in Lawrence's fiction, women seem a far more self-sufficient group than they do in *Wuthering Heights*. Brontë's women have little to say to each other, and Nelly, who stands as the nexus of all communications, is always ready to betray what she has learned, to turn speech into pain. What is suggested of an untrammelled and triumphant femaleness is seen in peripheral communications directed to no sister, but simply released into the void: Cathy's writing in the margins of religious texts, the negation of Edgar and Heathcliff written into the son Isabella names after them and marks for destruction. When men fail to read the female through the feminine in *Wuthering Heights,* the female remains untouched in her sublime solitude, though the woman's body may die. If men are hurt in the transaction, Brontë seems unconcerned. Brontë's power comes to her directly from what her works identify as the female within. But Lawrence, as a male author writing for women, needs to connect with what is female in his woman precursor. He is as dependent as Cyril on understanding woman and, so, releasing the essential female power that will give his existence meaning. His only means to power, in the literary territory he wishes to inhabit, is through interpretation of the female voice.

Cyril's future is foreshadowed by the lives of his natural father and Annable, who briefly acts as a father to him. Cyril says his mother "turned away" from her husband "with the scorn of a woman who finds that her romance has been a trumpery tale" (4). Annable's wife, too, turns away from marriage when the "Romance of a Poor Young Man" she creates to contain their passion begins to bore her (177). Both men are incapable of replacing their wives' feminine fictions with anything more satisfactory, so they lose their wives, who are finally too strongly female to be contained by the pretty stories society allows them to tell. The cast-off husbands go into decline and die. Cyril's only real hope, the novel suggests, would be to create a story that could satisfy a woman by expressing her full nature. Instead he is able only to create the brief homosexual shelter of the idyllic episode called "A Poem of Friendship." While this "poem" delights him, it can do nothing to structure his life or give it significance. In the next chapter, its mood gives way to those created by a book by "the squire's lady" and Emily's "legend," both of which work together to determine the futures of the main characters (260, 268). These metafictional references to the task of writing show Lawrence's awareness of his inability (in Keith Sagar's words) "to transcend Cyril's vision," as the inclusion of the failed attempt to unite with Emily shows his recognition that he is still unable to join his work successfully to Brontë's (*D. H. Lawrence* 17). His voice remains that which speaks only from and to maleness, which, in a stunning reversal of the usual valorization of such communications, he ranks hardly higher than the silence of death.

Since Lawrence chose to give away the authority of voice that his gender conveys, seemingly in the hope of speaking from the center of truth he found embedded in *Wuthering Heights,* it is not surprising that his failure to comprehend the book fully made him angry at the author as a woman. Lawrence seems enraged that the same woman who creates an untamable Heathcliff and holds him up to us as the living embodiment of nature's force all turned in adoration toward woman can then dispose of him to make way for the advent of a more manageable indoor version. In diminishing Brontë into a type of Jessie Chambers, Lawrence seems to be avenging himself upon her for allowing conventionality the apparent victory in a novel that would otherwise have been a tribute to uncompromising fierceness, for giving her readers a glimpse of the heaven in which male passion and female passion meet and fully natural life is attained, and, then, denying that it is possible in life after childhood. She becomes for him, in the simplest psychological terms, a figure of the withholding mother.

Lawrence's railing against such mothers in *The Lost Girl* illuminates his own understanding of the Oedipus myth as a description of the male condition.

> Wretched man what is he to do with these exigeant and never-to-be-satisfied women? Our mothers pined because our fathers drank and were rakes. Our wives pine because we are virtuous but inadequate. Who is this sphinx, this woman? Where is the Oedipus that will solve her riddle of happiness and then strangle her?—only to marry his own mother! (60)

That interpretation can be an aggressive act is blatantly obvious here. Interpreting the sphinx is the foreplay to killing her. But, as in *Kangaroo,* understanding forces union, and the man who sets out to make the withholding mother yield must end by marrying her. In literary terms, the question Lawrence puts to the sphinx is not "What do women want?" but "What do I mean in her language?" The primary intention behind all of Lawrence's work seems to be the solution of the riddle of how the female voice assigns meaning to men, but, ironically, like the Oedipus in his complaint, he fights with his (literary) mother only to return to her. Having wrested away the authority to define her and, so, himself, he nervously gives it back to find out if that was what she really meant (and meant him to mean). In his reworkings of material from *Wuthering Heights,* he vacillates between locating his own voice in relation to the meanings Brontë seems to assign to man and woman, and trying to speak in her voice to say what he wishes she had.

In her insightful article, "Potent Griselda," Sandra Gilbert demonstrates Lawrence's "preoccupation" with the Great Mother who is served by Dionysus. She discusses his mixed feelings about "both real mothers and Great Mothers," but might have added comment on his similar feelings about literary mothers (151). Ambivalence about Emily Brontë is evident in the novella to which she devotes most of her attention, *The Ladybird.* Parallel descriptions of characters immediately suggest *Wuthering Heights.* However, Count Psanek, who returns to Daphne against his will, just as Heathcliff returns to the married Cathy, and becomes her "vicar in wrath" (65), has the eloquence Heathcliff lacks. Heathcliff is taciturn even with Cathy. Psanek "can't stop talking" to Daphne, and even tells her, "I speak for me and you" (58, 63). Psanek's ability to express Daphne's unconscious thoughts is Lawrence's solution to the problem Brontë poses. Because Cathy is too ignorant of the connection between sexuality and love to understand that it is imperative to her own sanity and Heathcliff's that she not give herself to

Edgar, she never directly gives Heathcliff the authority to save her. Psanek speaks as (rather than merely symbolizing) the fierce female spirit hidden in woman. Unlike Heathcliff, he can, as he promises Daphne, "always be in the darkness of" her, while still communicating freely with her conscious self (104). This is necessary not just for Daphne's good, but because, as Gilbert shows, Psanek is no more of an autonomous individual than Heathcliff. Like Heathcliff, Psanek exists through the woman he loves; she must come to him "else he would die" (102).

Lawrence implies that Psanek is Daphne's weaker half. The mythic and fairy tale levels of *The Ladybird,* as Gilbert observes, refer to tales of female power to create men or bring them back to life, including the stories of Isis and Osiris, Demeter and Dionysus, Theseus and Ariadne, and Grimm's six swans and their sister (146–49). Alienated Psanek, "like a little ghost," scarcely seems to exist outside the dark connection Daphne allows him to have with her (97). On the story's mythic/symbolic levels, he seems to be a magic creature called into being by her need. In the same sense that Heathcliff is the fairytale answer to Cathy's request for a whip (Gilbert and Gubar, *Madwoman* 264), Psanek is the answer to Daphne's desperate subconscious call, as Lawrence's repeated references to "calls" and "summonses" at the story's climax suggests. Psanek, in turn, like the forgotten wild part of Daphne, calls her "into the underworld" of their dark, silent communion, the subconscious world in which she finds "her soul" (or female essence) and, so, peace (103–04).

Like Heathcliff, Psanek acts primarily as the agent for what is repressed in his beloved. Daphne, "remains silently master," forcing Psanek to express her secret anger to her father and husband (95). Lawrence rejects the realistic level of *Wuthering Heights,* in which Brontë shows that the world will not allow female wholeness, only to adhere more tenaciously to the spirit of Brontë's novel: her assertion that despite the world's demands, female passions are infinitely valuable, are the only transcendent things on earth. As Psanek is the answer to Daphne, speaking what she cannot, Lawrence tries to make himself act as an answer to Brontë. In his characteristic polemical style, he asserts the worth of female passion and expresses female rage against the conventional world. Here his ambivalence emerges. The two main narrators of *Wuthering Heights,* behind whom Brontë glides, evading interpretation, are put aside. Lawrence offers a revision that reduces *Wuthering Heights* to myth and ignores its many comments on specific crimes against women in a specific time and place. Cathy and Heathcliff's rage against the world is separated from its economic and political causes and presented *only* as protest against woman's eternally re-enacted entrapment in a socially constructed femininity. Moreover, Daphne, unlike Cathy, cannot express her anger directly. Man, who is often little more than an artistic convenience to Brontë, becomes an existential necessity to woman in Lawrence's interpretation of Brontë. Thus, Lawrence becomes the rather self-important answer to a call that he himself projects as coming from Brontë.

Certainly, Lawrence's aggressive appropriation of the female voice, in this instance, goes against any attitude one might associate with feminism. But aside from his comical insistence on having it call for him, he seems bent upon using it to disrupt his own speech, in a pattern mimicking the intrusions of female influence into his creative processes. Lawrence's "female" voice becomes, at some points, almost indistinguishable from a feminist voice of resistance to patriarchal discourse. Although it is clear from a great many of Lawrence's poems and essays that he was attracted by the idea of women's rage cured into quiet submissiveness, he seems unwilling to dramatize such a resolution in his fiction. Even when he sets the stage to show it, in what are often called the male leadership stories, the conflict between the sexes is projected beyond the novels' closings; the angry voices of his women seem likely to continue being heard. When Lawrence "returns to tenderness" with *Lady Chatterley's Lover,* he also turns to *Jane Eyre,* apparently determined to show that Jane should have been mated to the wrathful Heathcliff rather than buried in Victorian niceness with the safely crippled Rochester. In fact, what is surprising about Lawrence's rewriting of Charlotte Brontë's story is its revelation that what really disturbed him about *Jane Eyre* was the taming of Jane, the resolution of her rage rather than the means by which it is resolved.

The figure who represents Jane's rage is given an important role in the second version of *Lady Chatterley's Lover, John Thomas and Lady Jane.* David Higdon has convincingly demonstrated that Lawrence's Bertha Coutts, the estranged wife of the gamekeeper, was derived from Bertha Mason (294–96). Their lives, habits, and attitudes are remarkably similar and Bertha Coutts is even described as being "like a mad-woman" (298). But, while *Jane Eyre* tells us very little that can excite sympathy for Bertha Mason, Connie blames Parkin's insufficiencies for driving her rival "evil-mad" (298). Connie's musings about the marriage-maddened Bertha recall Cathy Earnshaw, who also "fought against even the love in her own soul" (Lawrence, 299). Lawrence, like Emily Brontë (and Jean Rhys), finds the explanation of the wife's insanity in her situation as wife—in the situation of any wife—subject through marriage to the demands of a patriarchal order that denies her femaleness. Moreover, Lawrence, like Brontë, keeps this specter of female rage alive.

If Bertha represents Cathy's angry ghost, Connie is no civilized and repressed Catherine Linton. Like Cathy (or Jane in her childhood), the Connie of *John Thomas and Lady Jane* exults in her own rage. Her anger, again like that of both other heroines, arises from her condition as a woman. "She [is] angry, angry at the implied insult to womanhood" not once but often throughout the novel (333). Like Cathy and Jane, she finds an angry, rebellious lover, but unlike them, she understands that his fury is "part of her own revolt" (275). The intermingling of angry voices destroys the false "paradise of wealth and well-being" available to Connie at Wragby Hall, but destroys nothing in the two lovers except the artificial genders built up around their true selves by society (245). Yet the Eden left is still contained within the male order and seems to depend on open female revolt against it.

Implicit in Lawrence's responses to *Wuthering Heights* is his reading of it as a parable about the importance of man and woman to each other and nature to both. To the extent that Brontë's concerns go beyond the material world, Lawrence seems uninterested in them. Lawrence saw his own power and authority as so closely connected to nature and the body that he could not embrace any vision of noncorporeal bliss. But he does not, like Bloom, equate the author and her heroine. To Lawrence, Cathy represents the aspect of Brontë that needs the body, no matter how imprisoning marriage and pregnancy have made it seem to her, to make possible revitalizing contact with the natural world and so must always run the risk of finding the walls of femininity taking form around her. While he is more than content to treat Brontë as a disembodied, ahistorical female voice, he interprets Cathy's longing to escape the body as the mark of sexual failure not as the inevitable inclination of a great spirit.

However, Bloom is right to observe that the energy in *Wuthering Heights* is not the sort that can find satisfactory expression in earthly activities. It is impossible to imagine Heathcliff and Cathy chastely warming each other and then drawing apart refreshed like Joe Boswell and Yvette Saywell in *The Virgin and the Gipsy,* or planning to work a little farm like Mellors and Connie Chatterley. Lawrence's impulse to rewrite the novel to allow Heathcliff's and Cathy's passion a happy consummation in the world is naïve. Brontë's feminism is of another sort than that which proposes worldly solutions. Despite her enumeration of injustices in property laws, she seems ultimately above concern with social change, although not above gender chauvinism. In *Wuthering Heights,* she values woman's natural passions above all else, and disdains everything, including woman's own fertility, that interferes with the expression of those passions. What gives Cathy Earnshaw stature is her refusal to accept any compromise, her refusal to control herself in any way.

In this unusually high valuation of female passion, lamentable from a liberal humanist standpoint, Brontë and Lawrence meet in a kind of feminism. Both writers break from culturally inscribed dichotomies as well when they make males figure both nature and culture, and posit woman as the universal subject finding a self in reference to the pull of each. One might even call Lawrence's understanding of *Wuthering Heights* feminist because his variations on its theme show that he evaluates the male characters exclusively according to their usefulness to women. Like Brontë, he sees tragedy as the violation of woman's connection to the natural world and man as important only in so far as he affects woman.

Lawrence, however, begins to move back across the border between gendered texts when he goes from finding an ideology through Brontë to speaking as/for her. In apparent reaction to his recognition of the necessity of the female voice and audience to his own existence as an author, he insists upon the necessity of man to woman. His high valuation of female passion is always accompanied by implied or explicit exhortations to men to interpret it for the women who feel it. If his women generally found their female voices issuing from the throats of men, as Daphne does, Lawrence would make us understand Brontë's feminism only by contrast. The confrontation between their texts would have the look of war and its crossfire would show us the hard outlines of a textual gender-specificity without shading. Instead, Lawrence's virtual compulsion to give voice to female anger, which resists appropriation and undercuts his meanings even as he speaks them, makes the border waver. Although Lawrence's "new heaven and earth" have in common with the old one masculine domination of discourse and control of the physical dimension, in this respect, the world of Lawrence's fiction is almost always a return to the world of *Wuthering Heights* before the first sighting of the Lintons: female anger and revolt flourishing in the interstices of patriarchal power.

Notes

1. Miller identifies this as one of her primary goals. ("Arachnologies: The Woman, the Text, and the Critic" 288).

2. There was no time in Lawrence's life when he did not rely heavily on comments from women he knew to shape his work. Occasionally his response to women's criticism was remarkably submissive. He completely rewrote *The White Peacock* on Jessie Chamber's recommendation (Chambers, 117). He asked Helen Corke "to cut out any prolix passage" from the final draft of *The Trespasser* (Corke, 232). When Mabel Dodge Luhan expressed annoyance with his first essay on the Hopi snake dance, he wrote a completely new version (Luhan, 268). And at Frieda's demand, he rewrote the ending of *The Boy in the Bush* in a way that he felt destroyed its artistic integrity (Brett, 128–29).

3. See Gilbert and Gubar's *The Madwoman in the Attic* for a full discussion of Edgar as a figure for patriarchal law (280–82).

Works Cited

Basch, Françoise. *Relative Creatures: Victorian Women in Society and the Novel.* New York: Schocken, 1974.

Baym, Nina. "The Madwoman and Her Languages: Why I Don't Do Feminist Literary Theory." In *Feminist Issues in Literary Scholarship.* Edited by Shari Benstock. Bloomington: Indiana University Press, 1987. 45–61.

Bloom, Harold. Introduction. *The Brontës.* Edited by Harold Bloom. New York: Chelsea, 1987. 1–11.

Brontë, Charlotte. "Biographical Notice of Ellis and Acton Bell." In *Wuthering Heights.* 1850. Edited by William M. Sale, Jr. New York: Norton, 1971. 3–8.

———. *Shirley.* 1849. Edited by Andrew and Judith Hook. Harmondsworth: Penguin, 1974.

Brontë, Emily. *Wuthering Heights.* 1847. Edited by William M. Sale, Jr. New York: Norton, 1971.

Brett, Dorothy. *Lawrence and Brett: A Friendship.* 1933. Santa Fe: Sunstone, 1974.

Burwell, Rose Marie. "A Catalogue of D. H. Lawrence's Reading from Early Childhood." *The D. H. Lawrence Review* 3 (1970): 193–330.

Chambers, Jessie [E. T.]. *D. H. Lawrence: A Personal Record.* Edited and with an introduction by A. J. Bramley. New York: Barnes, 1965.

Corke, Helen. "The Writing of *The Trespasser.*" *The D. H. Lawrence Review* 7 (1974): 227–39.

de Beauvoir, Simone. *The Second Sex.* Translated and edited by H. M. Parshley. New York: Bantam, 1961.

Fetterley, Judith. *The Resisting Reader: A Feminist Approach to American Fiction.* Bloomington: Indiana University Press, 1978.

Gaskell, Elizabeth. *The Life of Charlotte Brontë.* 1857. Edited by Alan Shelston. Harmondsworth: Penguin, 1975.

Gilbert, Sandra M. "Potent Griselda: 'The Ladybird' and the Great Mother." In *D. H. Lawrence: A Centenary Consideration.* Edited by Peter Balbert and Philip L. Marcus. Ithaca: Cornell University Press, 1985. 130–61.

Gilbert, Sandra M., and Susan Gubar. *The Madwoman in the Attic: The Woman Writer and the Nineteenth-Century Literary Imagination.* New Haven: Yale University Press, 1979.

———. *No Man's Land: The Place of the Woman Writer in the Twentieth Century.* 2 vols. to date. New Haven: Yale University Press, 1988–9.

Griffin, Susan. *Woman and Nature: The Roaring Inside Her.* New York: Harper, 1978.

Higdon, David Leon. "Bertha Coutts and Bertha Mason: A Speculative Note." *The D. H. Lawrence Review* 11 (1978): 294–96.

Homans, Margaret. *Bearing the Word: Language and Female Experience in Nineteenth-Century Women's Writing.* Chicago: University of Chicago Press, 1986.

Jacobus, Mary. *Reading Woman: Essays in Feminist Criticism.* New York: Columbia University Press, 1986.

Jehlen, Myra. "Archimedes and the Paradox of Feminist Criticism." *Signs* 6 (1981): 575–601.

Lawrence, D. H. *The First Lady Chatterley.* 1944. Harmondsworth: Penguin, 1973.

———. *Four Short Novels.* 1923. New York: Viking, 1974.

———. *The Fox. Four Short Novels.* 111–80.

———. *John Thomas and Lady Jane.* Harmondsworth: Penguin, 1972.

———. *Kangaroo.* 1923. New York: Viking, 1960.

———. *Lady Chatterley's Lover.* 1928. New York: Bantam, 1968.

———. *The Ladybird. Four Short Novels.* 41–111.

———. *The Lost Girl.* 1920. Harmondsworth: Penguin, 1977.

———. *Mr. Noon.* Edited by Lindeth Vasey. Cambridge: Cambridge University Press, 1984.

———. Introduction. *The Mother.* By Grazia Deledda. Traveller's Library. Cape: London, 1928. Reprint. In *Phoenix: The Posthumous Papers of D. H. Lawrence.* 1936. Edited by Edward D. McDonald. New York: Penguin, 1978. 263–66.

———. *The White Peacock.* 1911. Harmondsworth: Penguin, 1950.

———. *Women in Love.* 1920. New York: Compass-Viking, 1966.

Luhan, Mabel Dodge. *Lorenzo in Taos.* New York: Knopf, 1932.

Miller, Nancy K. "Arachnologies: The Woman, the Text, and the Critic." In *The Poetics of Gender.* Edited by Nancy K. Miller. New York: Columbia University Press, 1986. 270–301.

Moers, Ellen. *Literary Women.* Garden City: Doubleday, 1977.

Moi, Toril. *Sexual/Textual Politics: Feminist Literary Theory*. New York: Methuen, 1985.
Pratt, Annis. "Woman and Nature in Modern Fiction." *Contemporary Literature* 13 (1972): 466–90.
Sagar, Keith. *D. H. Lawrence: Life into Art*. New York: Viking, 1985.
———. "The Originality of *Wuthering Heights*." In *The Art of Emily Brontë*. Edited by Ann Smith. London: Vision, 1976. 121–59.
Schor, Naomi. "Dreaming Dissymmetry: Barthes, Foucault, and Sexual Difference." In *Men in Feminism*. Edited by Alice Jardine and Paul Smith. Methuen: New York, 1987. 98–110.
Schneider, Daniel J. *D. H. Lawrence: The Artist as Psychologist*. Lawrence: University of Kansas Press, 1984.
Sedgwick, Eve Kosofsky. *Between Men: English Literature and Male Homosocial Desire*. New York: Columbia University Press, 1985.
Showalter, Elaine. "Towards a Feminist Poetics." In *Women Writing and Writing about Women*. Edited by Mary Jacobus. New York: Barnes, 1979. 22–41.

"To Write What Cannot Be Written"[1]: The Woman Writer and Male Authority in John Hawkes's *Virginie: Her Two Lives*

Peter F. Murphy

The relation of a woman's writing to authoritative male discourse has dominated much of feminist literary theory over the past ten to fifteen years.[2] The debate has focused on sexual difference, female identity, and the woman writer. In *Virginie: Her Two Lives*, John Hawkes confronts this relationship head-on. Relying on a female narrator for the first time in his fiction, Hawkes examines ways in which women writers resist the patriarchal control exercised by one man. In this case, the man is an instructor, a professor of love.

Formally similar to Virginia Woolf's *Orlando, Virginie: Her Two Lives*, tells the story of a young girl who lives during two different historical periods: 1740 *ancien régime* France and 1945 post–World War II Paris. In 1740, Virginie helps the aristocratic Seigneur operate a school for women and in 1945 she and Bocage, a Parisian taxi driver, run a surrealist bordello. Seigneur's school instructs women of the lower classes to become erotically receptive women, especially in ways that will accommodate the tastes of a decadent French nobility. Bocage, on the other hand, assembles a group of prostitutes for his evenings of entertainment. From Seigneur's allegorical "Land of Love" to Bocage's satirical "Sex Arcade," Virginie maintains her innocence. Throughout her continued exposure to bizarre sexual episodes in both Seigneur's voluptuous world and Bocage's sensual underworld, Virginie remains committed to writing her journal, to telling her story, and, in this way, to unraveling her own deep, sexual ambivalence.

As the implied male author of *Virginie*, Hawkes confronts two provocative situations for a feminist male writer: his relationship to Seigneur, the male protagonist/pornographer and to Virginie, the narrator of the story and a woman writer. Hawkes uses the ambiguous, ambivalent, and ultimately (from a feminist viewpoint) suspect figure of Seigneur to explore the dilemmas of male heterosexuality. At the same time that he speaks through Seigneur and thus re-inscribes masculinist, misogynist discourses, Hawkes attempts to speak the feminine in a positive, even feminist sense. He uses Seigneur to explain the possibility as well as the contradictions of male liberation vis-à-vis feminism. For Hawkes, Seigneur represents a comic surrender to Hawkes's own phallocentrism. This ironical distance permits Hawkes to conceptualize women and, at the same time, decons- truct pornography. Unlike the majority of male writers who have explored this potentially misogynistic terrain, Hawkes exposes the fascination men have with pornography without evasion, guilt and shame, or aggression. Through the male voice in this novel, Hawkes confronts the confusion of male heterosexual desire in an attempt to understand the frustration of the woman writer as the subject of male authority. Virginie exemplifies this contradiction and allows Hawkes to examine the depth of this dilemma.

An ironic perversion of a Sadeian discourse, *Virginie* can be read as a feminist text. Hawkes's parody of de Sade invites the male reader into the text by exposing many of the contradictions informing male heterosexuality. Seigneur's lessons to the women at his school abound with aspects of the traditional male heterosexual role: voyeurism, pornography, submission-domination, and incest. The satirical tone of Hawkes's novel allows the male reader to see the asburdity of these fantasies while at the same time recognizing the magnitude of his own complicity in them. The difficulty men experience in their struggle to transcend the socially prescribed role of masculinity bears some similarity to the frustration of the woman writer. Writing through the feminine may be a way for Hawkes to understand the dynamics of his own dilemma as both a heterosexual male and a relatively unknown author.

As a fairly unknown author himself, Hawkes may identify with the plight of his female protagonist. In this way, he explores the frustration of both writing what cannot be written and, more to the point, writing what will not be read. By writing the feminine, Hawkes tries to transcend the silence of the male body which is implicit in Seigneur's behavior toward the women.

The point of Hawkes's novel, however, may be that while it is helpful for men to write in the feminine voice, to undertake that difference, it is just as important for them to write critically about their own sexuality. As Cixous makes clear, "men still have everything to say about their sexuality and everything to write" (247). By writing through the feminine, male authors can examine the fantasies as well as the realities of male heterosexuality. In *Virginie: Her Two Lives*, Hawkes explores the unconscious dreams of men as perceived by women. This powerful deconstruction of male desire reveals the contradictions of men in love.

The first section of *Virginie: Her Two Lives*, entitled "Her Poem," introduces the reader to what will become a primary force in the novel: the power of the written word, and in particular, a woman's written word. In this brief section three male lovers argue about who the beloved woman cares for the most. Is it her delicate glance, her holding of the man's hand, or her surreptitious nudge of the lover's foot under the table that signifies her love? All three men are convinced that each of these gestures carries the strongest indication of her love. At the end of the debate, however, the lady tells them that none of these signs is the most powerful; rather, it is to a fourth lover, "who each day receives [her] letter" (5), that she gives her love. Thus, the written word, the power of discourse, supersedes other forms of expression.

This initial thematization of the importance of women's writing pervades the novel, which includes a second section entitled "Her Journals" and a closing, one page section, entitled "Her Final Entry." In "Her Journals" Virginie records her experiences with Seigneur and Bocage as well as those with the many women with whom she becomes more and more intimate. She fills these diaries with reflections on her life as a woman and, of greater consequence, on her life as a woman writer. She explores the relationship between women and writing, the power that that relationship encompasses, and the frustration, even impotence, that that relationship engenders.

The authority of personal experience and its importance for women's writing has obtained a crucial position in much feminist literary criticism. Unlike scientific criticism which "struggles to purge itself of the subjective" (Showalter, 1979, 38), a feminist poetics celebrates the authority of female subjective experience. In many ways, Virginie's life consists of the traditional roles women have assumed throughout history: She takes care of all the others and, in 1740, for example, she "forgot about [herself] as usual and again found [all] her happiness in that of others" (35). In 1945, she explains:

> I was mistress of our house. I fed *Maman*, I washed Bocage's back . . . and on the wet floor beside the iron tub, knelt like the faithful busy attendant that I was. . . .
> I fired the stove, boiled water, wore my apron, handled the heavy spoon as long as my arm, on hands and knees regarded the reflection of my face in the stones I polished. (68)

The fatigue that comes from this kind of responsibility affects Virginie's writing ability as it has that of many women writers. In her early feminist classic, *A Room of One's Own*, Virginia Woolf identified this problem as a key to the difficulty faced by women writers. And, more recently, Adrienne Rich has characterized the exhaustion caused by domestic work as "that female fatigue of suppressed anger and loss of contact with my own being; partly from the discontinuity of female life with all its attention to small chores, errands, work that others constantly undo" (1979, 43). Virginie struggles against these distractions and fatigue to write her story. From the opening paragraph of the novel when she reflects, "Mine is an impossible story . . . I do not write . . . I do not exist" (9–10) to the end of the novel when she states "from its ashen niche I drew forth my journal, which no one allows or encourages me to read aloud, nor ever shall" (191), Virginie reflects constantly on the difficulty, even the impossibility, of being a woman writer.

Virginie seems aware of the likelihood that her journals may not be read when, in her reverie over the ecstasy of writing, she points out: "I am thankful I have the power of solacing myself with dreams of creations which neither I nor anyone shall ever see" (191). The recurrent image of Virginie's journals burning up and thus the impossibility (literally) of their being read, even some time in the future, exemplifies the hopelessness of the woman writer. Historically, women's writing has been denied and ignored, so Virginie's belief that her writing will also be disavowed is not unreasonable.

Seigneur retains his position of power by assigning to all the women at his school the keeping of a journal. He has them read sections of their journals which he interprets and/or criticizes. Seigneur's students, like so many women writers, experience "the need to provoke masculine response [as] the controlling factor in [their] writing" (Showalter, 1979, 33–34). At the end of Colère's story of the three sisters sitting by a stream talking about love, for example, she "appealed . . . to . . . Seigneur . . . to release her from ignorance, muteness and humiliation" (108). She needs Seigneur's approval, his acknowledgment of her abilities and intelligence. Without his endorsement, she remains silent and disgraced.

When she relates the complete story, Colère confirms Cixous's observation that "every woman has known the torment of getting up to speak. Her heart racing, at times entirely lost for words, ground and language slipping away. . . . A double distress, for even if she transgresses, her words fall almost always upon the deaf male ear, which hears in language only that which speaks in the masculine" (251). For Colère, "the open book trembled in her hands. Her voice was faltering. But she commenced to read" (103). Throughout her brief oration, Colère interrupts her story several times, repeats what she has just said, and stammers along. Seigneur focuses exclusively on the form of Colère's story when he reminds her that the writing of poetry is forbidden at his school. Echoing Plato's infamous concern over the power of the poet in the ideal state, Seigneur's restriction also anticipates Cixous's observation that "poetry involves gaining strength through the unconscious and because the unconscious, that other limitless country, is the place where the represented manages to survive" (250). Even though she is under the sway of Seigneur, Virginie's story begins with an effort to undermine one of his basic tenets: that women should always write in prose and never in poetry.

Hawkes's parody of de Sade in the character of Seigneur is exemplified by Seigneur's power to determine which female qualities will be represented at his school. His pupils signify the "five qualities of true womanhood: . . . anger, wit, voluptuousness, delicacy and magic" (30). These characteristics inspired the name Seigneur gives to each of them: *Colère, Bel Esprit, Volupté, Finesse,* and *Magie,* respectively. At first glance, anger (*Colère*), as an indispensable quality of women, seems incongruous with the traditional male heterosexual fantasy. Wit, voluptuousness, delicacy, and magic are consistent with this conception of the ideal woman, but anger does not fit. Men want women to be charming, sexy and docile, not hostile or rebellious. As the women's education unfolds, however, the significance of anger becomes clearer. Anger, as "the hallmark of women's writing,"[3] inspires Seigneur's students. At his school, the proud woman, the woman with a will of her own, becomes *La Noblesse*, the educated woman. Ironically, though, the first graduate of Seigneur's school introduced in the novel, shows no gratitude for his training, forgives nothing and, in fact, disdains her instructor. Empowered by her ability to write, La Noblesse rebels against the restraints Seigneur imposes upon her and her "sisters."

One of Seigneur's many poignant lessons teaches pride, "the heart of womanhood" (61). Having just learned about innocence, Magie learns self-esteem. The proud woman appears as a recurrent misogynist fantasy in literature written by men. The teaching of self-esteem, however, represents a radical variance on this theme. Women's pride usually relates to their vanity. Self-worth emphasizes individual power which depends not on a man's perception of a woman but on her own sense of value. Hawkes's vivid representation of the male fascination with female pride exposes the contradictory nature of Seigneur's lesson.

In an attempt to demonstrate his own power, Seigneur pulls two teeth out of a horse's mouth right in front of Magie. When he gives her the gift of these teeth, Seigneur tells her:

> She who is able to receive the gift, no matter the nature of that gift, is proud. . . .
> It is pride that makes a woman loved, or makes her desired, and the greater a
> woman's pride the more she is loved. . . . The amount of pain implicit in the gift
> is the only measure of a woman's pride. The greater the pain the more valuable
> the gift and the fiercer her pride. And the extent of her pride is the only measure
> of a woman's worth. (61)

This scene reveals women's socialization to bear the pain of others rather than accept a gift for themselves. Women are socialized to sacrifice for the sake of others, especially children and animals. As if echoing Tillie Olsen's observation that "women are traditionally trained to place others' needs first, to feel those needs as their own" (35), rather than see the horse harmed again, Magie offers herself to be injured. Women must confront their tendency to support others at the sacrifice of themselves and Magie must learn to respect herself first, to care for and to appreciate her own needs and desires. This self-consciousness manifests itself most clearly in a woman's writing by which, according to Cixous, a woman invents a "new insurgency." Though Seigneur's lessons (like all patriarchal education) emphasize women's docility and other traditional features of the feminine as a gender role, by learning to write the women learn to rebel against Seigneur's regimen. Magie's education, as that of all the women, inspires her to speak and thus enter into history.

Seigneur's power to name the women and to educate them exemplifies male authority. This patriarch and master describes his lessons at great length. He warns a new initiate of his cruelty and perversity. Echoing de Sade, Seigneur explains that "the regimen of true eroticism is strenuous" (29). But Hawkes's elaborate description of the women's training extends his parody of Sadeian discourse. By stating directly and without literary embellishment the objectives of Seigneur's lessons, Hawkes confronts yet one more male heterosexual fantasy:

> [The] person of true womanhood: a person, that is, indomitable in taste, speech, intelligence and the art of love, . . . You shall be trained in music as well as in the multitudinous forms of the erotic embrace; you shall know the beasts of farmyard and field . . . and you shall be expected to write in a journal, in prose but never in verse. (29)

Like the female characters in the novels of Jane Austen and Charlotte Brontë, women in this novel learn to sing, play the piano, and do needlework. The women weave the "Tapestry of Love" which, when unveiled at the end of the novel, reveals, ironically, the significance of Seigneur's vision. Unlike Emma and Jane Eyre, however, the women in *Virginie* learn how to make love. This knowledge empowers the women in their quest for liberation from the control of male heterosexuality and the history of social institutions reinforcing its omnipotence. These institutions and social assumptions make women indifferent to their own sexual desires. For Seigneur, a woman who can express her sexual passion transcends the experience of a woman manipulated by the sexual demands of her husband. While this may seem to be just one more male lesbian fantasy, Hawkes makes it clear that the women in the novel find each other attractive in spite of Seigneur's stress on "compulsory heterosexuality" (Rich). Like writing, sexuality empowers in ways that the teacher may not anticipate. The women's liberation in this novel occurs in opposition to the restrictions placed upon them by the patriarch, and Seigneur's lessons work against his goals as frequently as they do for them.

At times, however, Seigneur deviates from much of the male tradition controlling women's self-expression, a tradition characterized by Joanna Russ as one committed to promulgating "the idea that women make themselves ridiculous by creating art, or that writing or painting is immodest" (25). Seigneur believes quite strongly in the importance of women writing and being creative. Frequently, though, Seigneur employs "the trick [of making] the freedom as nominal a freedom as possible and then . . . develop[ing] various strategies for ignoring, condemning or belittling the artistic work that results" (Russ, 4–5). Seigneur maintains his position of power by belittling the women's ability to write well and their capacity to understand the subtle meanings of their stories. When Finesse tells her enigmatic story about fidelity between Arnaud and Celestine, Seigneur prefaces her tale by saying "I hope you have improved your style of writing." When she finishes her story, Seigneur "interpret[s] it more concretely" for the women (172–73).

The women in Seigneur's autocratically run school are more complacent than the women at Bocage's bordello. When, for example, the women at Seigneur's school "were exempt, [one] hour, from the obligations imposed upon them by

Seigneur, [they] talk[ed] to each other in soft voices" (96). In contrast, the women of Bocage's brothel actively oppose his restrictions and ideas. When he tells the women he is going out to procure "the indispensable element: men" (36) they laugh at him and applaud mockingly.

By 1945, two hundred years after Virginie's first life in the novel, a far greater feminist heritage exists. In postwar France, just four years before the publication of de Beauvoir's *The Second Sex*, women have begun to question men's indispensability. Bocage shares these doubts. Though he informs them one evening that they are too thin (an observation against which they rebel vociferously), Bocage remarks that a woman's desire is not prompted by or dependent on a man.

Seigneur, for all his radical ideas about women's power in love, retains many traditional views on femininity. For him, La Noblesse, the woman who successfully completes his lessons on love and womanhood and thus embodies all his art, shall be able "to command flowers and the entire universe of love" (146). But Seigneur's fantasy of female desire goes awry almost from the beginning. Not only does the novel open with a poem, the one literary genre Seigneur excludes from the writing options of his students, but the first woman introduced from his school is the highly rebellious La Noblesse.

Seigneur's instruction and the lesson of women's history confirm the potential that education has to empower women, especially when that education emphasizes the ability to write. As Seigneur's women gain knowledge of themselves and their plight as women under patriarchal authority, they rebel against his regulations and demands. His emphasis on women writing and women telling their stories empowers the women beyond his expectations. Their eventual rebellion against his authority confirms Cixous's assertion that "writing is precisely the very possibility of change" (249). By the end of the novel all the women at Seigneur's school rebel and burn him alive.

Before they kill him, though, he manages to unveil the "Tapestry of Love" to Virginie, who observes that the image of the erect penis dominating the tapestry "is a magnificent mirage." Seigneur agrees with this assertion and carries it one step further to point out that so "are the man, the woman, the labyrinth itself. The scepter is the emblem of them all! and just as indestructible! and as much a mirage!" (205). Both indestructible and an illusion, the phallus remains a symbol of power. The tapestry and Seigneur's conception of male sexuality are both confining and liberating. Unlike Lacan, for whom "the phallus can play its role only when veiled" (288), for Hawkes (and Seigneur) the phallus must be unveiled, must be exposed, in order for one to understand its power and, at the same time, begin to transcend that illusory omnipotence. On this point, Hawkes seems to be in complete agreement with Jane Gallop who believes that "contrary to phallic veiling, feminine discourse reveals the sex organ" (31).

By the end of the novel, Seigneur becomes a pathetic character precisely because he believes himself to be indispensable to the women. He is convinced that in his absence they would not understand their sexuality and could not become the kind of educated, sexually informed women that he wishes to create. A Pygmalion figure par excellence, Seigneur never quite understands female sexuality, even though he spends most of his life teaching the subject. Through Seigneur, Hawkes seems to be saying that men can't understand female sexuality and shouldn't try to. Men need to deconstruct their own sexuality, to examine the problematic nature of their own desires and needs.

The French feminist concept of *jouissance* offers one provocative way into the problematics of writing about sexuality and invites both women and men into the dialogue. Kristeva's belief that "men, too, have access to the *jouissance* that opposes phallogocentrism" (Jones, 363) positions John Hawkes as just such a male writer. The men's crying out in ecstasy during their orgasms exemplifies the "giving, expending, dispensing of pleasure without concern about ends or closure" that *jouissance* emphasizes (Jones, 375). The women at Seigneur's school also learn this "radically violent pleasure . . . which shatters—dissipates, loses—[the] cultural identity [and] ego" (Heath, 9), but for the men the lesson is a more difficult one to grasp.

Men still have a lot to learn about their own sexuality, a sexuality that, according to one woman at Bocage's bordello, should encompass "generosity, virility, wisdom, and a sense of humor" (85). The irony of her observation is that Seigneur possesses none of these characteristics. He is selfish, celibate, at times stupid, and rarely even smiles, much less laughs outright. Bocage, on the other hand, manifests many of these qualities.

Over time, almost all of the women in Virginie's life gain a critical under-standing of men, but Virginie herself remains innocent of these insights. While Virginie may have more power and freedom than any of the other women at the school, she is more dependent upon Seigneur to make sense out of her life; she has fallen in love with him. In the context of her writing, Virginie realizes that Seigneur is "the figure thanks to whom [she] had found [her] voice and [her] soul as well, which were forever his" (207). This dependence on male authority is as fatal for Virginie as it has been for women throughout literary history.

Virginie commits suicide at the end of the novel by jumping onto Seigneur's funeral pyre. Her suicide is due not solely to her dependence upon Seigneur as one individual man, but rather her frustration as a woman writer confined by what Cixous calls "the phallocentric tradition." The patriarchal monopoly of language, a control that pervades the way we think and write, "dominates nearly the entire history of writing" (249). In particular, the history of women's writing has been victimized by male domination. Russ's observation that "without models, it's hard to work; without a context, difficult to evaluate; without peers, nearly impossible to speak" (95) highlights the dilemma Virginie experiences with her own writing.

Virginie's despair as a female author and her inability to become a woman, in the sense that Seigneur and Bocage think of that identity, has nothing to do with being too young to lose her virginity to a man. Rather, her frustration arises from the fact that she finds women as attractive and sexually stimulating as she does men. As the Radclyffe Hall of the eighteenth century, Virginie possesses a strong ambivalence about her sexuality and her writing. Hints of Virginie's sexual attraction to women abound in the novel. What Sally McConnell-Ginet refers to as the "interactive and dynamic process of fruitful differentiation in a context of feminist community" (164) provide Virginie with a dynamic context in which to think and write. The women in this novel share a bisexual and, at times, lesbian desire. The women's sexuality informs much of their behavior and, in particular, their writing. While this woman–to–woman love assists them in overcoming male heterosexual dominance, they must struggle to liberate themselves completely from Seigneur's authority. The recurrent suggestions of a bisexuality in the novel (not just Virginie's but the other women's as well) counter an interpretation of the text that maintains that the source of Virginie's frustration and ultimate death is her inability to become a mature heterosexual woman.

If Virginie had succeeded in "writing herself [and] return[ing] to the body which has been more than confiscated from her" (Cixous, 250), she might have been able to overcome her decision to commit suicide. When she asks herself, "had I too some story I could tell?" (162), Virginie, like so many other women, strives "to write what cannot be written" (Jacobus, 13) of her life under the domain of male power. Her frustration over the impossible hurdles placed in the way of her creativity makes Virginie's reaction to this difficulty one of "intense despair" (Russ, 37). Her decision to commit suicide exemplifies the ambivalence many women feel about male authority. Virginie dives onto Seigneur's funeral pyre rather than live without him. At the same time, though, her frustration at not being able to write and, more importantly, not being read, reminds her of the omnipotence of this male authority. She decides upon suicide as the only viable option to a life of silence.

While this ending may seem to reassert the same old pattern of fiction written by men, Hawkes, I believe, confronts the reality of women's choices. Virginie's suicide is not an endorsement of oppressive male power but the recognition of its destructive potential. Hawkes's struggle to write through the feminine forces him to provide an accurate representation of the woman writer's options in 1740 and in postwar France, and even today, for that matter, when the choices for women remain limited. The woman writer still struggles to secure a room of her own, a receptive publisher, and an audience who takes her seriously. If, as Showalter maintains, "the task of feminist critics is to find a new language, a new way of reading that can integrate our intelligence and our experience, our reason and our suffering, our scepticism and our vision" (1979, 30–40), male writers (novelists as well as critics) are not excluded from this directive. Men need to write a critical literature about their own experience and their own vision. In order to write the male imaginary, men need to deconstruct their own sexual fantasies. They need to confront their personal relationship with pornography, their homophobia, and their desire to be submissive and/or dominant. In order to re-envision male heterosexuality men must explore honestly and vividly their sexual fantasies about women. In the guise of the female narrator, a male novelist can initiate a space in which to speak critically about his fears and desires, as Hawkes has done in *Virginie: Her Two Lives.*

For Cixous, "woman must write woman, and man, man. . . . It's up to him to say where his masculinity and femininity are at" (247). The importance of this insight has been recognized by male feminist writers as well. Most recently, Paul Smith, the co-editor of *Men in Feminism*, has stressed that men must assume "the responsibility of speaking their own bodies. . . . [They] have everything to say 'about' [their] sexuality" (37). Hawkes's fiction provides a way into this undertaking. *Virginie: Her Two Lives* poses crucial questions about the relationship between male and female sexuality (not only heterosexuality but bisexuality and lesbianism) and how that relationship can be informed by a feminist perspective. His novels invite an ongoing dialogue between men and women that can result in more men writing what cannot be written about their fantasies, doubts, and humiliations.

Notes

The author wishes to thank Anne Bertholf, Michael Boughn, Paul Hogan, John Kolaga, Thaïs Morgan, Susan Pearles, Neil Schmitz, and Carole Southwood for their critical contributions to this essay.

1.   Mary Jacobus. "The Difference of Views." *Women Writing and Writing About Women.* New York: Barnes & Noble, 1979, p. 13.

2.   In 1975, Robin Lakoff initiated the inquiry into a separate language for women. Since that time, Sally McConnell-Ginet, Mary Vetterling-Braggon, Philip Smith and others have explored the ramifications of such a possibility. Dale Spender's *Man Made Language* (1980) examined the difference between male and female speech. Carol Gilligan's study, which showed that a women's voice and ethical values develop quite differently from a man's, has been followed by the examination of women's ways of knowing in Mary Field Belenky, et. al. The literature addressing the question of sexual difference, female identity and the woman writer is vast (see Abel, Berg, Eisenstein and Jardine, Gardner, Jacobus, Rodenas, Showalter, and Spender).

3.   In her book, *Literary Women: The Great Writers*, Ellen Moers stresses the importance of anger in the history of women's writing, suggesting that it is the reason "why chattel slavery was a woman's literary subject in the epic age." I am indebted to Joanna Russ for this observation (Russ, 107).

Works Cited

Abel, Elizabeth, ed. *Writing and Sexual Difference*. Chicago: University of Chicago Press, 1980.
Belenky, Mary Field et. al., eds. *Woman's Ways of Knowing: The Development of Self, Voice and Mind*. New York: Basic Books, 1986.

Berg, Temma et al., eds. *Engendering the Word: Feminist Essays in Psychosexual Poetics.* Champaign, IL: University of Illinois Press, 1989.

Cixous, Hélène. "The Laugh of the Medusa." 1976. In *New French Feminisms.* Edited by Elaine Marks and Isabelle de Courtivron. New York: Schocken Books, 1980. 245–64.

de Beauvoir, Simone. *The Second Sex.* France, 1949. New York: Random House, 1952.

Eisenstein, Hester and Alice Jardine, eds. *The Future of Difference*, Boston: G K. Hall & Co., 1985.

Gallop, Jane. *The Daughter's Seduction: Feminism and Psychoanalysis.* Ithaca, NY: Cornell University Press, 1982.

Gilligan, Carol. *In A Different Voice: Psychological Theory and Women's Development.* Boston: Harvard University Press, 1982.

Hawkes, John. *Virginie: Her Two Lives.* New York: Harper & Row, 1981.

Heath, Stephen. Translator's Note. *Image–Music–Text*, by Roland Barthes. New York: Farrar, Straus and Giroux, 1977. 7–11.

Jacobus, Mary. "The Difference of Views." In *Women Writing and Writing About Women.* Edited by Mary Jacobus. New York: Barnes & Noble, 1979. 10–21.

Jones, Ann Rosalind. "Writing the Body: Toward an Understanding of *l'Écriture feminine*." In Showalter, ed. *The New Feminist Criticism*, 361–77.

Lacan, Jacques. "The Siginification of the Phallus." *Écrits: A Selection.* New York: W. W. Norton, 1977. 281–91.

Lakoff, Robin. *Language and Woman's Place.* New York: Harper & Row, 1975.

McConnell-Ginet, Sally. "Difference & Language: A Linguistic Perspective." In Eisenstein & Jardine, ed. *The Future of Difference*, 157–66.

———— et. al., eds. *Women and Language in Literature and Society.* New York: Praeger Publishers, 1980.

Moers, Ellen. *Literary Women: The Great Writers.* New York: Oxford University Press, 1976.

Olsen, Tillie. "Silences in Literature." 1965. *Silences.* New York: Dell, 1983.

Rich, Adrienne. "Compulsory Heterosexuality and Lesbian Existence." In *Women: Sex and Sexuality.* Chicago: University of Chicago Press, 1980. 62–91.

————. "When We Dead Awaken: Writing as Re-Vision." In *On Lies, Secrets, and Silence.* New York: W.W. Norton, 1979. 33–49.

Rodenas, Adriana Mendez. "Tradition and Women's Writing: Toward a Poetics of Difference." In Berg et. al. eds. *Engendering the Word*, 29–50.

Russ, Joanna. *How to Suppress Women's Writing.* Austin, TX: University of Texas Press, 1983.

Showalter, Elaine. "Feminist Criticism in the Wilderness" (1980). In Abel, ed. *Writing and Social Difference*, 9–35.

————, ed. *The New Feminist Criticism: Essays on Women, Literature and Theory.* New York: Random House, 1985.

————. "Towards a Feminist Poetics." 1979. In Jacobus, ed. *Women Writing and Writing about Women*, 22–41.

Smith, Paul. "Men in Feminism: Men and Feminist Theory." In *Men in Feminism.* New York: Methuen, 1987. 33–40.

Smith, Philip. *Language, the Sexes and Society.* London: Basil Blackwell, 1985.

Spender, Dale. *Man Made Language.* London: Routledge and Kegan Paul, 1980.

————. *The Writing or the Sex? or why you don't have to read women's writing to know it's no good.* New York: Pergamon Press, 1989.

Vetterling-Braggon, Mary, ed. *Sexist Language: A Modern Philosophical Analysis*. Totowa, NJ: Littlefield, Adams and Co., 1981.

Woolf, Virginia. *Orlando*. New York: Harcourt Brace & Jovanovitch, 1928.

———. *A Room of One's Own*. New York: Harcourt Brace & Jovanovitch, 1929.

SECTION TWO: THE GENDERING GAZE

Diderot and the Nun: Portrait of the Artist as a Transvestite

Béatrice Durand

> *Quand on écrit des femmes, il faut tremper sa plume dans l'arc-en-ciel et jeter sur sa ligne la poussière des ailes du papillon; comme le petit chien du pèlerin, à chaque fois qu'on en secoue la patte, il faut qu'il en tombe des perles.*
>
> —Diderot, *Sur les femmes*

Mystification is at the origin of Diderot's *The Nun*. In 1759, his friend, the Marquis de Croismare left Paris to settle on his Normandy estate. Diderot and his Parisian friends, who missed the Marquis, tried to persuade him to return to Paris by rekindling his interest in a young nun who had been persecuted and forced to enter a convent against her will. In 1758, the Marquis de Croismare had already expressed his concern for her when she attempted to renounce her vows. He had repeatedly petitioned the court in her favor, but she had nonetheless lost her trial that same year. Recalling the Marquis's interest, Diderot tried to make him come back to Paris by sending him desperate letters, supposedly written by the nun, describing her intolerable life in the convent. An exchange of letters ensued in which Diderot continued to assume the identity of the nun. The Marquis de Croismare was indeed moved by her suffering, but rather than returning to Paris himself, he invited the nun to his Normandy estate.

In the early 1760s, Diderot rewrote the nun's "memoirs" as a novel that he eventually published in installments in Grimm's *Correspondance littéraire* in 1770. Diderot took his opportunity to publicly reveal his mystification in the *Préface-annexe* of *The Nun*. The Marquis de Croismare is said to have laughed at the revelation. *The Nun* was not published in book form until 1796, eight years after Diderot's death.[1]

Many interpretations of *The Nun* are character studies that assume Suzanne's autonomy and coherence as a "paper-being" and trace her psychological development throughout the text.[2] Instead, I shall approach her as a projection, a feminine image that Diderot has constructed to hide behind *and* to identify with. Suzanne is explicitly designated as a woman. Diderot's account of her life creates a strong narrative illusion of her femininity. But even if her character is credible, "Suzanne" is not a woman who speaks and writes, but a man assuming a mask, the false identity of a woman.[3] She is the image of the feminine that a male author must project in order to disguise himself as a woman.

The desire for impersonation might have different motivations. Diderot could use his character to break into the feminine world of the convent and offer his male readers the pornographic spectacle of intimacy between women. Or he could write under Suzanne's identity in order to explore for himself, and by means of fiction, how it feels to be a woman. At this point, deciding between the two hypotheses seems impossible. The fact that Diderot continued to work on *The Nun* as a novel after the correspondence with the Marquis de Croismare ended at least shows that his interest in the nun's character, his enjoyment in assuming a woman's identity, went far beyond a joke: It very soon became a literary game, the writing of a borrowed gender.

I shall therefore read *The Nun* as the product of a male imagination, focusing on two aspects of transvestism in the novel, as well as in its pre-text (the letters exchanged with the Marquis and the *Préface-annexe*). First, I shall consider the devices of impersonation that mystified the Marquis and that made the illusion of a female autograph plausible or at least recognizable.[4] Secondly, I shall discuss the relationship between the male author and the female character he created, and the significance of this literary cross-dressing or "cross-writing."

Cross-writing

The Nun belongs to a "feminine" novel tradition, consisting of first person narratives that assume a woman's perspective, texts written by women as well as by men. Diderot's letters to the Marquis de Croismare and the novel subsequently written out of these letters are typical of eighteenth century "heroine's texts."[5] In addition to her name, Suzanne has many traits which enable the reader to identify her as a feminine subject.

The most obvious of those features, which she herself emphasizes in her attempt to apologize for it, is her simple and spontaneous style: "*je peins une partie de mes malheurs, sans talent et sans art, avec la naïveté d'un enfant de mon âge et la franchise de mon caractère*" (40).[6] Marivaux's Marianne similarly apologizes for writing in a conversational style, something considered typically feminine.[7] As opposed to masculine writing style, acquired through rhetorical training in college, feminine style is coded as freer from rhetorical constraint and closer to speech. Diderot creates for Suzanne a style to be decoded as "feminine" by the eighteenth-century contemporary reader:

> Monsieur, si vous avez été autrefois mon protecteur, que ma situation présente vous touche et qu'elle réveille dans votre coeur quelque sentiment de pitié! . . . Hélas! Monsieur, si vous saviez l'abandon où je suis réduite, si vous aviez quelque idée de l'inhumanité dont on punit les fautes dans les maisons religieuses, vous m'excuseriez! Secourez-moi, monsieur, secourez-moi! (213)
>
> Monsieur, j'ai reçu votre lettre. Je crois que j'ai été fort mal, fort mal. Je suis bien faible. Si Dieu me retire à lui, je prierai sans cesse pour votre salut; si j'en reviens, je ferai tout ce que vous m'ordonnerez. Mon cher monsieur! Digne homme! Je n'oublierai jamais votre bonté. (218)

Through its hesitations, pathetic repetitions and emotional qualities, this "*style naturel*" underscores not only Suzanne's inexperience and helplessness, but also her femininity.

To be intelligible, the impersonation of a feminine voice must conform to clichés, *topoi* that are marked as feminine. These clichés are not only to be found on the stylistic, but also on the narrative level. In eighteenth-century France, a woman, unless a widow, had no legal autonomy: as a girl, she was subjected to her father's authority, as a married woman, to her husband's. Practically speaking, however, there was room for an interpretation of the law that was not too literal, especially in aristocratic circles. Yet, in telling the story of Suzanne's life, Diderot seems to take an ironic pleasure in resorting to *topoi* that enhance her subjection. Like Cinderella, Suzanne has to suffer the hatred of less gifted sisters because she is an illegitimate child. The sisters are spoiled, while she is persecuted. They end up being honorably married, while she is forced to enter the convent. This forced religious vocation is also a narrative *topos*, used here by Diderot in the most caricatural way, to emphasize her total subjection to the church authority. As an illegitimate daughter first, then as a nun,—two statutes which deprive her of any rights and legal recourse—Suzanne takes on in a nearly redundant way, the worst aspects of feminine destiny.

Her body language is also coded as feminine:

> J'avançais vers la supérieure des bras suppliants et mon corps défaillant se renversait en arrière. Je tombais, mais ma chute ne fut pas dure; dans ces moments de transe où la force abandonne insensiblement, les membres se dérobent, s'affaissent, pour ainsi dire, les uns sur les autres, et la nature, ne pouvant se soutenir, semble chercher à défaillir mollement. Je perdis la connaissance et le sentiment. (108)

In the medical discourse of the eighteenth century, the female body was subject to various affections and disorders that constituted an anatomically based system of clichés of feminine behavior.[8] The elements of body language Suzanne mentions (*"défaillir mollement," "perdre connaissance," "être en transe"*) belong to this pathology and were certain to be recognized as such by readers who shared a similar code.

The Limits of Impersonation

According to male transvestites who have been interviewed, one of the biggest satisfactions in cross-dressing is to "pass," to make oneself credible as a member of the opposite sex, or, at least, to enjoy the fantasy that one is able to do so. In conforming to the code of feminine voice and gestures, Diderot and his male friends successfully "passed": They were rewarded for their efforts by the response they received from the Marquis. The *Préface-annexe* describes the impersonators' jubilation:

> "Nous passions nos soupers à lire, au milieu des éclats de rire, des lettres qui devaient faire pleurer notre bon marquis; et nous y lisions, avec ces mêmes éclats de rire, les réponses honnêtes que ce digne et généreux ami lui faisait."   (210)

Apparently, Diderot and his friends acted Suzanne's part, miming femininity with great talent. The general maxim of theater, as stated by Diderot in the *Paradoxe sur le Comédien*, also applies to the female impersonator:

> le talent consiste . . . à *rendre* si scrupuleusement *les signes* que vous vous y trompiez. Les cris de la douleur sont notés dans son oreille. Les gestes de son désespoir sont de mémoire, et ont été préparés devant une glace. Il [le comédien] sait le moment précis où il tirera son mouchoir et où les larmes couleront. . . . Ce tremblement de la voix, ces mots suspendus, ces sons étouffés ou traînés, ce frémissement des membres, ce vacillement des genoux, ces évanouissements, ces fureurs, pure imitation, *leçon recordée d'avance*, grimace pathétique, singerie sublime dont l'acteur garde le souvenir longtemps après l'avoir étudiée, dont il avait la conscience présente au moment où il l'exécutait, qui lui laisse, heureusement pour le poète, pour le spectateur et pour lui, toute la volonté de son esprit, et qui ne lui ôte ainsi que les autres exercices que la force du corps. (133, my emphasis)

In defining the actor's job, Diderot describes precisely what he did in his attempt to pass for a woman with the Marquis de Croismare: He had to reproduce the peculiarities of the feminine epistolary style. In fact, he only reproduced its signs, for impersonation is only possible through signs that are produced and similarly interpreted by actors and spectators, writers and readers. In order for the Marquis de Croismare to be fooled by Diderot's writing as a woman, both the author and the victim of his mystification had to share the same idea of the "feminine."

Gender impersonation is not possible without stable and somehow caricatural signs of sexual difference. Resorting only to the coded signs of gender, it is doomed to be parodic, it can only mimic. Cross-writing reaches its limits here, since it cannot reach the feminine beyond those coded signs. According to Diderot's own definition, the good actor should not indulge in identification with the character he plays. This limit is the condition for mastery, for the success of impersonation.

Destroying Narrative Illusion: The Letters Versus the Novel

The constraints of impersonation were too narrow and Diderot quickly exhausted the limited joys of impersonation as a social game. What soon fascinated him was not merely to "pass" or to master the role of femininity, according to his own definition of successful acting, but to identify with it. Thus, while turning *The Nun* into a novel, he did precisely what he criticizes in the *Paradox*: He became involved with his female character to the point that he lost control of the game of impersonating a woman:

> Un jour qu'il était tout entier à ce travail, M. d'Alainville, un de nos amis communs, lui [Diderot] rendit visite et le trouva plongé dans la douleur et le visage inondé de larmes. "Qu'avez-vous donc? lui dit M. d'Alainville; comme vous voilà!—Ce que j'ai? lui répondit M. Diderot, je me désole d'un conte que je me fais." (210–11)

The *Préface-annexe* not only records the bursts of laughter that accompanied the writing of the nun's letters, but also Diderot's later and quite different reaction as he was working on his book. While writing the novel, as opposed to the letters, Diderot explored the forbidden side of theater, exploring the femininity from within. He writes in the same way he read Richardson, identifying with Clarissa, the main female character and *"pren[ant] malgré qu['il] en ait un rôle dans [son] ouvrage."*[9]

The *Préface-annexe* points out the different nature of these two texts: While the letters were an exercise of mastery, the novel becomes an exercise of identification. While fooling the Marquis de Croismare was a collective and amusing undertaking, as recorded in the *Préface-annexe*, the writing of *The Nun* is an individual enterprise in which the suffering Diderot himself imposed on his female character moved him to tears. A male writer, creating for his female character the most unjust destiny, exposing her without defense to the tortures of her convent mates (the virtuous and good-hearted Suzanne is a remote ancestor of Sade's Justine), may be suspected of sadism. But this sadism turns to masochism, since Diderot seems to delight in identifying with the suffering he invents for her. One aspect of femininity Suzanne would give him access to, through his masochistic identification with her, would be passivity, or even victimization.

However, publishing *The Nun*, along with the letters and the *Préface-*

annexe that publicly reveal the whole joke, Diderot destroys the "illusion" that, presumably, is the goal of the impersonator and the fiction author. Roland Desné in his introduction to the Garnier-Flammarion edition of *The Nun* analyzes the function of the *Préface-annexe:*

> La Préface-annexe n'est donc pas une simple postface. Elle est aussi 'préface' à une appréciation en toute connaissance de cause des pouvoirs du roman. Par là et comme il le fera dans le roman anti-roman de *Jacques le Fataliste*, en imaginant, au fil du récit, un dialogue entre l'auteur et le lecteur, Diderot ébauche une théorie du roman conçu déjà comme l'art du 'mentir-vrai' selon le mot d'Aragon. (32)

The *Préface-annexe* tells us that *"ceci est un conte"* (a title that Diderot will give to a later short story). It warns the reader that Suzanne is a character born out of the author's fantasy. Moreover, a careful reader will notice the male impersonator's double play, which, under the pastiche of feminine style, ironically appears in the frequent narrative inconsistencies that Diderot did not even bother correcting, as if this self-exposure were part of his attack against the narrative illusion.[10]

In fact, *The Nun* calls for two types of reading. Since the *Préface-annexe* is added to the edition of the novel as a *"postface,"* Diderot's explanation of his gender game is read after the novel itself, so that a naïve and pitying reading of the story is always possible. Readers may still be fooled by this first contact with the text, exactly as the Marquis had been by Diderot's initial letters. After being enlightened by the *Préface-annexe*, one becomes aware of Diderot's duplicity or total honesty. By displaying the backstage,[11] Diderot forces us to accept a different reading pact. Between the correspondence with the marquis and the novel, Diderot's concerns have evolved. The question is now not only how to make other people believe that this is a woman speaking, but why it is tempting to pretend one is a woman. Diderot's writing of the letters and the way the marquis interpreted them, as well as a "naïve" reading of the novel constitute a first hermeneutic unit, in which the reader deciphers the signs of the feminine. The *préface/postface* to the novel, along with the interpretative work the reader may consequently perform, is a second unit, which displays the more complex relationship between the male author and his fictional female character. A critical interpretation of the text cannot but accept the conditions imposed by the second "reading pact." I shall now explore the textual and ideological effects produced by this reading pact.

The Author and His Mask

"La Religieuse *ou comment l'esprit ne vient pas aux filles*"[12]: Suzanne's repeated ignorance of sexual matters, her incredible naïveté, her very refusal to recognize manifestations of lesbianism among her convent sisters is a striking example of the narrative inconsistencies many critics have pointed out. None of her claims of "innocence," if innocence means ignorance of sexual sin, is plausible in the narrative context, since she has been repeatedly warned or "enlightened." For instance, this is how she reacts to the accusation of "impurity":

> on me supposa des desseins, des actions que je n'ose nommer, et des désirs bizarres auxquels on attribua le désordre évident dans lequel la jeune religieuse s'était trouvée. *En vérité je ne suis pas un homme, et je ne sais ce qu'on peut imaginer d'une femme et d'une autre femme, et moins encore d'une femme seule.* . . . Il faut qu'avec toute leur retenue extérieure, la modestie de leurs regards, la chasteté de leur expression, ces femmes aient le coeur bien corrompu: *elles savent* du moins qu'on commet seule des actions déshonnêtes, *et moi, je ne le sais pas; aussi n'ai-je jamais très bien compris* ce dont elles m'accusaient, et *elles s'exprimaient en des termes si obscurs,* que *je n'ai jamais su* ce qu'il y avait à leur répondre. (103, my emphasis)

The very mention of what she doesn't know, but would known if she were a man, a lesbian, or a practitioner of solitary pleasure cannot but refer to Suzanne's knowledge of sexuality. It reveals either her bad faith—if she were to be interpreted as an autonomous character—or else, if we interpret her as an impersonation, the presence of the male author using her as a mask. Her creator imbues all that she says with ambiguity: Her allusion to the sexual knowledge of the other women is nothing else than Diderot's appearance behind the mask. Similarly, while the tender attitude of the mother superior troubles her, Suzanne is unable to recognize the nature of her embarrassment, because this understanding is denied to her by the narrative manipulation:

> Le premier soir j'eus la visite de la supérieure; elle vint à mon déshabiller. Ce fut elle qui m'ôta mon voile et ma guimpe, et qui me coiffa de nuit; ce fut elle qui me déshabilla. Elle me tint cent propos doux, et me fit mille caresses qui m'embarassèrent un peu, je ne sais pas pourquoi, car je n'y entendais rien, ni elle non plus; et à présent que j'y réfléchis, qu'aurions nous pu y entendre? (144)

The emotions Suzanne feels, despite her ignorance and virtue, do not in fact lead to sexual enlightenment. Suzanne's character is set up to contradict Condillac's knowledge theory: In her case, sensation is never followed by knowledge.[13] Even at the end of her life in Arpajon, though she has witnessed or heard of many sexually-ambiguous situations and feelings and has on many occasions expressed her own doubts, Suzanne, when questioned remains, or at least she claims to have remained, completely unaware of "the language of the senses":

> —Mais dites-moi, quelle impression fait sur vous la présence d'un homme?
> —Aucune. S'il a de l'esprit, je l'écoute avec plaisir; s'il est d'une belle figure, je la remarque.
> —Et votre coeur est tranquille?
> —Jusqu'à présent, il est resté sans émotion.
> . . .
> —Et vos sens ne vous disaient rien?

—Je ne sais ce que c'est que le langage des sens.
—Ils en ont un cependant.
—Cela se peut. (163)

As an ironic apostle of Condillac's doctrine, the mother superior tries to elicit from Suzanne what she thinks of as the language of nature. It is worth noticing that in the above dialogue, Suzanne clearly lacks such a language. Although she is not totally deprived of perceptions (she notices when a man has a *"une belle figure"* or *"de l'esprit"*), those perceptions never acquire a sexual connotation. She is denied the possibility to elaborate her superficial impressions and translate them in sexual terms by the narrative manipulation. Seeing that she can't elicit these feelings from Suzanne, the mother superior offers in a rather authoritative manner to teach her the "language of the senses":

—C'est un langage bien doux; et voudriez–vous le connaître?
—Non, chère mère; à quoi cela me servirait–il?
—A dissiper votre ennui.
—A l'augmenter peut-être. Et puis que signifie ce langage des sens, sans objet?
—Quand on parle, c'est toujours à quelqu'un; cela vaut mieux sans doute que de s'entretenir seule, quoique ce ne soit pas tout à fait sans plaisir.
—Je n'entends rien à cela.
—Si tu le voulais, chère enfant, je te deviendrais plus claire.
—Non, chère mère, non. Je ne sais rien et j'aime mieux ne rien savoir, que d'acquérir des connaissances qui me rendraient peut-être plus à plaindre que je ne le suis. Je n'ai point de désirs, et je n'en veux point chercher que je ne pourrais satisfaire.
—Et pourquoi ne le pourrais–tu pas?
—Et comment le pourrais–je?
—Comme moi.
—Comme vous! Mais il n'y a personne dans cette maison . . .
—J'y suis chère amie; vous y êtes.
—Eh bien! qui vous suis–je? Que m'êtes–vous?
—Qu'elle est innocente!
—Oh! il est vrai chère mère, que je la suis beaucoup, et que j'aimerais mieux mourir que de cesser de l'être. (163–64)

The mother superior's attempts to teach Suzanne the "language of the senses" literally fall on a deaf ear. One by one, with wonderful patience and persuasion, the mother superior answers all of Suzanne's objections regarding the lack of a possible love "object." But Suzanne resists the enlightening lesson with a firmness that, by its grotesque lack of verisimilitude, betrays Diderot's narrative trick. His construction of the character endows her with a systematical *"volonté de ne pas savoir."*

Earlier in the account of her life, Diderot had given Suzanne a vague understanding of the sexual situation at the convent and the reader could believe that she would understand. Describing the mother superior, she says: *"Elle baissa les yeux, rougit et soupira; en vérité,* c'était comme un amant" (155, my emphasis).

The perverse or ironic narrator puts ambiguous words in her mouth. But this ambiguity is directed towards the reader. It is a clear sign of the narrator's game over the head of the character. Suzanne herself remains unaware of this ambiguity. She is always on the verge of "understanding," but never takes the final step. In the end, enlightening situations, sensations and conversations with her various directors of consciousness should leave her without doubts: *"Je me confessais, je me tus, mais le directeur m'interrogea, et je ne dissimulai rien. Il me fit mille demandes singulières, auxquelles je ne comprends rien encore à présent que je me les rappelle"* (180). If this were not enough, she eventually has the revelation of the mother superior's "evil" nature:

> Je descendis sur la pointe du pied et je vins me placer doucement à la porte du parloir, et écouter ce qui se disait là. *Cela est fort mal*, direz–vous. . . . Oh! pour cela, oui, cela est fort mal, je me le dis à moi-même, et mon trouble, les précautions que je pris pour n'être pas aperçue, les fois que je m'arrêtai, la voix de ma conscience qui me pressait à chaque pas de m'en retourner, ne me permettaient pas d'en douter; cependant la curiosité fut la plus forte. . . . Le premier mot que j'entendis après un assez long silence me fit frémir; ce fut "Mon père, je suis damnée. . . ." Je me rassurai. J'écoutais, le voile qui jusqu'alors m'avait dérobé le péril que j'avais couru se déchirait lorsqu'on m'appela. Il fallut aller, j'allai donc; mais hélas! je n'en avais que trop entendu. Quelle femme, monsieur le marquis, quelle abominable femme! (198)

But even here, Suzanne's sexual knowledge has not been acquired through experience or personal reflexion. It is somehow arbitrarily imposed on her by Don Morel's authority. Suzanne accepts him as a moral reference, but her acceptance is passive, it is not the result of maturing. Moreover,—and this is probably the most unlikely aspect of the whole narration—this theatrically staged revelation has no effect on Suzanne's own account of her life: She is writing that story after leaving the convent, supposedly from the point of view of this final revelation. But she is made to write as if it had no effect on her understanding.

Suzanne's innocence or, rather, the text's failure to turn the character's experiences into meaningful awareness, is a narrative manipulation performed by the author at his character's expense. Not "knowing" what she is talking about enables Suzanne to be the innocent and unwilling accessory to sexual license in the text. She doesn't need a sexuality of her own, not even a clear perception of anyone else's, since any conscious awareness of what is going on would morally bind her. She would be forced to flee any situation loaded with sexual significance. Instead, she "depicts" with the greatest faithfulness, or, rather, Diderot lets her express, that which is, in fact, his own sexual fantasy about female homosexuality, without subjecting her to the feelings of guilt that would arise from moral consciousness:

> Imaginez un atelier de dix à douze personnes, dont la plus jeune pouvait avoir quinze ans, et la plus âgée n'en avait pas vingt-trois; une supérieure qui touchait à la quarantaine, blanche, fraîche, pleine d'embonpoint, à moitié levée sur son lit,

avec deux mentons qu'elle portait d'assez bonne grâce, des bras ronds comme s'ils
avaient été tournés, des doigts en fuseau et tout parsemés de fossettes, des yeux
noirs, grands, vifs et tendres, presque jamais entièrement ouverts, à demi fermés
comme si celle qui les possédait eût éprouvé quelque fatigue à les ouvrir, des
lèvres vermeilles comme la rose, des dents blanches comme le lait, les plus belles
joues, une tête fort agréable enfoncée dans un oreiller profond et mollet, les bras
étendus mollement à ses côtés, avec de petits coussins sous les coudes pour les
soutenir.   (171–72)

The white female flesh preferred and the insistence on "embonpoint" here seem
to be directly taken from a painting by Boucher.[14] Suzanne's "*naïveté*" is a pretext
for letting her watch and describe several licentious scenes of sex between women.
She sometimes notes gestures with a precision close to the pornographic: "*Une
autre avait pris ma place en mon absence sur le bord du lit de la supérieure, était
penchée vers elle, le coude appuyé entre ses deux cuisses, et lui montrait son ouvrage; la
supérieure, les yeux presque fermés, lui disait oui ou non sans presque la regarder, et
j'étais debout à côté d'elle sans qu'elle s'en aperçût*" (173). Observation of such details
presupposes a narrator conscious of their sexual significance as well as their
pornographic nature. Again, Diderot is ironically appearing here behind the mask
of his female character. In fact, Suzanne's innocence seems to be the prerequisite
for the text's pornographic effect, for which there is no better medium than her
sexual "innocence": In order to ensure the voyeuristic pleasure of both writer and
readers, Suzanne must not understand the sexual contents of the scenes she
describes, but merely transcribe them. She is a transparent, blank screen on which
Diderot inscribes the object of his desire and of his curiosity, that is, both the
female body and the intimacy between women.

One has to raise the question of Suzanne's morality. Some critics have
"accused" her of duplicity, arguing that, by claiming her innocence and being, at
the same, time involved in situations whose meaning, had she understood it, would
ruin this innocence.[15] It has also been argued that she is playing an unconscious
double game in seducing some of the people who approach her without accepting
the consequences of this seduction. In my opinion, Suzanne, as a character, has so
little psychological consistency, is so clearly a construct produced by the fantasy of
her creator, that she cannot be held accountable for any moral conduct or give
matter to psychological analysis.

I would rather argue that Suzanne has only a narrative function, quite similar
to Mangogul's magical ring in *Les Bijoux indiscrets*, which allows its possessor to
become invisible and to hear what men always wanted to know about women
without daring to ask directly. "Suzanne," likewise, is the eye of a masculine spy
in the world of feminine sexuality. Of course, since Diderot did not actually live in
a convent under a fake feminine identity, his voyeurism is not literal. The act of
spying is performed only in a fantasy, through the writing of fiction. But even
though the possibility of spying is given only in the fantasy, it allows the male
imagination to explore many situations among women from which men are, by
definition, excluded.

Seducing as a Woman

One of these mysteries, always beyond man's sight, is the feminine way of seduction. Not that men cannot be seductive. But Don Juan's seduction of women is conceived as a conquest, whereas feminine seduction might be perceived (at least by men) as a paradoxical form of passive, natural capture. Suzanne seduces everyone, Madame de Moni and the superior at Arpajon, her lawyers and various "*directeurs de conscience*" within the novel, the Marquis de Croismare and the gullible reader outside the text, and, possibly, as suggested in the *Préface-annexe*, Diderot, her very creator, who was, after all, found weeping over her pathetic sufferings by a male friend.

Whatever she does, sings, or says, Suzanne always produces a very strong effect, but it seems she seduces everyone without effort, even without intent. For instance, when asked by the grand vicar to carry out Christian acts of faith, love, hope, and charity, Suzanne describes the effect of her devotion on the assembly:

> Je ne me souviens pas vraiment en quels termes ils [ces actes] étaient conçus; mais je pense qu'apparemment ils étaient pathétiques; car j'arrachai des sanglots de quelques religieuses, les deux jeunes ecclésiastiques en versèrent des larmes, et l'archidiacre étonné me demanda d'où j'avais tiré les prières que je venais de réciter.
> Je lui dis:
> "Du fond de mon coeur; ce sont mes pensées et mes sentiments." (113)

Spontaneously, without any intention, Suzanne, produces a pathetic effect on the audience, carefully orchestrated by her creator, although her seduction is said to be nothing but a natural emanation from her person.

Her mere fact of telling the story of her life is also seductive. The near absence of autobiographical concerns in Diderot's work has been noted.[16] However, the autobiographical gesture is not only present but quite obsessive in *The Nun*, even if it is framed by a fiction: Suzanne constantly tells her life to the Marquis de Croismare, to her successive mothers superior, to her various confessors, and to her lawyer. Each time, though in different ways, her interlocutors are seduced. This is how the amorous mother superior reacts to the account of Suzanne's suffering in her former convent: "*Je m'aperçus alors, au tremblement qui la saisissait, au trouble de son discours, à l'égarement de ses yeux et de ses mains, à son genoux qui se pressait entre les miens, à l'ardeur dont elle me serrait et à la violence dont ses bras m'enlaçaient que sa maladie ne tarderaient pas à la prendre*" (160). Her lawyer, Monsieur Manouri, falls in love, too. Pity is what makes her seduction so powerful: Under the veil of pity, the interlocutor makes room for sadistic attraction. Suzanne herself can resort *à volonté* to the power emanating from her life's account and tell her story again and again, since she has legitimate reasons to want it known outside the convent. She is not responsible for the suffering imposed on her; neither is she responsible for its erotic appeal to others. Thus, Suzanne/Diderot is allowed to perpetuate the autobiographical/seductive game. The mother superior recognizes this universal power of seduction:

> Quelquefois en me regardant, de la tête aux pieds, avec un air de complaisance que je n'ai jamais vu à aucune autre femme, elle [the mother superior] me disait: "Non, c'est le plus grand bonheur que Dieu l'ait appelée dans la retraite; avec cette figure là, dans le monde, *elle aurait damné autant d'hommes qu'elle en aurait vus, et elle se serait damnée avec eux.* Dieu fait bien tout ce qu'il fait." (152, my emphasis)

Attributing her own feelings to all men, she grants that Suzanne would literally cause any man's damnation. Suzanne is always *en train de se faire désirer* and leads the mother superior to literally die of love while claiming she cannot do anything about the other women's desire for her: "*Cette supérieure*, que je ne pouvais ni soulager ni m'empêcher de plaindre, *passa successivement de la mélancolie à la piété, et de la piété au délire*" (189, my emphasis). The desire Suzanne provokes in others is, of course, never answered, as if Diderot made her a vestal. Again, the systematic game Diderot performs under Suzanne's identity is a narrative trick, aimed here at illustrating the effects of seduction, at displaying and "studying" its symptoms in the character who feels desire, not in the character who inspires it.

Diderot's attitude towards his character is double: He both produces the mechanisms of feminine seduction and tries its effects on himself. He *is* Suzanne, innocently and passively enjoying an absolute power over whoever approaches her (and this might well be "Suzanne's" revenge for all the evil done to her). Weeping over the story he has made up for her, he also falls a consenting victim to her power. At this point, it seems that Diderot in the text might both identify with Suzanne (his spy disguise) as well as with the mother superior (who yields to the seduction).

Unlike Marivaux, who pictures Marianne as a universal seducer, partly to reveal her tricks, and to put himself out of the reach of the seduction exercised by women, it seems to me that Diderot does not denounce seduction as deceitful. Instead, he merely acknowledges its power by studying its effects, if not by yielding to it. The text is concerned with both perspectives: the seducer's and the seduced's.

Male Voyeurism versus Female Homosexuality

Through Suzanne's narrative account, Diderot is able to penetrate yet another feminine secret and realize yet another masculine fantasy: His disguise allows him to violate the intimacy of the "*gynecée*." Again, this intrusion is literary, that is, performed in the imagination. While the letters only tried to imitate Suzanne's voice, Diderot/Suzanne, in the novel's phantasmic projection, is living intimately among women and is able to capture one of the most hidden aspects of the feminine: female homosexuality.[17]

If Suzanne is the narrative puppet that gives Diderot phantasmic access to the feminine world of the convent, the object of the text's true curiosity is not Suzanne herself, but what Suzanne enables the male writer/reader to "see": the "secret" of the convent. Diderot's voyeurism, to which Suzanne is only instrumental, focuses, in fact, on the other female characters, such as the three successive mothers superior.[18] It is by analyzing these characters (rather than Suzanne, whose relationship to her own gender is, as I have shown, only suggested through theatrically coded signs) that we can understand Diderot's true approach of the feminine, and especially his fantasy about female homosexuality.

Diderot's phantasmic construction of the feminine in his characters rests on the traditional anatomical "pretext." In a review essay that Diderot wrote in 1772 for Grimm's *Correspondance littéraire* on Thomas's *Dissertation sur les femmes* two years after the publication of *The Nun*, he seems to comment on his own characters:

> La femme porte au-dedans d'elle-même un organe susceptible de spasmes terribles, disposant d'elle, et suscitant dans son imagination des fantômes de toute espèce. . . . C'est de l'organe propre à son sexe que partent toutes ses idées extraordinaires. La femme, hystérique dans la jeunesse, se fait dévote dans l'âge avancé; la femme à qui il reste quelque énergie dans l'âge avancé, était hystérique dans sa jeunesse. . . . Rien de plus contigu que l'extase, la prophétie, la révélation, la poésie fougueuse et l'hystérisme."[19]   (255)

The three mothers superior offer three different versions of hysteria: The mystic fervor of the first, the sadism of the second, and the nymphomania and homosexuality of the third can be interpreted as the outlet of hysterical dispositions. Diderot's attitude towards the feminine, as represented in these characters, is ambivalent. By definition, out of anatomical reasons, women are—or tend to be—hysterical. "Hysterism," to translate Diderot's own term, is women's access to genius. The devotion in the first superior is always represented in a very positive manner: Madame de Moni clearly conforms to Diderot's idea of the inspired "genius." But "hysterism" can also lead to the worst perversion, as in the second (sadistic) superior, who embodies a dark and fearful side of the feminine.

Homosexuality in the third superior is ambivalent. The discourse about it operates on different levels. On the first and most familiar level, it can be read as a perversion of the "natural," that is, heterosexual, direction of sexuality. The convent plays the role of a political and social hypothesis, designed to prove, in a paradoxical demonstration, the benefits of society: the convent illustrates the terrible consequences of arbitrary seclusion from society.[20]

But the novel's superficial political critique is challenged by the fascination exercised on the author as a man by female homosexuality, to which his disguise gives phantasmic access. Towards the end of the novel, when Suzanne is trying to placate a sister (who is jealous because she is no longer the superior's favorite and accuses Suzanne of taking her place), a significant grammatical shift shows precisely the discrepancy between these two discourses:

> Et nous nous séparâmes, elle pour aller se désoler dans sa cellule, moi pour aller rêver dans la mienne à *la bizarrerie de la tête des femmes.*
> Voilà l'effet de la retraite. L'homme est né pour la société. Séparez-le, isolez-le, ses idées se désuniront, son caractère se tournera, mille affection ridicules s'élèveront dans son coeur, des pensées extravagantes germeront dans son esprit, comme les ronces dans une terre sauvage. Placez un homme dans une forêt, il y deviendra féroce; dans un cloître, où l'idée de nécessité se joint à celle de servitude, c'est pis encore.   (153–54)

Suzanne/Diderot shifts from a consideration of female specificity ("*la bizarrerie de la tête des femmes*") to a generic concern ("*l'homme*", here, mankind).[21] The general discourse about mankind and the effects of seclusion from society picks up, in a rather artificial way, on Suzanne's reflexion about "*la bizarrerie de la tête des femmes.*" In this socio-political diatribe, the feminine suddenly functions as something representative of mankind, and homosexuality stands for a perversion that arises when social instincts are denied. The political concern seems to be superimposed on a deeper curiosity about the feminine and fails to account for it.

Some critics have read *The Nun* as a strong rejection of female homosexuality. Among these is Chantal Thomas: "*La 'maladie' lesbienne renvoie Diderot à une double horreur. Celle de son abstraction physiologique et celle de la clôture qui la favorise.*"[22] In her interpretation of the novel as a whole, Thomas identifies the text's point of view with the condemnation carried out by political fable and by the church's representatives, the Pères Hébert and Lemoine, sent to the convent to reestablish order. I would be more apt to argue that the text's point of view, if there is one, can not be the unchallenged opinion of church speakers. I agree with Elisabeth de Fontenay when she suggests that the mother superior is not guilty because she is a lesbian, but because she rules arbitrarily and tyrannically over the convent: "*Elle abuse du pouvoir que l'église lui a donné. . . . Elle exerce un véritable droit de cuissage sur les novices promises à l'époux divin.*"[23] Pierre Saint-Amand also noted the euphoric atmosphere of Arpajon, under the third superior: "*c'est une assemblée de femmes réconciliée avec elle-même. . . . C'est la joyeuse utopie d'une communauté de femme que Diderot anime sous nos yeux. La mère supérieure, objet d'adoration, est celle qui permet ce rassemblement.*"[24]

In the context of the convent, the precise description (by the blind Suzanne) of the mother superior's orgasm seems at first sight very provocative and almost frightening, especially for Suzanne who will interpret this excess as an "illness": "enfin il vint un moment, je ne sais si ce fut de plaisir ou de peine, où elle devint pâle comme le mort; ses yeux se fermèrent, tout son corps s'étendit avec violence, ses lèvres se fermèrent d'abord, elles étaient humectées comme d'une mousse légère; puis sa bouche s'ouvrit, et elle me parut mourir en poussant un grand soupir" (155). However, in the article "*Jouissance*" of the *Encyclopédie*, Diderot describes sexual pleasure in similar terms, but without any negative connotation: "le coeur palpite, les membres tressaillent; des images voluptueuses errent dans le cerveau; des torrents d'esprit coulent dans les nerfs, les irritent et vont se rendre au siège d'un nouveau sens qui se déclare et qui tourmente; la vue se trouble, le délire naît; la raison esclave de l'instinct se borne à le servir et la nature est satisfaite."[25] Far from carrying any negative judgment, this article is a challenge to the traditional Christian discourse about sexuality as excess. In *The Nun*, Diderot plays ironically with the unexpected effect of this description, applied to a woman and in the context of the convent. Beyond the first impression of shock and pious condemnation, something in the ironical interaction of various points of view represented in the text (the priests', the mother superior's) allows the reader, if not to accept, at least to consider seriously the mother superior's claim that her feelings towards the young nuns are innocent: *"On ne va à confesse que pour s'accuser de ses péchés et je n'en vois pas à aimer bien tendrement une enfant aussi aimable que Sainte-Suzanne"* (186). The confessor will, of course, try to persuade Suzanne of the *"noirceur du crime"* (185). His point of view, however, is not that of the text. In the light of the excerpt from the *Encyclopédie*, one is entitled to think that the text's point of view endorses, to some extent, the mother superior's claim that her desires might be innocent, and questions, in a very radical way, the current sexual moral. On the other hand, the mother superior embodies the fearful excess of unmastered sexuality: she will literally die of love.

Suzanne, in a way, could be reproached for the neutrality that Diderot had criticized in Thomas's *Dissertation sur les femmes* in his review for the *Correspondance littéraire*: *"[Thomas] n'a pas senti. Sa tête s'est tourmentée, mais son coeur est demeuré tranquille. . . . il a voulu que son livre ne fût d'aucun sexe. . . . C'est un hermaphrodite, qui n'a ni le nerf de l'homme, ni la mollesse de la femme.*[26] Because she is, finally, an instrumental figure or a pretext, Suzanne is "neutral," degendered, and desireless. In contrast—according to Diderot's observations on femininity in his review essay—the mother superior is supremely feminine: *"J'ai vu l'amour, la jalousie, la superstition, la colère, portés dans les femmes à un point que l'homme n'éprouva jamais"* (252). If womanhood gives feelings their most extreme expression, female homosexuality seems a redundant form of femininity. As such, it provokes the same ambivalent feelings of fascination and fear as the feminine itself does.

One could argue that Diderot's grotesque and excessive female characters are misogynistic creations. I had indeed started working on this paper with the purpose of digging out the male stereotypes on which the male impersonator had based his performance. I also intended to show how the impersonator misses what is supposed to be his goal (total identification with the other gender) because he is caught up in stereotypes.

What Diderot's construction of the feminine owes to the contemporary stereotypes about the feminine is rather obvious. What, in my opinion, proved to be much more interesting, was his use of impersonation: Even if deeply involved in the game, Diderot never disappears as a male subject under the mask of the feminine character. The projection in the feminine world remains consciously and, for those who pay attention to the subtleties of the narration, explicitly bounded in male fantasy. His obvious presence as a male in the text, his constant destruction of the narrative illusion that make impersonation possible, is probably Diderot's fairness towards the feminine: He always acknowledges the masculine origin of his curiosity about, or desire for, the feminine. He does not use literary impersonation in order to achieve a total, utopian identification with the feminine. He does not try to deliver any knowledge about the feminine, but tries to come to terms with the complexity of his own fantasies about the other gender.

Notes

1.   On the genesis and history of *The Nun*, see Georges May, *Diderot et la Religieuse* (New Haven: Yale University Press; Paris: PUF, 1954). See also Jean Cartrysse, *Diderot et la mystification* (Paris: Nizet, 1970), 42–43.

2.   On other nuns in fiction, see for example Jeanet Whatley, "Nun's Stories," *Diderot Studies* 20 (1981): 299–320; Jeanne Ponton, *La Religieuse dans la littérature française*, (Québec: Presses de l'Université Laval, 1969).

3.   Henceforth, Suzanne's name should be understood not as a reference to an autonomous "paper being," but as the designation of a narrative instance. "She" is a feminine character conceived and formulated by a man.

4.   On this notion, see *The Female Autograph*, edited by Domna C. Stanton (Chicago: The University of Chicago Press, 1987), esp. "Autogynography: Is the Subject Different?," 3–21.

5.   Cf. Nancy K. Miller, *The Heroine's Text* (New York: Columbia University Press, 1984).

6.   All quotations refer to the Garnier-Flammarion edition of *La Religieuse* (Paris: 1968).

7.   Cf. Marivaux, *La Vie de Marianne* (Paris: GF, 1978). Marianne writes the way she speaks: *"mais je vais comme je puis, je n'ai garde de songer que je fais un livre, cela me jetterai dans un travail d'esprit dont je ne sortirai pas; je m'imagine que je vous parle, et tout passe dans la conversation"* (71).

8.   On female pathology, see, for instance, Marie-Claire Vallois, *"Politique du Paradoxe: tableau de moeurs/tableau familial dans la* Religieuse *de Diderot" Romantic Review*, 76:2 (1976): 62–171: *"L'écriture autobiographique suit ici la logique et la rigueur de l'écriture médicale"* (166). See also Yvonne Kniebieler, *"Les Médecins et la nature féminine," Annales* 4 (1976); *"Le discours médical sur les femmes: constantes et ruptures," Romantisme* (1976); see also Michel Delon, *"Le Prétexte anatomique," Dix-huitième Siècle*, 12 (1980): 35–48.

9.   *Eloge de Richardson*, in *Oeuvres esthétiques*, (Paris: Garnier, 1959), 30. On Diderot's absorption in the nun's story, see also the two letters respectively written to Madame d'Epinay and Damilaville during the summer of 1760: *"je suis après ma Religieuse. Mais cela s'étend sous la plume et je ne sais plus quand je toucherai la fin." "Je me suis mis à faire la Religieuse et j'y étais encore à trois heures du matin. Je vais à tire d'aile. Ce n'est plus une lettre, c'est un livre"* (quoted by May, 41–42).

10.   On this narrative problem, see May, 203–07; see also Roland Desné, 29–32; Walter E. Rex, "Secrets from Suzanne: The tangled motives of *La Religieuse*," *Eighteenth Century* 24:3 (1983): 185–98.

11.   Some commentators, such as Naigeon, criticized Diderot for revealing his "secrets of fabrication" (see R. Desné, 32). See also Herbert Dieckmann's critique of Naigeon's critic, "The *Préface-annexe* of *La Religieuse*," *Diderot Studies* 2 (1952): 3–23.

12.   I borrow this formulation from Elisabeth de Fontenay, *Diderot ou le matérialisme enchanté*, (Paris: Grasset, 1981), 153.

13.   Condillac's *Essai sur l'origine des connaissances humaines* (Paris, 1746) argues (against Descartes and his theory of "innate ideas") that ideas arise from the progressive elaboration of perceptions.

14.   In the 1761 *Salon*, Diderot criticized Boucher on artistic and ethical grounds. This critique conflicts with masculine sensuality expressed in *The Nun* behind the mask of Suzanne (*Salons*, edited by J. Szenec [Paris: Flammarion, 1967], 38–40): "*Son élégance, sa mignardise, sa galanterie romanesque, sa coquetterie, son goût, sa facilité, sa variété, son éclat, ses carnations fardées, sa débauche doivent captiver les petits maîtres, les petites femmes, les jeunes gens, les gens du monde, la foule de ceux qui sont étrangers au vrai goût, à la vérité, aux idées justes, à la sévérité de l'art.*" Cf. also Pierre Saint-Amand, *Séduire ou la passion des Lumières* (Paris: Méridiens-Klincksieck, 1987), 52: "*A ces épisodes, Diderot accorde un investissement esthétique. Ils se succèdent devant nos yeux comme des tableaux.*"

15.   In addition to Fontenay, see May, 205; Saint-Amand, 50–51 shows how Suzanne, despite her denegation is consenting to the mother superior's game. Also see Rex, 185–98.

16.   Cf. Jean-Claude Bonnet, "*L'écrit amoureux ou le fou de Sophie*," *Colloque International Diderot* (Paris, 1985), 105–14. According to Bonnet, the love correspondance with Sophie Volland is Diderot's only autobiographical writing. In a sense, the writing of *The Nun* also bears an autobiographical trace.

17.   On Diderot's representation of homosexuality and its literary precedents, see May, chapters "*Diderot sexologue*", 98–114, and "*Influences littéraires: Héroïnes lesbiennes et héroïnes cloîtrées*," 115–41. In the next chapter, "*Quelques modèles authentiques*," 142–60, May recalls the possible influence on *The Nun* of Diderot's suspecting a lesbian love affair between Sophie Volland and Madame Legendre, Sophie's sister. But he concludes his study by saying that the character of the mother superior is essentially an imaginary creation, rather than a transposition into fiction of Diderot's actual knowledge about lesbianism.

18.   See Saint-Amand, 52–53: "*la supérieure d'Arpajon, le personnage homosexuel de l'histoire brille admirablement dans la galerie des meilleurs personnages de Diderot. . . . Ce n'est pas Suzanne, trop réglée, qui est une créature diderotienne, mais la turbulente supérieure d'Arpajon.*"

19.   *Sur les femmes*, edited by Assézat-Tourneux (Paris, 1876), II, 250; published in the *Correspondance littéraire* in 1772. Also see Delon, 35.

20.   See May (100), who compares the *Letter on the Blind*, in which Diderot uses the hypothesis of blindness in order to think about vision, and *The Nun*, in which he uses the hypothesis of seclusion from society in order to think about society itself. On the same problem, see Henri Coulet, *Le Roman Français jusqu'à la Révolution* (Paris: Armand Colin, 1967), 502.

21.   For a discussion of generic and non–generic uses of grammatical gender, see Paula A. Treichler and Francine Wattman Frank, eds., *Language, Gender, and Professional Writing* (New York: MLA, 1989), 114–18.

22.   Chantal Thomas, *"Les Femmes folles de leur soeurs,"* *La Quinzaine littéraire* 418 (*Mars* 1984): 7.

23.   de Fontenay, 153.

24.   Saint-Armand, 144–45, n.5.

25.   *Encyclopédie* article *"Jouissance"*, t. 8, 885, b. See also Georges Benrekassa, *"L'article 'Jouissance' et l'idéologie érotique de Diderot"*, *Dix-Huitième Siècle* 12 (1980): 9–35.

26.   *Sur les femmes*, 252.

"This Kind": Pornographic Discourses, Lesbian Bodies and Paul Verlaine's *Les Amies*

Barbara Milech

I

In 1867 Paul Verlaine gathered together into a small book entitled *Les Amies* (*The Women-Friends*) six sonnets on the subject of lesbian love. The collection is often discounted as juvenile, derivative, or licentious. A. E. Carter's summation especially emphasizes that last term:

> Verlaine's sonnets have a lascivious charm. Like most works of this kind, they are voyeuristic; the spectacle of two sprigs of girlhood in amorous abandon is of high erotic potency. Although the result is pretty enough in an exhibitionistic way, it cannot compare with Baudelaire's verse which, as in everything he wrote, invests the subject with an intense and tragic grandeur.[1]

Of particular interest here is Carter's lack of specificity as to just what "this kind" means. On the one hand, in discussing Verlaine's poetry critically and comparing it to that of Baudelaire, he suggests that Verlaine's work is literature. On the other hand, his conviction that it possesses "high erotic potency" and little redeeming (Baudelairean) value suggests that it is pornography. The two seemingly exclusive classifications of pornography and literature are, however, not so much reconciled as set aside by Carter's dismissal of the poems as immature, that is, charming and pretty, even if highly potent. His operating assumption seems to be that pornography is non-literature in the sense that it is immature literature, something that true men of letters grow out of. This is not an uncommon critical assumption; for example, Steven Marcus in his often cited *The Other Victorians* sees pornography as "immature" because it is culturally a primitive form and psychologically an expression of uncivilized instinct.[2]

A similar indeterminacy as to whether or not *Les Amies* is literature or pornography also marks the publishing history of Verlaine's sonnet sequence. The well-known pornographer Auguste Poulet-Malassis first printed the book in late 1867 in Brussels, listing the author's name as "Pablo de Herlagnez" (a homophone of Paul Verlaine) and the place of publication as "Ségovie." The books were seized at the Franco-Belgian border, condemned by a correctional tribunal in Lille on the same day (6 May 1968) as Baudelaire's *Les Épaves* (*The Wrecks*), and Poulet-Malassis received a fine and a prison sentence. This part of its publication history identifies *Les Amies* as pornography. However, one of the six poems, "Sappho," had been published earlier in the literary magazine *Le Hanneton* (August 1867), and the entire collection later appeared in the *Revue indépendante* (October 1884). Finally, more than twenty years after its first appearance, *Les Amies* was republished in book form, as part of Verlaine's *Parallèlement* (*In Parallel*, 1889 and 1894). In these instances the poems were treated as literature, as having a value beyond "erotic potency." Thus it seems that the same book can sometimes be pornography, sometimes literature.[3]

Implicit in the publishing history and criticism of *Les Amies* are perennial questions about pornography and literature, as well as less often addressed questions about the representation of lesbian love in general. Why should Verlaine, a young man about to be married and starting a career in poetry, publish lesbian poems through a pornographic publishing house? What is the relationship between the central image of women in these nineteenth-century poems and the recurrent figure of the lesbian in those present day "adult" magazines and videos purchased and viewed mostly by middle-class, middle-aged, married men?[4] How do the categories of literature and pornography apply to Verlaine's book and to such magazines and videos? How do both kinds of texts position women as subjects of representation and as readers?

Such questions invoke the eponymous reader of Teresa de Lauretis's *Alice Doesn't*.[5] What Alice doesn't do is take for granted oddities in the representations of a patriarchal wonderland, the silences and gaps in its critical, explanatory models. Instead, she "begin[s] an argument"[6] with the images, metaphors, codes and practices, through which she not only apprehends literary and social meanings, but through which she also lives her own subjectivity. Alice is, in Judith Fetterley's phrase, a "resisting reader."[7] She pays attention to moments of slippage or discomfort in her own readings. Such a moment occurs when a woman encounters the lesbian bodies of *Les Amies*. Should she read them "liberally" as erotica—and, if so, as heterosexual, lesbian, or homosexual erotica? Should she read them literarily, as allegories of some human condition, say, the loss of love and union? Should she read them historically, as exemplars of a particular nineteenth-century social and literary milieu? Should she read them psycho-biographically, in terms of Verlaine's known bisexuality? These are the somewhat incommensurate readings encouraged, even produced, by the currently available critical models.[8] What I wish to do here is to interrogate these several, conventional readings from a perspective that owes much to Foucauldain and feminist theory, and that asks what meanings the image of the lesbian couple might have within the representational systems of our culture.

II

Foucault's *History of Sexuality* speaks directly to the questions posed by *Les Amies'* double identity as pornography and literature, and by its pivotal image of the lesbian couple.[9] The central argument of that work is that at a certain point in western history sexuality began to be regarded as an essence of self rather than as one of a number of important human behaviors. Foucault argues that this shift occurred when Christianity equated sex with sin, thereby transforming a social behavior regulated by ethical norms into a spiritual condition governed by moral laws. In the Christian period before the eighteenth century, this newly sexualized concept of the self was defined, supervised, and regulated by civil and canonical law, and by the church's pastoral institution of confession. Confession, with its imperatives of self-examination and self-revelation, is of most interest to Foucault. In Christian confession he sees the model for the "moral technologies" of the modern period—technologies through which the individual even more completely interiorizes sexuality as a fundamental truth of self.[10] Chief among these technologies were the medical, juridical, pedagogical, and psychiatric discourses that developed from the eighteenth century onward. Like the confessional, each of them functioned, then as now, as an institutional incitement to individuals to speak the truth of sex contained within the self, as a "determination on the part of the agencies of power to hear it spoken about, and to cause *it* to speak through explicit articulation and endlessly accumulated detail."[11] Together these moral technologies created a set of discourses on sexuality, a set of knowledges that are also technologies of power, that is, kinds of suasion which permeate society and the individual, operating from below and inside rather than from above and outside.

The pastoral institution of confession, then, was displaced in the eighteenth century by *"scientia sexualis"*—a set of discourses whose purpose is to know sexual being rather than to codify sexual practice, as in an *ars erotica*.[12] Foucault ties the development of sexology to the rise of the bourgeoisie throughout the eighteenth and nineteenth centuries. Where the older aristocratic era legitimated itself through inherited rank and property, the new middle class located its power and identity in its collective health and generative potency: in heredity, not inheritance. So, where the aristocratic era organized and controlled sexuality by focusing on the marriage relation and any breaches to it which might affect inheritance, the new bourgeois moral technologies designated procreative heterosexual marriage as natural, and then focused on any sexuality which was "essentially different."[13] What resulted from this interrogation, according to Foucault, was a "new *specification of individuals*."[14] The unconscious project of *scientia sexualis* was the eugenic one of ensuring the collective health and potency of the hegemonic social body. To accomplish this, the bourgeoisie needed to identify and exclude so-called unnatural, that is, non-heterosexual and non-procreative, sexualities; thus, a discursive repertoire of perverse sexual types was constructed. The masturbatory child, the hysterical woman, the prostitute, the sadomasochist, the homosexual—"It was time for all these figures, scarcely noticed in the past, to step forward and speak, to make the difficult confession of what they were. No doubt they were condemned all the same; but they were listened to."[15] By the same token, each of these perverse figures became not only an agent of forbidden acts, but also "a personage, a past, a case history, . . . a type of life," a subjectivity constituted by the very discourses that spoke through them.[16]

Foucault's analysis of the discourses of sexuality in modern European cultures (*scientia sexualis*) provides a way of understanding the institution of pornography as we know it today—and as Verlaine knew it in the nineteenth century. The etymology of the word "pornography" gives one kind of evidence for thinking that it, too, was part of the rise of *scientia sexualis*. Derived from the Greek *pornographos*, meaning a painter of whores, the word was coined in Europe toward the end of the eighteenth century, and, at first, referred to a moral, civic or scientific discussion about prostitutes.[17] For example, in 1769 the French novelist Nicholas Edme Restif de la Bretonne proudly called himself *le pornographe* in a book of that name, which benignly purported to be a "project for the regulation of prostitutes"; similarly, in the first half of the next century, the label "pornography" was used to describe works of medical writers like Alexandre-Jean-Baptiste Parent-Duchâtelet, social reformers like William Acton, art historians like C. O. Müller, and curators of newly unearthed priapic antiquities such as the collection from Pompeii at Naples.[18] Such writers took great pains to distance themselves and their work from identification with a whore-painting or whore-writing whose intention was neither moral nor civic. But their investigations and treatises did much to help create the genre they disavowed. Despite their concern, and, in part, as a result of their very efforts, by the end of the nineteenth century the word "pornography" had come to mean not the scientific depiction of obscene sexuality but rather an obscene representation of sexuality.

In effect, the "new" discourse of pornography gravitated from the realm of science to that of literature during the late eighteenth and the nineteenth centuries. As pornography came to mean obscene representations, it became less a scientific than a legal question: less a struggle over the meaning of the word "pornography" and the institutional location and control of a discourse, and more a struggle over how whores or, by extension, all modes of sexuality could be licitly represented. In this struggle to define the boundary between licit and illicit representation, between literature and pornography, existing obscenity laws were put to work. Prior to the nineteenth century, these laws, for the most part, had proscribed obscene behaviors (and, to a lesser extent, obscene representations) as political or religious transgressions.[19] However, as bourgeois society came to regard sexuality as a truth of self, and became preoccupied with defining and controlling "unnatural" sexualities, obscene representations per se came under the scrutiny of revised laws whose motivation was not so much narrowly political and religious as broadly civic and moral. For example, in 1857 England legislated the Obscene Publications Act; in the same year France applied an 1819 law condemning "outrage to public and religious manners and to good morals" in the benchmark trial of Gustave Flaubert's *Madame Bovary*;[20] and in 1897 the Roman Catholic Church revised its *Index Librorum Prohibitorum*, previously concerned mostly with doctrinal matters, specifically to ban obscene books (although "classics" were authorized for use in education, that is, for young males).

These new and differently focused obscenity laws were part of the ideological shift Foucault describes in *History of Sexuality*. Moreover, they reflect changes in the production, distribution, and consumption of literature in the eighteenth and nineteenth centuries. Improved technologies for cheaply reproducing and circulating books, pamphlets, and illustrations made depictions of obscene sexualities much more available: As Kendrick remarks, "the most remarkable facts about hard-core pornography before the nineteenth century are how little of it there was and how obsessively those few works fed off one another."[21] Moreover, an increase in literacy among poor people, children, and women meant that pornography potentially was more widely accessible; it could no longer be confined securely to the comedies, satires, "private editions," or the drawings and paintings of the nobleman's or gentleman's personal library. It was under the pressure of such ideological, technological, and sociological changes that the law and the courts reconstructed the category of pornography. By the end of the nineteenth century, pornography designated those representations of sexuality considered obscene because of a tendency to corrupt (a definition that foregrounds reader or viewer response). Who especially might be corrupted was identified, explicitly, as that population of women, children, and workers that had gained greater access to books and museums; implicitly, what had to be protected was bourgeois morality.

From a Foucauldian perspective, then, the genre of pornography is an historically contingent phenomenon. However, most legal and literary definitions of pornography treat it as a transhistorical category—one that unproblematically includes ancient priapic art and statuary, Martial's epigrams, Arentino's tales and the imitations and "figures" (illustrations) they inspired, Sade's narratives, Victorian "classics" like *My Secret Life*, and contemporary pornographic magazines and videos. Such approaches generally define pornography according to one or more of four criteria: authorial intention, presented content, elicited response, and ascribed value.[22] Yet none of these differentia itself withstands what might be called the test of history: authorial intention is always indeterminate; what is considered sexually explicit, or even sexual, varies from time to time and place to place; sexual response is conditioned by situation, gender, class, nationality, and sexual orientation; and, not least, what value is given to such representations depends upon the assumptive worldview of the viewer/reader/definer. As Morse

Peckham remarks in *Art and Pornography*, "definitions of pornography are controlled by the interests of the definer because definitions of anything must be controlled by the interests of the definer."[23]

For Peckham, the necessary subjectivity of all definitions is the problem. When he gives a definition of pornography, therefore, he does not adopt an historical perspective but rather seeks for objectivity by applying, in a strict fashion, the single criterion of content: "Pornography is the presentation in verbal or visual signs of human sexual organs in a condition of stimulation."[24] But Peckham's definition is no more successful than the "subjective" ones he criticizes. In the first place, the definition fails in its own terms, for although it is clear from Peckham's discussion generally that he would not count, for example, medical texts or self-help sex manuals as pornography, his definition nonetheless includes them. More importantly, when Peckham discards the criteria of intention, response, and value as too subjective, he sets aside not just several definitional problems but history as well.[25] Peckham's definition is, as he claims, an operational one; it allows us to categorize texts and to specify an identity between modern pornographic works and earlier ones: among a Martial, a Sade, and a porn video, an identity of content exists. Still, it is also an essentialist one, oblivious to the fact that genres are not transhistorical entities, to be defined by their presented content only, but rather culturally specific semiotic codes and practices through which texts are produced and received.[26] As such, the criteria of intention, response, and value necessarily must be taken into account in some way. True, the *particular* uses of a given generic code by *particular* individuals—the intentions, responses, and values of individual activity—may not be determinable, predictable, or objective. But, as Foucault's analysis of *scientia sexualis* demonstrates, the purposes and values/ meanings of the discourses that condition those activities are identifiable. Thus, when Foucault describes the "explosion" of discourses on sex from the mid-eighteenth century onwards, and remarks that it inevitably generated an "increase in 'illicit' discourses, that is, discourses of infraction that crudely named sex by way of insult or mockery of the new code of decency,"[27] he explains what historians of pornography like Marcus, Kendrick, and Kearney assert when they trace the first developments of the genre as we understand it today to Arentino in the sixteenth century.

Once pornography is understood in this way, in historical rather than essentialist terms, the intimate relationship between pornography and "literature," as those genres developed in the eighteenth and nineteenth centuries, is more evident. Not only do their systems of production, distribution, and reception overlap, but also, more importantly, both are centrally concerned with the representation of *desire*. In Foucault's terms, both are institutional imperatives and occasions to construct one's subjectivity in terms of one's sexuality. The relationship between them, therefore, is not oppositional, with pornography being the obverse or underside (Marcus' immature form) of literature. For a discourse necessarily includes by exclusion, and literature helped to construct what it excluded—pornography.

Scientia sexualis produced the normative and the perverse individual; beyond the domain of science, literature spoke of the former and pornography of the latter. Literature operated within the field of a morality that articulated the bourgeois norm of monogamous heterosexuality, of procreative married sex. Its objective was the health of the hegemonic social body, its purpose moral education, and its central instructional model the romantic or married couple as a single androgynous subjectivity. Reciprocally, pornography functioned in the field of bourgeois immorality, realizing through subversion and parody that which bourgeois morality silenced and excluded. Its central figure was the perverse adult—the libertine, harlot, or homosexual who uncouples the bourgeois ideal subject. With this uncoupling, the male is restored to his position of dominance in a discourse in which woman is no longer the Complement of the One but rather, simply, the object of man's desire and locus of all he fears; woman becomes that which is controlled and needs to be controlled. Then as now, bourgeois literature and pornography, both obsessed with the heterosexual couple and the question of whether its unity should be strengthened or broken, represent male erotic desire primarily to men, so that their masculinity may be confirmed, even as their sexuality is supervised and channelled.

III

If the relationship between literature and pornography is understood in this way, then it becomes clear how Paul Verlaine's *Les Amies* can be sometimes pornography, sometimes literature. Indeed, the sonnets are poised on the (constructed) border between literature and pornography, held there by two further discourses in which the poems participate—the long tradition of men writing about lesbian women, and nineteenth-century Decadent writing. The first of these, the Sapphic tradition, has two variants, one of which centers on two, often interrelated, representations of woman: woman as poet, and woman as lover who commits suicide because of unrequited love for a younger man. The focus on the lesbian woman as a poet derives from Plato's invocation of Sappho as the tenth Muse, and the representation of her as deranged lover owes much to Ovid's account of the legendary story of Sappho and Phaon (*Heroides* XIV). These two classical representations comprise what might be called the respectable variant of the tradition of Sapphic writings, for in the Platonic model the lesbian woman's sexuality is ignored, while in the Ovidian one her sexuality is tolerated because it is non-procreative, and only a prelude to heterosexual love.

The second or libertine and "obscene" variant of the Sapphic tradition centers on the figure of an older woman who seduces a younger girl. Elaine Marks notes that in classical and European literature after Sappho this image "was discarded,

except for its pornographic, comic value."[28] Its pornographic value derives from
the explicit depiction of lesbian sexuality as, in Lillian Faderman's words, "a sterile
game, the sight [of which] serves only as an aphrodisiac to the male spectator."[29]
Its comic or satiric value is associated with the depiction of the "virile" lesbian
lover, the woman who through her dress, behavior, or sexual practices usurps
male prerogative, and, so, must be punished through invective, denigration, and
representations of violence upon her body.[30]

Verlaine's *Les Amies* draws on both strands of the Sapphic tradition. Its final
poem, "Sappho," belongs more to the respectable variant of this literary discourse
and, for this reason, could be separately published in a literary journal. Three of
its four main narrative events—Sappho's display of sexual frustration, her fury at
Phaon's indifference, and her suicide—recapitulate Ovid's story and reiterate the
heterosexual assumption that lesbian loving is only an apprenticeship or foreplay
to heterosexual coitus.[31] The fourth event of the sonnet—Sappho's recollection of
former loves sung in verse—invokes the Platonic model of Sappho as disembodied
Muse. Yet, at the same time, the libertine version of the Sapphic tradition is also
alluded to in the opening image of Sappho as a she-wolf. Within a Christian
register of symbolism, the image symbolizes selfishness, solitariness, treachery, and,
at the same time, connotes an unnatural, bestial, voracious female sexuality.[32]
When these meanings are fused with the representation of the woman poet, they
activate the libertine attitude toward the "virile" woman who deserves punishment
for her usurpation of male roles and prerogatives. Indeed, Sappho's suicide is, in
one sense, such a punishment.

There are, however, elements in Verlaine's "Sappho" that are anomalous to
the received literary tradition. The most important of these is Sappho's recollection
of former loves sung in verse, which, with "remorse unremitting" (7), she
remembers as pure and shining with "youthful glory" (8).[33] Coming as it does at
the volta, or turning point, of a *sonnet renversé*, this moment of recollection and
regret for having been "forgetful of the Rite" (4) can be seen to motivate Sappho's
suicide: if so, Sappho dies for lost lesbian love, not for unrequited heterosexual
love. This counter-traditional reading finds some support in the final stanza.
Sappho is called to leap to her death by "*la Moire*." In the classical literary context,
"*la Moire*" is usually read as *Moira* or Fate: it is Sappho's fate as lesbian to be
fatally overcome by unrequited heterosexual love. However, "*la Moire*" is also the
silk-like shimmering of the night sea in the light of the moon, that is, Selena.
Thus Verlaine's poem permits a second reading, concurrent with the received one,
in which Selena, goddess of the feminine principle,[34] calls Sappho to her suicide
and thereby avenges the female lovers and lesbian loves forgotten by Sappho in
her passion for Phaon, but still remembered in her verse. If this reading is
accepted, then Sappho and her verse signify not only Plato's bodiless Muse and the
pornographer's virago, but also a positively valued lesbian sexuality: The loves of
Sappho are embodied in her verse, which will speak to and perhaps awaken
virgins who sleep, in the sense of being uninitiated into lesbian rites.

Similar departures from the Sapphic tradition can be traced in the other five poems of Verlaine's *Les Amies*: *"Sur le Balcon"* ("On the Balcony"), *"Pensionnaires"* ("Room-mates"), *"Per Amica Silentia"* ("Through Friendly Silence"), *"Printemps"* ("Spring") and *"Été"* ("Summer"). These sonnets belong more to the book's libertine literary variant, illustrated by the condemnation and destruction of it upon its first publication. The seduction of a younger by a (somewhat) older woman is portrayed in *"Pensionnaires"* and in the paired poems, *"Printemps"* and *"Été*. Further, the five sonnets insist on lesbian loving—in the images of the rumpled bed behind the two women in the first; of one girl kneeling before and mouthing another in the second; of the "tangled voices" (9) coming from the bed in the third; and of two women speaking to one another during the sexual act in the fourth and fifth. Finally, the libertine variant of the Sapphic tradition is traceable in the representational structures of the poem—most noticeably in the first and third sonnets—in the voyeuristic perspective and paternalistic voice, which suggest both the mystery and otherness of lesbian love.[35] Nevertheless, Verlaine's sonnets do reorient the Sapphic tradition. The voyeuristic speaker does not mock, satirize or otherwise punish the depicted lovers in these poems. Rather, the lovers are apostrophized as "dear and Lonely Ones," possessed of "faithful hearts" and "sublime souls," whose "noble vow" is a "glorious Stigma" (respectively in *"Pensionnaires,"* 12, *"Sur le Balcon,"* 8, and *"Pensionnaires,"* 11, 14). Similarly, no particular emphasis is given to the convention of the sterility of lesbian love, and there is no overt suggestion that such love is merely a prelude to heterosexual love. Through such reinflections of the tradition, Verlaine invites the reader/spectator to identify with the women's coupling, and same-sex love is positively valorized. Even more so than "Sappho," therefore, these five sonnets idealize the "unnatural" and "perverse" lesbian pair, representing them as a "strange couple who pity all other couples" (*"Sur le Balcon,"* 10).

Verlaine's departures from the Sapphic tradition can be ascribed in part to the influence of the Decadent movement.[36] The movement's slogan was *épater le bourgeois* (shock the conventionally minded); they revolted against the constrictions of bourgeois society and morality not by following the Romantic return to nature, but rather by cultivating the "unnatural." Some of the figures constructed by *scientia sexualis* make an appearance in Decadent literature, especially the lesbian couple, the androgynous esthete who submits his will to a woman, and the femme fatale who dominates him. Isabelle de Courtivron sees several interrelated male desires at play in these three Decadent types.[37] Their fascination with lesbians encodes the male writer's desires for a fully eroticized body, for a forbidden passivity, for an undifferentiated sexual experience; the androgynous hero in Decadent fiction projects homoerotic desire; the castrating character of the fatal woman embodies the phallic desire of her male author to be punished for wishing to be a woman, for drawing too close to the maternal body. In this way, according to de Courtivron, the recurrent lesbian figure of Decadent literature can be read as a metaphor for homosexuality. Unlike homosexuality, lesbianism was the "unnatural love" that *could* be spoken. And it could be spoken precisely because of a long tradition of patriarchal thought and literature that either could not conceive the possibility of women loving women or, if it did so, could only imagine it in one of two ways: trivial and titillating, or virile and punishable.

Les Amies both does and does not belong to the Sapphic tradition, for Verlaine appropriates the heterosexual representational system of Sapphism to signify not only patriarchal meanings (woman as signifier of man's poetic and sexual potency), but also the ideality of same-sex coupling and, thereby, covertly, of homosexual coupling. The convenience of this discursive strategy is that it distances the threat of homosexuality to masculine identity, sociality, and power at the same time that it coopts the heterosexual codifications of female bodies as beautiful, female friendships as innocent, and the loving couple as intimate. Thus the figure of the lesbian couple safely provides the male writer and his male audience with the illicit pleasures of the "immoral" (non-normative) and "unnatural" (non-heterosexual).

Verlaine's recordings of the Sapphic literary tradition participate in the radical-liberal political attitude that sees society as repressive and inimical to the individual's pursuit of freedom and happiness, to the rights of liberty and—to borrow the term of another radical-liberal, Roland Barthes—*jouissance*.[38] However, it would be a mistake to identify the transgression of bourgeois morality in *Les Amies* or in Decadence more generally with a rupture within patriarchy. Such a metaphoric use of the image of the lesbian couple finally submits female pleasure to the masculine gaze: The bodies, orgasms, and mutual bonding of the two women doubly confirm male potency, since all are represented by the text as existing only for masculine attention, heterosexual or homosexual. Though *Les Amies* can be seen to challenge and resist the discourses of bourgeois morality, Verlaine's poems still confirm the gender definitions and divisions upon which the structure of that morality rests.

IV

For the resisting reader, *Les Amies* and its critical reception exemplify a clash between two patriarchal interests—those of the moralist and those of the radical-liberal—both equally bourgeois. If, like the nineteenth-century bourgeois moralist, one imagines the social edifice as based upon the procreative couple, then a text like *Les Amies* is perverse and proscribable. But if, like the radical-liberal Decadent, one's commitment is to the individual's right freely to express himself and, therefore, his sexuality (since the liberal imagination is also a product of *scientia sexualis*), then it is the censorship of such a text that is unhealthy and perverse. In short, the clash between the interests of the bourgeois moralist and those of the bourgeois liberal is a product of a central conflict within bourgeois discourse between the ideology of the family and that of individualism. It is a conflict in which the class interests of women do not much figure.

From the trial of Gustave Flaubert's *Madame Bovary* in 1857 to that of Vladimir Nabokov's *Lolita* in 1957, this political conflict was played out in courts of law through the issue of a text's literary value: If a text's sociality could be demonstrated through its literary value, then any pornographic threat it might pose could be overlooked. In this way, the major ideological conflict between conservatives and liberals could be reconciled but, perforce, only temporarily. Legal paternalism, however, became increasingly less practical as the legal and social status of women and workers improved, and the conjunction of consumerist capitalism and multi-media communications made pornography not only more various and more available, but also more profitable. As a result, by the end of the 1960s, the courts effectively withdrew from the business of protecting the community (with the exception of the very young) from "immoral" or "obscene" representations. In the United States the majority opinion of the 1970 *Report of the Commission on Pornography and Obscenity* exemplified the general liberalization of attitudes toward pornography in the west during the mid-twentieth century. It recommended that "federal, state, and local legislation prohibiting the sale, exhibition, or distribution of sexual materials to consenting adults be repealed."[39] The long struggle between bourgeois moralists and liberals, illustrated by the history of Verlaine's *Les Amies*, ended in the latters' victory.

But even as the liberal position legally consolidated itself, it was challenged by the feminist critique of pornography that emerged in the 1970s. Not surprisingly, liberals, like Kendrick in *The Secret Museum*, perceived this challenge as a return of the repressive forces of bourgeois morality. However, in at least one of its major variants, the contemporary feminist critique is conducted more within the domain of bourgeois individualism than within that of bourgeois morality, in that it appeals to the rights of individuals to freedom from social discrimination and bodily harm. The argument of this variant, which could be called "activist," begins by questioning the liberal contention, exemplified by the 1970 *Report,* that pornography is essentially harmless to adults. It contends that, on the contrary, pornography is "graphic sexually explicit subordination of women,"[40] and is, therefore, harmful to some. This analysis is represented by activist groups like Women Against Pornography, in reports such as *Pornography and Sexual Violence: Evidence of the Links,* in writings like those collected in Laura Lederer's *Take Back the Night: Women on Pornography,* and in studies like Andrea Dworkin's *Pornography: Men Possessing Women.*[41] In the latter book Dworkin passionately argues that women's subordination is represented in the standard tropes of hardcore pornography: woman as a commodity; women enjoying humiliation, physical abuse, rape; women in postures of sexual submission and servility; women reduced to body parts; women as whores by nature; and women as filthy and animalistic. Dworkin's argument is encapsulated in the activist slogan "Rape is the Practice, Pornography the Theory," which focuses on the representations of violence in pornography, drawing both a symbolic and a causal link between these representations and women's condition in society. Dworkin's analysis, and others like it, is politically inflected; it is meant to serve as the theory for direct action that redresses woman's subordination in society.

The second variant of the contemporary feminist critique of pornography owes much to semiotic and poststructuralist discussions of the subject, and is illustrated by Susanne Kappeler's *The Pornography of Representation.*[42] Kappeler's thesis is that pornography fundamentally annihilates the woman as subject, both through what it represents and through how this is represented. In its images and masculinist ideological perspective, pornography either denies, ignores and/or elides woman's subjectivity by showing her as object or victim, or it appropriates and fakes her subjectivity by showing her pleasure to exist only because of and for man. Kappeler indicts, therefore, both pornography and literature, arguing that the feminist "develops her critique from within the realm of representation; her argument is not simply sociological, . . . and not simply 'moral,' according to the morality of the censorship lobby. Her argument is literary-political, a political critique of the literary, a critique of the politics of the literary and of representation."[43] Whereas Dworkin concentrates on the physical violence done to women in pornography and in society, Kappeler focuses on an ideological violence: Whatever woman's legal or constitutional status, she is *not* the subject of Western society's representations, not the individual referred to by even the liberal imagination. As the title of Kappeler's book suggests, this second type of feminist critique attends not so much to the category of pornography per se as to the structures of phallogocentrism generally. It therefore operates at some remove from the political activism of the first critique, but is still congruent in its apprehension—its understanding and fear—that there is someone who is harmed in and by our culture's representations of sexuality.

An important strand within this second, poststructuralist variety of the feminist critique draws on psychoanalytic theory in an effort to understand the structures of pornography in relation to desire. It deploys the re-reading of Freud initiated by Jacques Lacan, and, in this way, differs from more traditional Freudian analyses of pornography such as Susan Griffin's *Pornography and Silence: Culture's Revenge Against Nature.*[44] Like Kappeler, poststructuralist feminist writers define heterosexual pornography in terms of what is shown (women) and for whom (men), and they discuss pornographic representation in terms of codes of submission and fragmentation, of looking and knowing, and so forth. However, their interest further lies in how such codes, and the discourses to which they pertain, are *interiorized* by historical individuals. Their focus is not simply on those systems of power or representation as they exist externally to the subject, as Kappeler's largely is, but rather upon the subject's internal experience of them, especially on the level of the unconscious. In other words, the focus of such feminist psychoanalysis is on desire as it relates to patriarchal discourse, power, and systems of representation, all of which work to erase female desire.

Both the activist and the poststructualist feminist critiques shift the debate about pornography from an ethical to a political arena: The question is no longer, as it was in nineteenth-century France and England, who is harmed in the sense of being morally corrupted, but rather who is harmed in the sense of being physically hurt or psychologically diminished. Patriarchal representations of the lesbian couple highlight this issue. Poststructuralist feminists contend that the Sapphic literary tradition within pornography is a textual practice that invites the spectator/reader to identify with a masculine gaze and voice, and to fetishize the represented pleasures and potencies of the lesbian couple on display as "his" own. In this view, the represented pleasure of the lesbian couple in pornography is phallic, and belongs to those who exchange such icons in order to signify the interests and power of men. Thus, Verlaine's *Les Amies* is pornographic, not because it is non-literature, nor because it is "obscene" in the legal sense of the word, nor because it is the occasion of physical violence against women, but rather because it fetishizes female pleasure and desires, thereby erasing and eliding women's presence, difference, and subjectivity. Whatever "this kind" of writing is worth as poetry, *Les Amies* speaks both through and across the body of woman, but not about her nor to her.

Notes

1. A. E. Carter, *Verlaine: A Study in Parallels* (London: Oxford University Press, 1970), 40.

2. Steven Marcus, *The Other Victorians: A Study of Sexuality and Pornography in Mid-Nineteenth Century England* (London: Corgi, 1969), 289.

3. The point can be made in still another way, once more by using Verlaine: Jacques Borel, Octave Nadal and Henry de Bouillane de Lacoste, eds., *Oeuvre poétique complètes,* 2 vols. (Paris: Club du Meilleur Livre, 1959–60) could not decide whether or not to include Verlaine's quite scabrous poems, *Femmes* (1890 or 1891) and *Hombres* (1893 or 1894), in the so-called complete works, and, thus, did so in only a quarter of the 6000 copies of the edition.

4. According to *The Report of the Commission on Obscenity and Pornography* (New York: Random House, 1970), "[t]he profile of the patron of adult bookstores that emerges from these observations in different parts of the United States is: white, middle-aged, middleclass, married, males dressed in a business suit or neat casual attire, shopping alone" (159). The *Report* also indicates this profile extends to patrons of adult theatres and arcades.

5. Teresa de Lauretis, *Alice Doesn't: Feminism, Semiotics, Cinema* (London: Macmillan, 1984).

6. de Lauretis, 3.

7. Judith Fetterley, *The Resisting Reader: A Feminist Approach to American Fiction* (Bloomington: Indiana University Press, 1978).

8. Susan Sontag's influential apologia for pornography, "The Pornographic Imagination," in *A Susan Sontag Reader* (New York: Farrar, Strauss, Giroux, 1963), 205–34, encourages the "liberal" reading, as does Angela Carter's *The Sadean Woman and the Ideology of Pornography* (New York: Pantheon, 1978). A. E. Carter's *Verlaine* represents a

humanist approach, while his *The Idea of Decadence in French Literature: 1830–1900* (Toronto: University of Toronto Press, 1959) illustrates a literary-historical one, as does Joanna Richardson's *Verlaine: A Biography* (New York: Viking, 1971). Finally, Paul Schmidt's "Vision of Violence: Rimbaud and Verlaine," in *Homosexualities and French Literature: Cultural Contexts/Critical Texts,* edited by George Stambolian and Elaine Marks (Ithaca and London: Cornell University Press, 1979) deploys a fairly orthodox psycho-biographical framework.

9. Michel Foucault, *The History of Sexuality, Volume 1: An Introduction,* 1976 translated by Robert Hurley (New York: Random, 1978).

10. For a useful discussion of the notion of "moral technologies," see Ian Hunter, "After Representation: Recent Discussions of the Relation between Language and Literature," *Economy and Society* 13: 4 (November 1984): 409.

11. Foucault, 18, his emphasis.

12. Ibid., 57.

13. Ibid., 39.

14. Ibid., 42–43, his emphasis.

15. Ibid., 39.

16. Ibid., 43.

17. According to Walter Kendrick, *The Secret Museum: Pornography in Modern Culture* (New York: Viking, 1987), " 'pornography' first appeared in English print, in a translation of German art historian C. O. Müller's *Handbuch der Archäologie der Kunst* (1850). . . . The source of Müller's coinage was a unique instance in classical Greek of the word *pornographoi* ('whore-painters'), tucked away deep in the *Deipnosophistae* ('Learned Banquet') by the second-century compiler Athenaeus" (11).

18. Kendrick, 103–08.

19. The history of censorship laws is told from a liberal point of view in Kendrick's *The Secret Museum,* and from a Foucauldian perspective in Ian Hunter, David Saunders and Dugald Williamson, *On Pornography: Literature, Sexuality and the Law* (New York: St. Martin's Press, 1993).

20. Kendrick, 105–16.

21. Kendrick, 64.

22. Morse Peckham, *Art and Pornography: An Experiment in Explanation* (New York: Harper and Row), 42–43.

23. Peckham, 36.

24. Peckham, 47.

25. In this regard Patrick J. Kearney's definition of pornography as that which published *sous le manteau,* in *A History of Erotic Literature* (London: Macmillan, 1982), 7, is more useful, for it does not altogether ignore contextual determinants.

26. Important early structuralist/semiotic discussions of the theory of genre are Tzveton Todorov, *Les Genres du discours* (Paris: Seuil, 1978) and Gérard Genette, "*Genre, 'types,' modes,*" *Poétique* 8:32 (1977): 239–421. Also relevant is Jacques Derrida, "*La Loi du Genre*/The Law of Genre," *Glyph* 7 (1980): 176–233. More recent useful discussions that

take a semiotic/reader-reception approach include: Gunther Kress and Terry Threadgold, "Towards a Social Theory of Genre," *Southern Review* 21:3 (November 1988): 215–43; Ian Reid, ed., *The Place of Genre in Learning: Current Debates* (Geelong: Deakin University, Centre for Studies in Literary Education, 1987), and Alistair Fowler, *Kinds of Literature: An Introduction to the Theory of Genre and Modes* (Oxford: Clarendon Press, 1982).

27. Foucault, 18.

28. Elaine Marks, "Lesbian Intertextuality," in *Homosexualities and French Literature,* 356–57.

29. Lillian Faderman, *Surpassing the Love of Men: Romantic Friendship and Love between Women from the Renaissance to the Present* (New York: Farrar, Strauss and Giroux, 1979), 27.

30. See Faderman, ch. 3.

31. There are other classical myths that establish Sappho's heterosexuality, like the tale that she married Cerclyas and had a daughter by him named Cleis, after Sappho's own mother.

32. See, for example, Dante's *Inferno* (Canto 1), where the three beasts—the lion, leopard and she-wolf—represent progressively graver sins.

33. Translations of the poems in *Les Amies* given here are drawn from Brian Dibble, "Pseudonyms, Counterfeits and Translations: Paul Verlaine's *Les Amies,*" *The Phoenix Review* 1 (Summer 1986/87): 33–45.

34. Selene, Hecate and Artemis are substantially fused as deities connected with the moon. Artemis emphasizes virginity, chastity and/or a preference for women as companions but also fertility and childbirth; Hecate is more associated with the well-being of children; and Selene's *raison d'être* seems to derive from her conflation with the other two.

35. Bram Dijkstra, *Idols of Perversity: Fantasies of Feminine Evil in Fin-de-Siècle Culture* (New York and Oxford: Oxford University Press, 1986), 119–59, explores the nineteenth-century motif of woman as sexually self-sufficient or separate from male sexuality, that is, as virginal, self-absorbed, absolutely natural; he relates this motif to lunar, circular and narcissistic imagery—all present in *Les Amies*—and to representations of lesbianism.

36. For introductory discussions of French Decadence, see A. E. Carter, *The Idea of Decadence in French Literature,* and Richard Gilman, *Decadence: The Strange Life of an Epithet* (New York: Farrar, Strauss and Giroux, 1979).

37. Isabelle de Courtivron, "Weak Men and Fatal Women: The Sand Image," in *Homosexualities and French Literature,* 210–27.

38. See Roland Barthes, *Pleasure of the Text* (1973), translated by Richard Miller (New York: Hill and Wang, 1975).

39. *Report of the Commission of Obscenity and Pornography,* 57.

40. Catherine A. MacKinnon and Andrea Dworkin, "The Model Anti-Pornography Law," *MS.* (April 1988): 46–47. This model appears as part of Mary K. Blakely, "Is One Woman's Sexuality Another Woman's Pornography?" in the same issue of *MS.,* 37–47 and 120–23. It is based on earlier versions by the same authors, drafted for the Minneapolis and Indianapolis city councils.

41.   Minneapolis City Council Government Operations Committee, *Pornography and Sexual Violence: Evidence and Links,* The Complete Transcript of Public Hearings on Ordinances to Add Pornography as Discrimination Against Women, December 12 and 13, 1983 (London: Everywoman, 1988); Laura Lederer, ed., *Take Back the Night: Women on Pornography* (New York: Morrow, 1980); and Andrea Dworkin, *Pornography: Men Possessing Women* (New York: Perigee Books, 1979).

42.   Susanne Kappeler, *The Pornography of Representation* (Minneapolis: University of Minnesota Press, 1986).

43.   Kappeler, 136.

44.   Susan Griffin, *Pornography and Silence: Culture's Revenge Against Nature* (New York: Harper, 1981).

The Woman in the Mirror: Randall Jarrell and John Berryman

Christopher Benfey

A man looks at himself in the mirror and sees a woman's face. What are we to make of his surprise? If he has turned into a woman, why does he need a mirror to know it? And if he hasn't, who is the woman? Questions such as these are prompted by a reading of certain American poems of the fifties and early sixties, in which male poets assume a woman's identity. For "confessional" poets like Randall Jarrell and John Berryman, whose primary lyric impulse was autobiographical, this exchange of sexual identities was more than just the creation of "female *personae*." It involved, as I will argue, a probing of repressed and evaded aspects of the poet's own gender identity. If the resulting texts seem ultimately problematic, it is because a palpable fear of the feminine, and of appearing "effeminate," has disguised itself as empathy for woman's experience. These poets write from within certain culturally restrictive notions of the feminine, which mark their poems as unmistakably of a definite time and place.

But before turning to the texts, some earlier examples of the same scenario—of a man seeing himself as a woman in the mirror—drawn from a story by Sherwood Anderson and a case study of Freud's, should help define an approach to the issues of sexual identity posed in the later poetry of Jarrell and Berryman. Consider a passage from Anderson's extraordinary story "The Man Who Became a Woman" (1923). The narrator is a stable groom with a night off, a sensitive young man who is a bit at sea in the macho world of the racetrack where he works.

> The point is that the face I saw in the looking-glass back of that bar, when I looked up from my glass of whisky that evening, wasn't my own face at all but the face of a woman. It was a girl's face, that's what I meant. That's what it was. It was a girl's face, and a lonesome and scared girl too. She was just a kid at that.

Some of the ideas in this essay appeared, in much shorter and substantially different form, in "The Woman in the Mirror: Jarrell and Berryman." *Pequod* 23/24 (Fall 1988): 24–33.

When I saw that the glass of whisky came pretty near falling out of my hand but I gulped it down, put a dollar on the bar, and called for another. "I've got to be careful here—I'm up against something new," I said to myself. "If any of these men in here get on to me there's going to be trouble."[1]

Two kinds of glasses figure in this case: looking-glasses for women and whisky glasses for men. To each gender its own glass. For the young man, to drink another glass of whisky is to be more of a man—it is an elixir of virility—while to look in a mirror is to risk turning into a woman, as though the long history of mirrors as props of feminine *vanitas* had become a threat to this man's masculinity.[2] But the groom's very effort to "be a man" seems to invite the opposite: to bring on his repressed feminine side, with its "lonesome and scared" girl's face.

Freud was one of Anderson's many passing intellectual fascinations, especially during the twenties, when this story was written; he may well have been familiar with Freud's case study of the distinguished fin-de-siècle jurist, Dr. Daniel Paul Schreber, for whom "the idea of being transformed into a woman was the salient feature and earliest germ of his delusional system."[3] Schreber, as he reported in his *Memoirs,* often stood in front of the mirror "wearing sundry feminine adornments," and was " 'bold enough to assert that any one who should happen to see me before the mirror with the upper portion of my torso bared . . . would receive an unmistakable impression of a *female bust.*' "[4] But whether Anderson knew the case study or not, the cross-gender scenarios are remarkably similar, and Freud's analysis provides a starting point for making sense of these mirror scenes.

The Schreber case became the basis for Freud's theories regarding psychosis. Following his pioneering analysis, this case has inspired such a voluminous commentary, both Anglo-American and (after Lacan's work on Schreber during the fifties) French, that its subject has been called "by far the most famous mental patient ever."[5] While much of the commentary centers on the nature of psychosis, for our purposes it is the more recent (and mainly French) work centering on sexual identity that will prove most helpful.

Analyzing Schreber's desire to be a woman, Freud himself arrived at precisely the etiology we would expect: "suppressed homosexual impulses"; "the appearance in [Schreber] of a feminine (that is, passive homosexual) wish-fantasy."[6] But to later critics, the very narrowness of this interpretation—with its quick equation of the feminine with the passive homosexual, and its limited conception of the "normal" oedipal process—has been responsible for the liveliness of debate in succeeding analyses of the case.

It may seem, in particular, that Freud has put blinders on his insight from *Three Essays on the Theory of Sexuality* that we are all bisexual, that each person is part male and part female.[7] Might the "feminine wish-fantasy" be an attempt, by poet or patient, to explore aspects of the self that our culture shies away from? Some recent contributions to the literature on the Schreber case have, in fact, taken this line. The French psychoanalyst Janine Chasseguet-Smirgel argues that a culture that places undue emphasis on virility can unwittingly foster precisely such a return of (repressed) femininity in men—as in Germany in the 1890s or, as here, the United States in the 1950s.[8] Similarly, Jean-François Lyotard, in an essay on Schreber's "vertiginous sexuality," stresses the bisexual possibilities of Schreber's "psychosis." Thus, Schreber imagines an afterlife in which "one [would] be finally delivered from the difference between the sexes," and quotes Mignon's song from *Wilhelm Meister: "Und jene himmlischen Gestalten/ Sie fragen nicht nach Mann und Weib"* ("And these celestial figures don't ask whether you are a man or a woman").[9]

That Schreber was a gifted writer (or *"Schreiber,"* in a much noticed pun) introduces the literary problem into the question of sexual identity. The American male poets of the fifties and early sixties—John Berryman, Randall Jarrell, Robert Lowell—achieved their most conspicuous successes with poems that seemed close, and often insisted on their proximity to autobiography, hence the popular use of the term "confessional" to describe them.[10] Berryman's *Dream Songs* (1965–69), Lowell's *Life Studies* (1959), Jarrell's *The Lost World* (1965) were all attempts to retrieve the past of the poets, often with the help of Freud—albeit a rather mechanical, fifties' version of Freud. But a striking and neglected feature of the work of these poets—neglected, no doubt, because it fits uneasily with a stress on autobiography—is their various attempts to assume a woman's voice. Given their confessional poetics, this practice of speaking as or for the opposite gender is more ambitious than merely the use of female personae. The magical and euphemistic word "persona" always masquerades as an explanation, but it hides more than it reveals; what it would mean to write without a persona is far from clear, since the poet is always inventing a self, and that self is always gendered. The distinction between the poet and the woman speaker seems, at critical points in the poems of Jarrell and Berryman, to break down, or to be put in question. The female speakers in these poems seem deeply uncanny, as though the primary aim of the poets was less to create believable women characters than to produce a truly bisexual poetry, a poetry in which male poets allow their femininity to speak.[11]

If persona derives from the Latin word for mask, Randall Jarrell found a perfect subject for a poem with a female speaker: the woman's face—that is, the mask assumed by the male poet. In several of Jarrell's most interesting and characteristic poems, a woman speaker looks into the mirror and sees that her face is getting old. Here the fantasy described by Sherwood Anderson and by Freud, of a man seeing himself in the mirror as a woman, has taken a further turn, as a male poet imagines himself *as a woman* confronting a mirror.[12] Frances Ferguson has read these poems as *mementi mori:* "The characters who see themselves mirrored [are forced] to recognize suddenly that they have changed irreversibly and that movement toward death is their fixed condition."[13] But equally arresting in these poems is their open confrontation with narcissism—though *whose* narcissism, the woman speaker's or the male poet's, is not always clear—and their somewhat less open confrontation with the male poet's own sexual identity.

"The Face" (1951) is, according to the poet's second wife Mary Jarrell, the poem in which "the idea of altering the gender of his feelings is first apparent."[14] The poem carries an epigraph from Jarrell's favorite opera, *Der Rosenkavalier: "Die alte Frau, die alte Marschallin!"* In a note at the beginning of his *Selected Poems* (1955), Jarrell explains that the Marschallin laments her age while looking in the mirror, but he says nothing about the gender of the speaker in his poem. Critics have always assumed that the speaker is a woman. John Crowe Ransom confidently called the poem "the tragedy of Everywoman as she stares and speaks into a mirror"—as though it isn't tough for a man to get old and lose his looks.[15] The poem begins:

> Not good any more, not beautiful—
> Not even young.
> This isn't mine.
> Where is the old one, the old ones?
> Those were mine.
>
> It's so: I have pictures,
> Not such old ones; people behaved
> Differently then. . . . When they meet me they say:
> You haven't changed.
> I want to say: You haven't looked.

Clearly Jarrell associated this speech with *Der Rosenkavalier* because of the shared lament over lost looks, but something else may have triggered the association. In Richard Strauss's opera, sexual identity is foregrounded and "in play." Sexual ambiguity is achieved by means of a Mozartean "pants role." The Marschallin's young male lover, Octavian, whom she decides to renounce while she is still beautiful (and not yet *"die alte Frau"*), is played by a female mezzo-soprano. At a crucial point in the drama the character Octavian disguises himself as a girl. The ensuing complication of genders—a female singer playing a man who dresses up as a girl—might well have seemed to Jarrell to correspond to his own lyric self-transformation into an aging woman. Jarrell, then, identifies with the Marschallin's dilemma, but it is the transformations of Octavian across gender that provide the analogy for the machinery of Jarrell's poem.[16] Aspects of the composition of the poem bear this out.

Sometimes Jarrell seemed to think that switching gender was simply a matter of switching pronouns, as though sexuality was more an issue of linguistic than of bodily difference. By concentrating on tricks of language, he could evade the deeper issues of gender identity, as well as his own ambiguous fascination with switching gender. Toward the end of his life, in 1965, Jarrell was preparing to write an essay on Emily Dickinson and he was particularly fascinated with the way Dickinson switched pronouns in her poems, which to him implied a change in the gender of her speakers. He reminded himself to "notice change in versions" of poem 446 (from "I showed her Hights she never saw" to "He showed me

Hights I never saw—") and poem 494 ("Going to Him! Happy letter!" and "Going—to—Her! / Happy—Letter!").[17] Along strikingly similar lines, and with kindred evasiveness, John Berryman once claimed "to know more about the administration of pronouns than any other living poet working in English or American."[18] As Berryman remarked, he had discovered "that a commitment of identity can be 'reserved' so to speak, with an ambiguous pronoun. The poet himself is both left out and put in." "Without this invention," he added, "I could not have written [Homage to Mistress Bradstreet]."[19] A certain ambiguity in the "administration of pronouns" is, then, a trick Berryman and Jarrell mastered early.

But what Jarrell switched in "The Face" wasn't a pronoun; it was an adjective. As Mary Jarrell remembers:

> In a letter to a former student at the Salzburg Seminar he described ["The Face"] as "a sad poem about the way one's face looks in the mirror when one grows old." In the copy he enclosed with the letter, the first line was, "Not good any more not handsome—" and continues with a man's soliloquy about his face.[20]

The adjective "beautiful," as well as the epigraph (*"Die alte Frau . . ."*), suggesting that the speaker is Hofmannsthal and Strauss's Marschallin, came later, when the poem was first published.

But it seems to me that Jarrell leaves the speaker's gender ambiguous: A man's face may be beautiful, too, and an epigraph does not necessarily identify the speaker. I suspect that Jarrell added the epigraph from Hofmannsthal's libretto because it made him uncomfortable—as though he were betraying an "unmanly" emotion—to lament his own lost looks. It probably seemed more fitting to him, more in keeping with societal assumptions about physical vanity, that a woman would worry about such things.

The speaker in Jarrell's "The Face" is profoundly double-voiced, with Jarrell's own lament about his appearance merging with, and disguising itself by, the hypothetical woman's voice he identifies with Hofmannsthal's Marschallin. There is an interesting biographical context for this doubling. In 1948 Jarrell wrote a letter to Elisabeth Eisler, whom he'd met and fallen in love with in Salzburg earlier that year:

> Hannah Arendt said something last night that gave me the feeling of being talked about by posterity. . . . She said to her husband about me, "He has affinities with Rilke, you know." Then, she added, "His face is a little like." Her husband looked at me and said quietly, in a surprised way, "Why yes, that is so." I sat, rather awkward and silent, and finally remarked what an odd man Rilke had been. They both laughed, and I did, too.
>
> I evidently was quite successful in writing "The Face" in a style quite different from my usual style for she said she would never have recognized it as mine.[21]

More than contiguity links these two paragraphs. In the second paragraph, it almost seems that Jarrell is saying that Hannah Arendt wouldn't have recognized *his face* as his own. He may want reassurance that he hasn't revealed too much of his own male, narcissistic fears in his poem "The Face." To look like Rilke, on the other hand, is to resemble one of the immortals, to be transported beyond fears of mere physical aging by being of the ages. But Rilke, of course, had an extremely peculiar face, one with a distinctly androgynous cast, and one of Rilke's best known odditites is that until he was old enough to go to school his mother dressed him as a girl and called him by his androgynous given name, René, which he later changed to Rainer. Here again, as with the ambiguous role of Octavian in *Der Rosenkavalier,* a certain covert theme of female impersonation seems operative in Jarrell's associations.

Jarrell's stylistic remark about "The Face" implicitly raises the issue of disguise, and, specifically, of disguised gender. To have a style "different from my usual [male, autobiographical] style," and yet one that is still "mine," is, in this case, to aim for a style that is uncannily ambiguous in gender, and perhaps, in Freud's terminology, bisexual.

If "The Face" registers, while it disguises, Randall Jarrell's anxiety about aging and losing his "looks," another kind of look, the look of the spectator or onlooker, is invoked in this and other poems by Jarrell. Indeed, in poems like "The Face" it is this look of the Other that determines the speaker's identity: "I want to say: You haven't *looked*." "The world goes by my cage and never sees me," says the female speaker in the title poem of Jarrell's book, *The Woman at the Washington Zoo.*[22] Jarrell's women are identified, given value, targeted, by "the look" of other people. Jarrell, who passed the "formative years" of his childhood in Hollywood, might not find it surprising that the most sophisticated recent thinking about women's sexual identity and the defining "look" occurs in feminist film criticism, where critics such as Laura Mulvey and Teresa de Lauretis—working from Freud's insights about the pleasure of the "gaze," or scopophilia—have located in the look of the camera and of male characters the defining strategy of "classical [Hollywood] cinema."[23]

But in Jarrell's mirror poems the look is self-directed, more narcissistic than exhibitionistic. He follows the logic of the cinema here, making male narcissism and male identity relatively self-contained and self-justifying, while condemning women to exhibitionism, dependent on the gaze of others. It is as though Jarrell (or his speaker) has regressed to the primary stage of Freud's scopophilic instinct, which "at the beginning" is, according to Freud, "auto-erotic: it has indeed an object, but that object is the subject's own body."[24] This regression would help explain how relatively prim and evasive Jarrell's poetry is about sexual acts. But one would have to modify an observation like M. L. Rosenthal's that "sexuality in itself seems hardly present as a factor in [Jarrell's] own thought and emotions or in those of his characters."[25] Sexuality and anxiety about gender are continually present, even if sexual activity tends to be repressed.

In Jarrell's much later and more famous poem "Next Day" (1965), everything turns on gestures of looking and overlooking.

> *Moving from Cheer to Joy, from Joy to All,*
> *I take a box*
> *And add it to my wild rice, my Cornish game hens.*
> *The slacked or shorted, basketed, identical*
> *Food-gathering flocks*
> *Are selves I overlook. Wisdom, said William James,*
>
> *Is learning what to overlook. And I am wise*
> *If that is wisdom.*

The female speaker in this poem, as in "The Face," is anxious about losing her looks. She wishes

> *That the boy putting groceries in my car*
>
> *See me. It bewilders me he doesn't see me.*
> *For so many years*
> *I was good enough to eat: the world looked at me*
> *And its mouth watered. How often they have undressed me,*
> *The eyes of strangers!*

She feels that she has been a popular product on the shelf, now unaccountably overlooked. As a result, like all of Jarrell's woman speakers, she looks in the mirror for confirmation:

> *I am afraid, this morning, of my face.*
> *It looks at me*
> *From the rear-view mirror, with the eyes I hate,*
> *The smile I hate. Its plain, lined look*
> *Of gray discovery*
> *Repeats to me: "You're old." That's all, I'm old.*

In this poem, more explicitly than in "The Face" or "The Woman at the Washington Zoo," aging and the loss of looks are understood as fear of death. And Jarrell allows himself, in the guise of a woman to express what he thinks are unmanly fears about death and the loss of beauty. Surely only a female impersonator would say, as the speaker of "Next Day" says, "my wish / Is womanish: / That the boy putting groceries in my car / See me." Do men consider their wishes mannish? But female impersonation is double-edged. To impersonate a woman is to use a female disguise for certain purposes—in Jarrell's case to explore anxieties that threaten a conventional masculinity. But the disguise itself can be a threat, for what could be more effeminate than to be a female impersonator?

In poems like "Next Day," Jarrell uses a version of the structure characteristic of many of his dramatic monologues, in which, as Frances Ferguson has noted, "the initially individual speakers borrow from dream lives obliquely related to their own, and the speakers merge so thoroughly with their dream counterparts that they create new amplitude for themselves in the act of speaking."[26] In Jarrell's woman-in-the-mirror poems, I would argue that the speaker is Jarrell himself and that the dream lives are those of women—not specific women, but the woman's voice, the femininity that he finds is a part of himself.

For the fear of death is not the only fear in these poems. What Jarrell is confronting is his capacity to speak as a woman, to let the repressed feminine speak through him ("the eventual return, by way of delusion, of this abolished femininity," as Chasseguet-Smirgel puts it),[27] which may be as threatening as death. The mirrors in all his woman poems are not there simply because women are reportedly vain and look in mirrors, but because Jarrell is noting a transformation for which he demands proof. To take on a woman's identity requires a change of face, and the mirror shows him the woman's face he has momentarily adopted. Perhaps there is also a measure of reassurance in this gesture, a confidence that the mirror is distorting his (male) image, and that he can return to his "real" identity. In one of his last poems, "The Player Piano," he addresses, in a woman's voice, the woman in the mirror:

> *Let's brush our hair before we go to bed,*
> *I say to the old friend who lives in my mirror.*
> *I remember how I'd brush my mother's hair*
> *Before she bobbed it.*

Still, the reader may leave Jarrell's poems with a certain disappointment with his efforts to let the feminine speak in his poetry. For it is finally a narrow view of the feminine that he gives voice to. His woman are obsessed with losing their looks. They peer in the mirror, they primp, they shop, they long for the world's (that is, men's) attention. His aging speakers confine their sexual longing to being noticed, looked at. Except for the displaced fantasies of sexual violence and violation in "The Woman at the Washington Zoo" and "Gleaning," Jarrell's treatment of women's bodies is superficial—a matter of faces and surfaces.

If Jarrell's female speakers are primarily concerned with appearance, as though sexual difference were superficial, John Berryman explores a deeper level of sexual difference. Jarrell is primarily interested in faces, while Berryman is drawn to bodies. His answer to the question of sexual difference is Dr. Johnson's: "I can't conceive, Madame. Can you?" In his *Homage to Mistress Bradstreet* (1953, 1956), Berryman adopts the guise of a seventeenth-century American woman poet, but—and the qualification is crucial—one he does not admire. "The question most put to me about the poem," he wrote in 1965, "is why I chose to write about this boring high-minded Puritan woman who may have been our first American poet but is not a good one."[28] Critics of the poem, more schooled in twentieth- than in seventeenth-century lyric, have tended to share Berryman's low estimation of Bradstreet. Thus Joel Conarroe, in his pioneering book on Berryman's poetry, writes of Bradstreet's "extraordinarily dull work" and her "derivative blandness," while J. M. Linebarger claims that Bradstreet "is remembered as the first poet in America rather than for the quality of her verse."[29] Berryman himself remarked that Anne Bradstreet concerned him "almost from the beginning, as a woman, not much as a poetess."[30] We may translate this misogynist distinction to mean that she interested him as a maker of babies, not as a maker of poems.

Berryman's Bradstreet poem arises from his disappointment with her verse, from his desire to give her what he thinks are better words than she gave herself. Before his voice, as he puts it in a note, "modulates" into hers, he complains in his "own" voice of

> all this bald
> abstract didactic rime I read appalled
> harassed for your fame
> mistress neither of fiery nor velvet verse   (stanza 12)

It is her body he means to appropriate:

> Out of maze & air
> your body's made, and moves. I summon, see,
> from the centuries it.   (3)

The main reason he has summoned this woman's body is to experience vicariously the act of giving birth to a child.

For this ambitious undertaking, Berryman researched the experience of childbirth by questioning all the mothers he knew, including his own, on the nature of labor and delivery. As one friend remembers:

> J. B. called me one afternoon and said he needed some advice: could be come over and ask me some questions: his "mistress was having a baby." I was in some confusion until it became clear that he was referring to his poem.
>
> He came over and I remember answering, to the best of my ability, his very specific and intense questions: how long did the strong labor pains last; what kinds of pains were they; what kinds of thoughts went through my head during labor; how the pains changed as labor progressed; and so on.
>
> He seemed to be trying to understand, as clearly as possible, *exactly* what a woman went through, both physically and psychologically in the course of giving birth—every step of the way. He tried to understand so clearly that he himself almost seemed to be trying to empathize.[31]

In effect, through his poem, Berryman becomes a woman who, after a barren stretch of five years—the time it took Berryman to write the poem—gives birth to a child. The specificity and ambition of the scene make it seem something more than simply a metaphor for male creativity.[32] Here is Berryman's description, through Anne Bradstreet's voice, of the birth of her baby boy:

> So squeezed, wince you I scream? I love you & hate
> off with you. Ages! Useless. Below my waist
> he has me in Hell's vise.
> Stalling. He let go. Come back: brace
> me somewhere. No. No. Yes! everything down

> *hardens I press with horrible joy down*
> *my back cracks like a wrist*
> *shame I am voiding oh behind it is too late.   (19)*

There is much to say about this scene, for example that Berryman thinks of childbirth as part fucking, part shitting.[33] More provocative than the believability of the scene (which I'm in no position to judge) is the gleeful, virtuoso feel of the passage. Berryman, like Joyce in his Molly monologue in *Ulysses* (who is as much as stylistic influence on the passage as the often cited Hopkins), conceives of the inner life of women as an uninterrupted verbal stream. Elsewhere, the poem is heavily, even obsessively, punctuated; thus, Joel Conarroe mentions "the unusually large number of caesurae," counting "an average of 12.7 punctuation marks in each stanza, which, in crude terms, comes to something between one and two per line."[34] The equation of male punctuation versus female lack is peculiar, to say the least. Could it be that Berryman and his male critics, in the face of the sheer physicality and otherness of childbirth, can bring themselves to focus on nothing more substantial than punctuation marks and their absence? (The word "caesurae," in this context, is particularly unsettling, and points to what is being repressed.) At the moment of birth, punctuation all but disappears:

> *hide me forever I work thrust I must free*
> *now I all muscles & bones concentrate*
> *what is living from dying?*
> *Simon I must leave you so untidy*
> *Monster you are killing me Be sure*
> *I'll have you later Women do endure*
> *I can can no longer*
> *and it passes the wretched trap whelming and I am me*
>
> *drencht & powerful, I did it with my body!   (20–21)*

This woman's peculiar mixture of pride and shame during the act of childbirth may have some historical accuracy; maybe women in Puritan America really felt this way. But one senses a certain distance in the scene, as though Berryman is willing to work out the scene rhetorically without committing himself emotionally to it.

Berryman considered the childbirth scene "the poem's supreme triumph," and his critics—male as well as female—have tended to agree.[35] But I would like to see more discussion of the scene that does not take, as its point of departure, amazement that a male poet could have taken upon himself such an ambitious task,[36] and that addressed instead Berryman's ambivalence toward childbearing and the politics of appropriation involved in his speaking for Anne Bradstreet. Berryman's critics have not advanced beyond admiration, however, and even women critics reading *Homage to Mistress Bradstreet* steer clear of a feminist critique. It is not surprising that a male critic like Berryman's biographer John Haffenden should find the representation of childbirth "almost unprecedented in literature" or that Joel Conarroe should praise "the magnificent twentieth stanza, part of a central passage to which everything in the poem is related, describing the moment of giving birth."[37] More unsettling is the sympathetic reading by Diane Ackerman, who, after quoting the same stanza, remarks: "This is vivid empathy of course; how many male poets have gone so alertly, so keenly, to the core of a female experience? Pain, relish, and disgust come together here to make a shocking, though far from sensationalist whole."[38] But Ackerman veers sharply away from the questions of gender raised by the passage: "It's not just a woman, a woman poet, it's a human being in a fit of being tweaked by body chemistry."[39] The pejorative emphasis of "just a woman" is unmistakable. Ackerman's attempt at universalizing the poem's subject in fact diminishes the complexity of Berryman's empathy; if the subject is "[just] a human being," why bother about the crossing of gender in the first place?[40]

When Berryman arrives at what for him must have seemed the less demanding moment of Bradstreet's approaching death, his/her voice sounds precisely like Jarrell's aging women:

> *The seasons stream and, somehow, I am become*
> *an old woman. It's so:*
> *I look. I bear to look. . . .*
>
> *My window gives on the graves. . . .   (50–51)*

This is the now familiar voice of the woman in the mirror, saying what mirrors always say (at least in these poems): You aren't the fairest of them all, and you will die.

Assuming the opposite gender in a poem seems to have had a similarly therapeutic value for Berryman and Jarrell. Both poets felt empowered to express certain things in a woman's voice that seemed forbidden to them as men. Jarrell's discomfort with his own male narcissism is matched by Berryman's unease about the profession of poetry for the male writer. In a perceptive and provocative aside, J. M. Linebarger has seized on this issue for Berryman:

> Most importantly, Berryman admired [Bradstreet] for overcoming "the almost insuperable difficulty of writing high verse at all in a land that cared and cares so little for it." Ironically, in Anne Bradstreet's time a woman was considered a domestic creature and insufficiently bright to compose verse; Berryman once complained [to a *Life* magazine interviewer] that in our time poetry is considered "effeminate." Both poets therefore had to face a culture that accused them of taking inappropriate masculine or feminine roles.[41]

Thus we may speculate that the promotion of masculinity during the 1950s, like the cult of virility that caused Schreber's discomfort during the 1890s, forced Berryman to abandon his habitually autobiographical poetics and find a more disguised means of expression for aspects of himself that he regarded as effeminate.

His merging of Bradstreet's poetic voice with his own allowed him to speak lyrically and without anxiety about the writing of poetry.

The biographical contexts of Jarrell's "The Face" and Berryman's *Homage* confirm this analysis. "The Face" was composed at a time of acute mid-life crisis for Jarrell, when he was entering an adulterous affair with a younger woman (the Salzburg student mentioned above) and worrying about his appearance. Berryman's poem also arose in a time of marital crisis, and aspects of the Bradstreet character were modeled on the real-life "mistress" that Berryman referred to as "Lise." During this period, too, Berryman's own ambivalence about fathering a child reached almost psychotic proportions. He reported in a *Paris Review* interview that his first wife, Eileen Simpson, had been admitted to "the hospital in New York for an operation, what they call a woman's operation, a kind of parody of child birth. Both she and I were feeling very bitter about this since we very much wanted a child and had not had one."[42] But Simpson had not, in fact, had a hysterectomy; the myomectomy she had, to remove a benign fibroid growth, was performed in order to *facilitate* pregnancy. Berryman's fears about his own inadequacy as a father came into play—because of his alcoholism and, perhaps, his sense that poetry was an unsuitable profession for a man. Consequently, he projected his own "unmanly" ambivalence about childbirth onto what he considered were the more suitable subjects of his real wife and fictional mistress.

While recognizing the undeniable aesthetic achievement of these poets, we must be willing to historicize their confining notions of woman's voice and female desire. Poems that appear, at first glance, to be sensitive and empathetic attempts to find an androgynous voice for poetry, and to allow a woman's voice to be heard at a time when the most influential and widely published American poetry was written by men, reveal, on closer analysis, new evasions, new repressions. For, what Jarrell and Berryman have done is to define a supposedly typical range of "feminine" experience: looking into the mirror, shopping, giving birth, and so on. The result is the opposite of a sensitive integration toward some ideal bisexuality. In speaking explicitly as a woman, the male poet may, in fact, be enforcing an even stronger distinction between the sexes.

What, then, is the task of criticism when interpreting men writing the feminine? One may wish that Berryman has chosen to impersonate a woman poet he admired—Emily Dickinson, perhaps?—but then his words for her would have had to compete with her own. One may wish that Jarrell had imagined himself changed into a woman who worried about things other than her looks, who did not see in every object her own approaching death. The work of the critic, however, is not to rewrite poetry but to understand it. The very limits of these poems are instructive in historicizing a particular moment in American lyric poetry. A poetry beyond sexual difference may be, as Mignon's song suggests, a poetry from beyond the grave. In the meantime, a questioning of the voices of women and of men, in male and female poets, will tell us about the limitations of our own engendered selves.

Notes

1. Sherwood Anderson, "The Man Who Became a Woman," in *The Portable Sherwood Anderson,* edited by Horace Gregory (New York: Penguin, rev. edition, 1972), 381. See also Sandra M. Gilbert and Susan Gubar, *No Man's Land: The Place of the Woman Writer in the Twentieth Century,* vol. 2, *Sexchanges* (New Haven: Yale University Press, 1989), 365–6, for a brief discussion of this and similar scenes of "sex-change." The authors detect in the Anderson scene "a nausea associated with the blurring of gender boundaries" (365).

2. See, on mirrors and feminine *"vanitas,"* John Berger, *Ways of Seeing* (New York: Penguin, 1973), 45–64. See also Jenijoy La Belle, *Herself Beheld: The Literature of the Looking Glass* (Ithaca: Cornell University Press, 1988). La Belle, in her exhaustive analysis of mirror scenes in nineteenth- and twentieth-century literature, finds a major historical shift in the meaning of the mirror. "In European literature through the eighteenth century, a woman looking in a mirror only rarely escapes its traditional emblematic meaning—vanity. But, in the works of a few acute novelists in the nineteenth century, we find writers investigating more than the *Vanitas* motif: we begin to see the psychological processes that come into play when a woman looks in the glass" (15).

3. Sigmund Freud, *Three Case Studies* (New York: Collier Books, 1963), 117.

4. Ibid., 130.

5. *Psychosis and Sexual Identity: Toward a Post-Analytic View of the Schreber Case,* edited by David B. Allison, Prado de Oliveira, Mark S. Roberts, Allen S. Weiss (Albany: State University of New York Press, 1988), 2.

6. Freud, *Three Case Studies,* 147. Clearly, the Anderson story has homoerotic aspects: by the end of the story two men do in fact, as the narrator fears, "get on to" him. In the darkness of the stalls, they mistake the sleeping groom for a girl.

7. Freud, *Three Essays on the Theory of Sexuality,* translated by James Strachey (New York: Avon, 1965), 28–31. See also Freud, *Civilization and Its Discontents,* translated by Strachey (New York: Norton, 1961), 52–53.

8. Janine Chasseguet-Smirgel, "On President Schreber's Transsexual Delusion," in *Psychosis and Sexual Identity,* 162. She finds in the Schreber case "the inability to integrate one's femininity because of a lack of narcissistic cathexis of maternal femininity or a reactive countercathexis of it, and the eventual return, by way of delusion, of this abolished femininity." Documentation of the cult of virility during the fifties goes beyond the boundaries of this essay, but it might involve such episodes as Norman Mailer's rewriting of *The Deer Park* to make its style more "masculine."

9. Jean-François Lyotard, "Vertiginous Sexuality: Schreber's Commerce With God," in *Psychosis and Sexual Identity,* 153.

10. For a critique of the term "confessional," see Robert von Hallberg, *American Poetry and Culture, 1945–1980* (Cambridge: Harvard University Press, 1985), 93.

11. Lowell, unlike Jarrell and Berryman, has a very literal way with his women speakers: they are often historical women married to famous men—Lady Raleigh, Marie de Medici—and it's the men who matter to Lowell. He often seems to be raiding his correspondence—with Jean Stafford (as Ian Hamilton has pointed out in his biography of Lowell) in *The Mills of the Kavanaughs,* and, explicitly, with Elizabeth Hardwick in *For Lizzie and Harriet.* When Lowell tries to embody, or be embodied by, a woman, one may feel that he is simply too resolutely and rigidly masculine for the task. As Jarrell remarked of Lowell's *Mills,* "You feel, 'Yes, Robert Lowell would act like this if he were a girl'; but who ever saw a girl like Robert Lowell?"

12. La Belle, in *Herself Beheld,* is concerned primarily with women writers: "I think it is significant that in my search for mirror scenes I have found precious few in which men use the mirror for acts of self-scrutiny" (9). This is precisely the use that men make of mirrors in the scenes that I am concerned with, but with the added complication that they imagine themselves *as women.* Thus they confirm La Belle's ratio: Only as women do they use the mirror for self-scrutiny.

13. Frances C. Ferguson, "Randall Jarrell and the Flotations of Voice," *The Georgia Review* 28 (Fall 1974): 433.

14. Mary Jarrell, "Ideas and Poems," *Parnassas* 5:1 (Fall/Winter 1976): 218.

15. Ransom, "The Rugged Way of Genius," in *Randall Jarrell: 1914–1965,* edited by Robert Lowell, Peter Taylor, Robert Penn Warren (New York: Farrar, Straus & Giroux, 1967), 173.

16. For an interesting discussion of the genesis of *Der Rosenkavalier,* see Herbert Lindenberger, *Opera: The Extravagant Art* (Ithaca: Cornell University Press, 1984). One anecdote addresses the complexity of gender in the opera. Hofmannsthal imagined the famous singer Mary Garden in the (male) role of Octavian. She never sang it, and remarked later that "Making love to women all night long would have bored me to death" (250).

17. I would like to thank Mary Jarrell for showing me Jarrell's marginalia in his volumes of Emily Dickinson's poems.

18. John Berryman, *The Freedom of the Poet* (New York: Farrar, Straus & Giroux, 1976), 327.

19. Berryman, *Freedom,* 326.

20. Mary Jarrell, "Ideas and Poems," 218.

21. Mary Jarrell, ed., *Randall Jarrell's Letters* (Boston: Houghton Mifflin, 1985), 206–07.

22. All quoted texts of Jarrell poems are from Randall Jarrell, *The Complete Poems* (New York: Farrar, Straus & Giroux, 1969).

23. See the essays in *Narrative, Apparatus, Ideology,* edited by Philip Rosen (New York: Columbia University Press, 1986), esp. Laura Mulvey, "Visual Pleasure and Narrative Cinema" (198–209) and Teresa de Lauretis, "Through the Looking-Glass" (360–72).

24. Sigmund Freud, "Instincts and Their Vicissitudes," in Philip Rieff, ed., *General Psychological Theory* (New York: Collier Books, 1963), 94.

25. M. L. Rosenthal, "Randall Jarrell," in Denis Donoghue, ed., *Seven American Poets*

from MacLeish to Nemerov: An Introduction (Minneapolis: University of Minnesota Press, 1975), 164.

26. Ferguson, 431.

27. Chasseguet-Smirgel, 162.

28. Berryman, *Freedom,* 328.

29. Joel Conarroe, *John Berryman: An Introduction to the Poetry* (New York: Columbia, 1977), 81, 82–83, J. M. Linebarger, *John Berryman* (New York: Twayne, 1974), 68–69. For a more positive view of Bradstreet's work, placing her in the tradition of women's poetry in America, see Wendy Martin, *An American Triptych: Anne Bradstreet, Emily Dickinson, Adrienne Rich* (Chapel Hill: University of North Carolina Press, 1984), 15–78.

30. Berryman, *Freedom,* 328.

31. John Haffenden, *John Berryman: A Critical Commentary* (New York: New York University Press, 1980), 23–24.

32. See, on the subject of male appropriation of metaphors of childbirth, Susan Gubar, " 'The Blank Page' and Female Creativity," in Elaine Showalter, ed., *The New Feminist Criticism: Essays on Women, Literature, and Theory* (New York: Pantheon, 1985), 292–313. Gubar discusses modern women writers who "were involved in the creation of a revisionary theology that allowed them to reappropriate [from male writers] and valorize symbols of uniquely female creativity and primacy" (307–08).

33. Or, as Haffenden says, "Childbirth is related to incontinence, for example, through the non-predicational collocation of 'shame I am voiding oh behind' " (*John Berryman,* 24).

34. Conarroe, 72.

35. Berryman, *Freedom,* 329.

36. For an exception see Carol Johnson, "John Berryman and Mistress Bradstreet: A Relation of Reason," *Essays in Criticism* 14 (October 1964): 390. Haffenden quotes Johnson on Berryman's "mistake" in "the preternaturally speedy and literal parturition recounted in the space of three stanzas" (24).

37. Conarroe, 72; Haffenden, *John Berryman,* 38.

38. Diane Ackerman, "Near the Top a Bad Turn Dared," *Parnassas* 7:2 (Spring/Summer, 1979): 144.

39. Ibid.

40. See also the appreciation by Sarah Provost, "Erato's Fool and Bitter Sister: Two Aspects of John Berryman," *Twentieth-Century Literature* 30:1 (Spring 1984): 69–79: "By projecting himself into Anne, he allowed himself to participate vicariously in this experience [of childbirth]. . . . When he suffered couvade with the laboring Anne, he was immersed in this powerful and rewarding event, while giving birth to the only kind of child he really wanted: the poem itself" (78).

41. Linebarger, *John Berryman,* 70. The *Life* article was in the July 21, 1967, issue of the magazine. For an interesting analysis of another poet's discomfort with poetry as an

"effeminate" occupation see Frank Lentricchia, "Patriarchy Against Itself—The Young Manhood of Wallace Stevens," *Critical Inquiry* 13 (Summer 1987): 742–86.

42.   John Haffenden, *The Life of John Berryman* (Boston: Routledge and Kegan Paul, 1982), 223.

William Faulkner as a Lesbian Author

Frann Michel

Gender is a representation, socially and historically variable, internally contradictory.[1] In mid-nineteenth-century America, middle-class white women were represented as asexual and spiritual, while black women were represented as danger-
ously sexual.[2] In the 1920s and 30s, Freud and others theorized female sexuality as
passive and masochistic, while popular magazines advertised the flapper's interest
in petting. In the 1980s, women were depicted as either guardians of emotional
intimacy or knife-wielding careerists.[3] But these representations exist in relation to
others: Women's ostensible spirituality confronts men's worldliness, black women's
allegedly animalistic sexuality faces white male rationality, theoretical female
passivity meets male activity, and so on. The hierarchical valuations of these
relations can serve to legitimate and perpetuate gender inequality, for gender is
also specifically a power relation. Despite variations in representations, white men
as a group continue to have greater access to social, political, and economic
power than women. Women who have claimed access to these powers are often
represented as masculine, while men who have lesser access to them are represented as feminine.[4]

William Faulkner's literary career began in an era when the destabilization
of gender relations was particularly visible, and his works, especially his early
works, reveal a preoccupation with male feminization, both authorial and charac-
terological.[5] Faulkner organizes the multiple feminizations entailed in his position
as author by coupling this position with a feminine text, presenting himself not
simply as a feminine author, but as a lesbian author. This duplicitous position is
ultimately undermined by its kinship with the discourse on female sexual inversion
current in the 1920s and by the degree to which the notion of male feminization
arises from female disempowerment.

Faulkner's experience of male feminization emerges from the historical
context of Southern white men's sense of diminished potency after the Civil War,
from men's sense of disempowerment following World War I, and from Faulkner's
own sense of emasculation at not having seen combat in the Great War.[6] Men

experienced the first two decades of the century as disempowering not only because for many of them the war was literally disabling (as it was, for instance, for the mute and wounded Donald Mahon, dead by the end of Faulkner's *Soldiers' Pay*), but also because the era was empowering for many women. In the first two decades of the twentieth century, women renewed their demands for the vote, for jobs, and for control over their own bodies. By the twenties, middle- and upper-class women had better opportunities for education and employment than women of the previous generation had had. The war provided job opportunities for those at home, and, in the ensuing years, women obtained the vote and continued their activity in political, reform, and service movements. Women's public prominence elicited charges of masculinity, indicating the relational, hierarchical pattern of gender relations. Women's increased prominence and power may have threatened a feminization of men insofar as it threatened male power over women and challenged the notion that power was a male prerogative.[7]

Faulkner's own experience of the male feminization attendant on the First World War occurred not because he suffered physical injury or shell shock, but because he did not, because he had no opportunity to prove his masculinity in active combat. Although Faulkner's service in 1918 in the Royal Air Force was all in Canada, he fabricated an increasingly elaborate set of lies about his military service, and in 1943 wrote to his nephew, "I would have liked for you to have had my dog-tag, R.A.F., but I lost it in Europe, in Germany. I think the Gestapo has it; I am very likely on their records right now as a dead British flying officer-spy" (*Selected Letters* 170). The motive for such deceptions is clearly a need to allay his anxieties about his gender identity; congratulating his stepson for enlisting in 1942, he stressed a man's need for "the public proof of his masculinity" offered by active duty (*SL* 166).

The social movement toward gender destabilization affected literary communities as well, of course. We can trace the authorial feminization marking Faulkner's early career both to the prominence of women writers in the South, and to the 1920s and 30s backlash that masculinized the literary canon. In an introduction to *The Sound and the Fury*, Faulkner notes that the male artist in the South finds himself choosing "between being an artist and being a man" (411). In a 1946 letter, Faulkner comments that in the South, " 'art' was really no manly business. It was a polite painting of china by gentlewomen" (*SL* 216). Since authorship was defined as feminine at least in part because of women's prominence in the literary marketplace, Faulkner's sense of authorship as feminine was not countered by any sense of participation in that marketplace as necessarily masculine, particularly because his was not initially successful participation. Complaining about not having been paid money owed him by the publisher of *The Marble Faun*, Faulkner wrote, "It never occurred to me that anyone would rob a poet. It's like robbing a whore or a child" (*SL* 35). Aside from the possible implication that the obvious role for a woman in the marketplace is that of prostitute, and aside from a privileged erasure of the sorts of abuses sex workers suffer, this comment suggests the persistence in the marketplace of the feminization connected with authorship, and, through the equation of whore and child, the powerlessness (notably, here, economic powerlessness) that prompts the characterization of authorship as feminizing.

Despite Faulkner's sense that writing in the South was no manly business, study of anthologies and college courses in the 1920s and 30s reveals that in reaction to marginal groups' claims for social, political, and economic equity, official historians of American literature were eliminating white women, as well as blacks and Native Americans, from the canon (Lauter). The masculinization of the canon, itself, in part, a response to women's empowerment, may, in turn, have exacerbated male authors' gender anxieties. In 1921, Joseph Hergesheimer (a then popular novelist) complained about the "feminine nuisance in American literature" and insisted that a truly vital, potent, masculine hero would seem "abnormal" by contemporary standards, a comment that suggests that he saw women's promi- nence in literature as having a feminizing effect on men, as though femininity were contagious (Hergesheimer, 719). The following year, Faulkner reviewed Hergesheimer's work, tracing the failure of his novels to a "fear 'of living, of [being] man' " and, specifically, to "sex crucifixion." Faulkner says, "What was, in Poe, however, a morbid but masculine emotional curiosity has degenerated with the age to a deliberate pandering to the emotions in Hergesheimer" ("Joseph Hergesheimer" 101). That a writer who was busily asserting his masculinity was criticized for not being masculine enough suggests a kind of competition for a scarce masculinity. That is, the more "masculine" literature became in reaction to the threat of female power, the greater the threat that a "normal" male would seem feminine by comparison. This extension of a heterosexual, masculine- feminine, metaphorics to male-male literary relations appears in the bond between Quentin and Shreve, when their narrative relationship is metaphorized as hetero- sexual, as a "marriage of speaking and hearing" (*Absalom, Absalom!* 316), with Shreve the "husband" to the "girl" Quentin (*The Sound and the Fury* 96, 201).

This anxiety about being feminized in relation to other men has obvious affinities with male homosexual panic. Certainly Faulkner was familiar with the work of the sexologists: A character in Faulkner's second novel, *Mosquitoes*, mentions "Dr. Ellis and your Germans" (208). Havelock Ellis argues that there is a "tendency for [male] sexual inverts to approach the feminine type" (Ellis, 287). Moreover, the sexologists suggested that "inverts" were particularly artistic. According to Ellis, "[t]here are . . . certain avocations to which inverts seem especially called. One of the chief of these is literature" (Ellis, 293).

Literature provides contact with a feminine artwork Faulkner describes as a "vase" in an introduction to *The Sound and the Fury*. He refers to contact as with the feminine "that ecstacy, that eager and joyous faith and anticipation of surprise which the yet unmarred sheets beneath my hand held inviolate and unfailing" ("An Introduction" 415, 414). Clearly, in presenting the object of creative desire as feminine, Faulkner draws on a long tradition of the artwork as feminine, text as female body. But rather than simply being part of a heterosexual metaphorics in which the male author deflowers his female page, this image may also participate in the contagion of femininity. Ellis cites "what is supposed to be a very common type of inversion, Oscar Wilde being the supreme exemplar, in which a heterosexual person apparently becomes homosexual by the exercise of intellectual curiosity and esthetic interest" (Ellis, 179). Faulkner's admiration for Wilde is clearly documented: In 1955 Faulkner tacitly acknowledged Wilde's influence (*The Lion in the Garden* 95); in 1925 Faulkner wrote to his mother that he had gone "particularly to see Oscar Wilde's tomb" in the cemetery Père Lachaise (*SL* 12). Faulkner must have been aware of the implications of the influence of feminine aesthetic objects; these implications were exemplified by Wilde, and their relevance for Faulkner would have been heightened by Wilde's importance to him.

These historical and literary-historical circumstances bring to light the fault lines inherent in male subjectivity as it is constructed in the bourgeois nuclear family in a male-dominated society in which women mother. Because male gender identity is achieved through repudiation of the mother and not through primary identification with a parent of the same gender, it is particularly fragile; behind male gender identity is always an identification with the mother, who turned out to be female (Stoller, 357–60). The pre-oedipal symbiosis and identification with the mother remains both attractive and profoundly threatening for the son. The original identification with a woman, from the perspective of the child who recognizes himself as male, as not like the mother, represents a threatening engulfment of the self (Chodorow, 106). But a feminine identification also represents a return to a pleasurable state of fusion and an identification with a powerful female figure.

If the transitional state between fusion and separation is the state most conducive to creativity, we can see why the identification of authorship with maternity provides a relatively available metaphor (Winnicott, 95–103). If the idea of writing as giving birth to the text is a traditional trope, part of its resonance is attributable to its echoing of psychological structures. When he was working on *Absalom, Absalom!*, Faulkner commented, "the book is not quite ripe yet; . . . I have not gone my nine months" (*SL* 83–84). Identification of authorship with motherhood allies the male author with a compelling creative power, but does not mitigate the association of the feminine with social and economic disempowerment.[8]

To escape the feminization of identification with and engulfment by the mother, the male child turns to a relation with the father. But the escape offered by the relation with the father entails the threat of castration by the father. In *The Sound and the Fury*, as John Irwin argues, Quentin Compson's reaction to the threat of castration is a suicidal desire "to return to a state in which subject and object did not exist" (Irwin, 43). Desire to escape the feminization entailed in castration by the father provides impetus for a nostalgia for a pre-gendered symbiosis with the mother.

These psychological structures parallel the discourses of Faulkner's historical circumstances. The attempt to escape feminization leads to an oscillation between two feminizing positions. To escape the feminization of identification with and engulfment by the mother, the male child turns to a relation with the father. To escape the feminization of castration by the father, he turns to a relation with the mother. Homologously, the male writer flees from a world of feminized literature, only to encounter an idealized standard of masculinity that threatens to leave him comparatively feminized. Identifying the act of writing with maternal power might promise an escape from the definition of femininity as powerlessness, as well as an escape from the new feminized relation to other males. But again, that identification defines the writer, in the larger context of the social valuation of women, as relatively powerless. So, for Faulkner as Southern, white, middle-class male, as son and as writer, masculinity proves impossible to achieve, feminization impossible to escape.

Faulkner's confrontation with male feminization demonstrates the social construction of masculinity, as Frank Lentricchia has argued Wallace Stevens's experience of feminization does.[9] Insofar as Faulkner contributes to a discourse on the feminine as creatively powerful, his works are potentially enabling for women and transformational for men. Insofar as his delineation of male feminization constitutes an ambiguation of gender, it might presage a liberation from restrictive and oppressive discourses of gender. But male feminization does not necessarily entail patriarchy's dismantling of itself from within, as Lentricchia suggests it does. The coding of male disempowerment as male feminization rests on and may contribute to the disempowerment and devaluation of women. Faced with the impossibility of identifying themselves as masculine, Faulkner, as writer, and a number of his male characters act to assert a masculinity by more or less violently disempowering female and feminine figures. Probably the most obvious example of this is the impotent Popeye's corn-cob rape of Temple Drake in *Sanctuary*, but one can see it operating also, for instance, in Joe Christmas's murder of Joanna Burden in *Light in August*, or, arguably, in the rape of the wilderness in *Go Down, Moses*.

The multiple vectors of male feminization in Faulkner's work are especially evident in his second novel, *Mosquitoes* (1927). Because it is about a group of artists, would-be artists, and hangers-on to the art world, who spend four days on a yacht off New Orleans discussing art and sex, *Mosquitoes* provides a rich source of information on Faulkner's ideas about authorship. Like much of Faulkner's work, it is problematic in more ways than one. Faulkner himself agreed with Malcolm Cowley's description of *Mosquitoes* as a very bad early novel: "I'll agree with Mr. Cowley because I was still learning my craft, but I think that some of the book, some parts of it, are funny" (*Faulkner in the University* 257).

The book's fragmentation and humor, its divisibility into "parts," may facilitate its overt expression of the gender anxiety associated with male authorship. The logical leaps and unclear referents in many of the characters' statements are often both a source of humor and an expression of the anxieties raised by the issues they discuss. Rather than distancing himself from the issues the book raises by working them into a coherent artwork, the author distances himself from the anxieties attendant on those issues by suggesting that it is all a joke. The characters' statements and behaviors are often patently absurd; they and their ideas are distinctly the objects of humor. But while the characters are ironized, the points they raise, including the connections between women and art, and women and artists, are made so often as to resist any ironic undercutting they might suffer.

Of course, it is in some sense a joke to call William Faulkner a lesbian author. I have not uncovered evidence that Faulkner was really a woman, and, as applied to Faulkner, the term "lesbian" does not signify the kind of affirmative, woman-centered erotics, politics, or poetics it signifies to many lesbians today.[10] Rather, Faulkner's "lesbianism" consists in a doubling of a version, or versions, of the feminine generated by a masculine ideology characterized by gynophobia, misogyny, and male gender anxiety. Faulkner's lesbian authorship should, however, call attention to the range of symbolic possibilities available even from Faulkner's apparently restricted position on the sex/gender map. Moreover, it should remind us that however firmly the heterosexual conceptuality of masculine/feminine is entrenched as the basis of Western symbolic systems, it does not constitute the only conceptual dyad available, even within the confines of phallogocentric symbolic systems.

If my description of William Faulkner as a lesbian author is a joke, then, it is his joke, and a serious one, an ironic shorthand for a real pattern in Faulkner's work. Faulkner presents himself as a lesbian author in the narrative of *Mosquitoes* not only by attributing to a lesbian character the authorship of poetry he later acknowledged as his own, but also by aligning his own desire with lesbian desire. Faulkner aligns himself with a woman character erotically involved with another woman, Mrs. Eva Wiseman (209). Despite Eva Wiseman's ambiguously gendered name and status as widow, she is not implicated in any of the book's numerous heterosexual romantic couplings, and she fits Ellis's account of the female invert as a masculine woman by virtue of sharing the male characters' profession, conversation, and desire. Eva Wiseman interrupts rather than participates in the novel's most explicit depiction of female-female sexual activity (*Mosquitoes* ts. 204–07), which Faulkner's publisher insisted on cutting from the book (*SL* 34). But her "dark intent speculation" about the incident apparently prompts her later pursuit of Jenny (ts. 208). Eva daydreams about "Jenny's soft body" (208), kisses Jenny on the mouth, and finds her dress "exciting" (166–67). One section of the novel breaks off with: "Mrs. Wiseman gazed at Jenny's finely minted hair, at her sleazy little dress revealing the divine inevitability of her soft body. 'Come here, Jenny,' she said" (146; ts. 239). Further, some of the strongest evidence we get of Eva's sexual feelings for Jenny appears in sentences whose perspective is ambiguously attributable to Eva or to the narrative voice: Jenny, in Patricia's dress, "stood before the mirror, bulging it divinely, smoothing the dress over her hips" (166).

The expressive adverb "divinely" indicates subjectivity, but it remains unclear whose subjectivity it is. Moreover, a "Faulkner" appears in the narrative and expresses his desire for this same Jenny pursued by Eva. In 1933, in *A Green Bough*, Faulkner published under his own name the poem attributed to Eva Wiseman in *Mosquitoes*.[11]

The presentation of female same-sex sexuality helps focalize the multiple feminizations found in the novel. Faulkner's lesbian identification is particularly useful precisely because it occurs on the metaphorical level of the relation between author and text, as well as on the narrative level of characters and plot. Both the creating artist and the work of art (like Keats's urn) are feminine. For Faulkner, as we will see, not only "creation, reproduction from within" is "feminine" (267), but also the object of creative desire: The author is always writing for some woman (207). If both the author and the object of the author's desire are feminine, then the author *qua* author is a lesbian. If the relationship between author and work is erotic (as, for instance, Roland Barthes suggests in *The Pleasure of the Text,* or as John Irwin argues of Faulkner's work), then that erotic relationship is carried out, if not between two females, then still between two feminines: Writing is a lesbian act. The dual femininity of author and work helps limit the author's femininity to his relation with his feminine work; this limiting removes the male author from a feminized position in relation to other males, and the lesbian identification with female power further effects an escape from the threat of being engulfed by a feminine other.

Clearly, *Mosquitoes* presents a female power as threatening, but just as clearly, it disarms that threat by arrogating female power to the male author. The character Dawson Fairchild says,

> There is a kind of spider or something. The female is the larger, and when the male goes to her he goes to death: she devours him during the act of conception. And that's a man: a kind of voraciousness that makes an artist stand beside himself with a notebook in his hand always, putting down all the charming things that ever happen to him, killing them for the sake of some problematical something he might or might not ever use. (267)

There's a lack of logical connection between the second and third sentences here; it's not entirely clear just what the antecedent is to the "that" that is a man. The equation of the "that" that the man is with a "voraciousness," however, aligns the male author with the consuming power of the female spider. In casting the male author in the role of devouring female, Faulkner avoids being devoured by her. Such identification, however, is shadowed by the reference to conception in which the male is not eater but eaten. John Irwin's reading of this image of the artist-as-spider as a "procreative devouring of the artist's masculine self by the feminine work of art" (Irwin, 165) reveals a subtext of male anxiety in this passage: Irwin supplies a connection the text avoids. While Irwin's reading preserves, with questionable justification, the notion of the author's "masculine self," it also suggests that the identification of the male writer as a powerful, devouring female originates in a male fear of being devoured by a powerful female.

Clearly, the image of the artist as spider owes a debt to the image of the artist as mother. But while male characters in *Mosquitoes* are quick to ally male artists with the generative power of maternity, they are also quick to distinguish between feminine male mothers and women themselves, to insist that the maternal metaphor is only a metaphor, albeit a compelling one. Fairchild says that the purpose of art is

> getting into life, getting into it and wrapping it around you, becoming a part of it. Women can do it without art—old biology takes care of that. But men, men . . . A woman conceives: does she care afterward whose seed it was? Not she. And bears, and all the rest of her life—her young troubling years, that is—is filled. Of course the father can look at it occasionally. But in art, a man can create without any assistance at all: what he does is his. A perversion, I grant you, but a perversion that builds Chartres and invents Lear is a pretty good thing. . . . (267)

This clearly links and opposes women and male artists. Male artists have the reproductive capacity of women, but can go women one better: Like all male mothers (the Old Testament God, Adam, Zeus, Victor Frankenstein), they give birth without the aid of women. By becoming like women, they have separated themselves all the more from women, have obviated women. Most peculiarly, this notion of art presents a way of being "part of" life, while excluding or obviating any human need and any connection with other human beings, male or female. The sculptor Gordon's thought that he is "crowned with stars" aligns him typologically with the Virgin Mary, a female mother notable for not having needed a human partner (33; and see Revelation 12:1).

Although male characters acknowledge that male artists may be like women, they resist the notion that women may be artists and artists may be women. When Eve Wiseman asks (rhetorically) whether there's anything other than love and death worth writing about, her brother Julius responds,

> "That's the feminine of it. You'd better let art alone and stick to artists, as is your nature."
> "But women have done some good things," Fairchild objected. "I've read—"
> "They bear geniuses. But do you think they care anything about the pictures and music their children produce? That they have any other emotion than a fierce tolerance of the vagaries of the child? . . . (205)

Julius's initial assertion here might suggest that love and death, as topics, are "the feminine of it," and thus that any writer who pursues these topics is feminine. If this is what he means, however, he certainly scorns such writers, and his subsequent assertion assigns women to the category of mother and excludes them from that of genius.

Although male characters insist that women are not artists, then, artists and art are repeatedly characterized as feminine. Indeed, one suspects that they insist women are not artists precisely because they believe artists are feminine. Fairchild says that "Genius" is

> that Passion Week of the heart, that instant of timeless beatitude . . . that passive state of the heart with which the mind, the brain, has nothing to do at all, in which the hackneyed accidents which make up this world—love and life and death and sex and sorrow—brought together by chance in perfect proportions, take on a kind of splendid and timeless beauty. Like Yseult of the White Hands and her Tristan with that clean, highhearted dullness of his; like that young Lady Something that some government executed, asking permission and touching with a kind of sober wonder the edge of the knife that was to cut her head off; like a redhaired girl, an idiot, turning in a white dress beneath a wistaria [sic] covered trellis on a late sunny afternoon in May.   (283)

Like the account of the artist-as-spider, this passage is characterized by a logical leap, a lack of clear reference. It's not entirely clear what the implied subject of this last fragment is: Just what are all these women "like"? The metaphor is internally readable. In each case, a woman of increasingly vague identity (Yseult has a name and a story, the nameless Lady has a title and a history, the redhaired girl has none of these) is paired with an image of increasingly vague masculinity (Tristan is male, governments are usually male and knives considered phallic, and wisteria blossoms might be ambiguously sexualized: feminine as flowers, they might be described as flaccidly phallic in shape). Each feminine/masculine image presents gender relationally, and the series suggests that the dissolution of identity connected with women inspires a dissolution of male gender identity.

But the application of the metaphor is more puzzling. Who or what is feminized? Is it the artist or the art? In relation to what is she/he/it feminine or feminized? The women in these images may be "like" the event of genius, in which case, the artist *qua* genius is, as the text suggests elsewhere, like a woman. They may also be like the beauty acquired by the accidents of the world in or during the event of genius. In that case, the products of artistic genius are feminine.

The beauty of artworks and the beauty of women are aligned through the description of both as "fecund and foul" (280; 82). Moreover, the object of creative desire is feminine in the sense that women seem to provide the impetus to men's creative action: Faulkner wrote *Mosquitoes* "for" Helen Baird. Dawson Fairchild believes the writer is

> always writing it for some woman, that he fondly believes he's stealing a march on some brute bigger or handsomer than he is; I believe that every word a writing man writes is put down with the ultimate intention of impressing some woman that probably don't care anything at all for literature, as is the nature of women. Well, maybe she ain't always a flesh and blood creature. She may be only the symbol of a desire. But she is feminine.   (206)

Significantly, the woman who provides the motive for art is not "always a flesh and blood creature." More strikingly, the activity of writing "for some woman" immediately becomes the activity of "stealing a march on some brute bigger or handsomer than he is." Against the dissolution of femininity, characters assert the tangibility of male-male bonds. Male bodies insinuate themselves as female bodies evaporate. The attempt to propitiate the intangible feminine functions in practical, social terms as competition between men. The male writer flees from the devouring feminine to the invisible feminine and an all male literary world.

Thus, at the same time as the author can be feminine in the sense of mothering the book, he is also potentially feminized in male-male authorial or narrative bonds. Fairchild talks about authorship by saying "It's a kind of sterility—words. . . . You begin to substitute words for things and deeds, like the withered cuckold husband that took the Decameron to bed with him every night" (172). Eve Kosofsky Sedgwick notes that cuckoldry (or rivalry) is a potentially sexualized power relation between men—one man cuckolds another, and the woman in the picture is just a kind of vehicle (Sedgwick, 49). Similarly, in Fairchild's formulation, using words, creating literature, becomes some kind of (inadequate, unsatisfying, possibly castrating) response to being subject to another man's domination.

Thus, while the novel symbolically or psychologically connects art or artists with women, it represents the world of art as socially male. Just as the literary canon of the 1920s was becoming more exclusively male, so, in *Mosquitoes,* art or being an artist, is related to a male homosociality. The male artists in the *Mosquitoes* yachting party (except for the "prehensile" and artistically constipated Mark Frost [278, 40], along with Major Ayers (who is planning to go into the laxative business), repeatedly retreat below deck for what seem to be alcoholic rituals of male bonding. On one of the men's forays onto deck, Eva Wiseman comments, " 'We haven't seen any gentlemen since we left New Orleans' " (65). Though the women have seen Mark Frost and Ernest Talliaferro, Mrs. Wiseman insists they don't count: not all men fit into the "man's world that" Julius says "we all prefer" (189). The more ideological freight gender carries, the less likely that individuals will successfully bear that freight. The more "being a man" means, the more possible for a man not to fit that meaning.

Faulkner's account of the male artist as a feminine male bears what must have been an uncomfortable resemblance to sexologists' accounts of the male invert as containing a more feminine psyche than usual. But despite—indeed, in part because of—this apparent congruence between the male artist and the male homosexual as feminine men, the active inversion, the actual same-sex sexuality Faulkner includes in the book is not between men but between women. We can thus see Faulkner's lesbian identification as a wedge, splitting the feminized male writer from the feminized male invert by presenting same-sex sexual activity as something that occurs between women. Because Faulkner doesn't split lesbianism-as-metaphor from lesbianism-as-sexuality, he can use it to split male feminization-as-metaphor from male feminization-as-homosexuality. By presenting the reader with female inversion and not male inversion, the novel distances the metaphorical (literary) femininity of the male writer from the putatively literal (sexual) femininity of the male invert.

Although Faulkner's identification with lesbian eroticism provides a focus for the multiple feminizations of the male author, and a defense against male homoeroticism, it also reemphasizes the author's alignment with devalued women. Just as the imaging of authorship as metaphorically maternal inspires a distancing of that metaphor from literal, biological maternity, so, more generally, the position of the lesbian male author is distanced from the position of actual women through a reassertion of women's actual disempowerment relative to men. In *Mosquitoes,* male characters and the novel itself display a disturbing tendency to focus on women's decapitation—what Hélène Cixous calls the backlash on women of the castration complex (Cixous, 43). The fascinated lingering over the prelude to a woman's decapitation in the image of "Lady Something" reflects not Dawson Fairchild's personal idiosyncracies, but a fantasy shared by other men in the book and by the author.

The image of a decapitated woman reappears near the end of *Mosquitoes* in an episode Faulkner evidently liked so much he salvaged it from the early fragment *Elmer.* The drunken Elmer dreams of "the naked headless body of a black woman: She is rigid, her limbs are as beautiful as if carved from ebony" (*Elmer* 92–93). In *Mosquitoes* the metaphorical ebony becomes literal in "the headless naked body of a woman carved of ebony" (281). Notably, the decapitation is carried out on an image of a black woman, someone not only even less socially empowered than a white woman, but also usually coded as more physical, and often more actively involved in raising white children than white middle- and upper-class women were in the South. Although both white and black women were artists, and although the neglect of race as an issue here indicates that white women as artists are in question, the reactive image of violence is directed at the more vulnerable target.

In some cases, removing the woman's head doesn't seem to be enough. Gordon's "dark" statue (274) is the "breastless torso of a girl, headless, armless, legless" (3). Gordon describes his statue as his "feminine ideal: a virgin with no legs to leave me, no arms to hold me, no head to talk to me" (15). By depriving the ideal woman of subjectivity and the power to act on it, the artist can reserve feminine subjectivity to himself, can identify with a feminine role without identifying with woman. As it happens, these deprivations also deprive women of life, not only by turning them into inanimate objects (works of art) but also by turning them into representations of women without life: decapitated or dismembered.

Faulkner's authorial femininity is strikingly overdetermined: by a historical male disempowerment and a decreasing distance in the hierarchical social relations between men and women, by the prominence of women writers in the South, by male authors' competition for a position of masculine superiority, by sexologists' discourse on aesthetic activity as feminizing, by the economic disempowerment attendant upon the uncertain profession of writer, by the prevalent trope of authoring as mothering, and by the psychological instability of male gender identity. In aligning himself with a lesbian position, emphasizing the contagion of femininity, Faulkner paradoxically helps define and limit that femininity.

But the dominant discourse on homosexuality in the 1920s, the discourse on inversion, preserved a heterosexually structured model of desire as inter-gender rather than intra-gender, thus preserving a notion of gender as relational, hierarchical. A male author who sees his social or economic disempowerment as feminizing may also, like Faulkner, see that feminization as creatively empowering, insofar as it allies him with metaphors of writing as maternity. But even as Faulkner embraces and accentuates his status as feminine author, he insists on distinguishing literary from biological maternity, intellectual from physical feminization, feminized male authors from actual women or female characters. The urgency of these divisions reminds us that the initial coding of male disempowerment as male feminization rests upon women's devaluation relative to men. The persistence of this structure, highlighted by the persistence of an inter-gender model of desire, prompts the male author writing as a woman to write simultaneously against women, in order to distance himself from the devalued position in which he finds himself. The complexity of this pattern of feminine identification and female disempowerment should help account for the double valence of women in Faulkner's fiction. More broadly, it should demonstrate the fallacy of Lentricchia's argument that male feminization constitutes an instance of patriarchy against itself. Male feminization does not in itself constitute a feminist progress; we need context-specific studies to determine its function in any given instance. Finally, we need to keep in mind that the very term "male feminization" indicates the extent to which women remain the measure of disempowerment.

Notes

1. For an extended discussion of gender as a representation, see de Lauretis, esp. 3–6: "The construction of gender is both the product and the process of its representation" (5).

2. For an example of the representation of women's spirituality, see Fuller: "The especial genius of Woman I believe to be . . . Spiritual in tendency" (115). For a discussion of white men's representations of Black women's sexuality, see Gilman on the "labeling of the black female as more primitive, and therefore more sexually intensive" (212).

3. Freud argued that the "suppression of women's aggressiveness which is prescribed for them constitutionally and imposed on them socially favours the development of powerful masochistic impulses" (76). Ryan discusses the flapper, 220–52. One recent argument for women's greater capacity for emotional intimacy can be found in Hite: "one might call 'male' behavior 'emotionally repressed,' and 'female' behavior 'gloriously expressive' " (37). For a representation of the homicidal businesswoman, see *Fatal Attraction*.

4. In 1922, Harold Stearns argued that while "men and women in America to-day share their intellectual life on terms of equality and perfect understanding, closer examination reveals that the phenomenon is not a sharing but a capitulation. The men have been feminized. . . . The young, independent college girl of today is in fact more likely to possess 'masculine' intellectual habits than is the average Y.M.C.A. director" (143–44). Smith-Rosenberg argues that the sexologists' category of the Mannish Lesbian focused more on social than sexual behavior (see esp. 265–81).

5. For discussions of the role of this destabilization in literary history, see Gilbert and Gubar, *No Man's Land, Vol. 1,* which discusses continuities in a battle of the sexes but also emphasizes the role of feminist movements in heightening instability and tension (for example 28–37); see also Lauter, whose study concentrates on the particularly problematic period of the 1920s and 30s.

6. Jones, for example, notes that following defeat in the Civil War, the Southern white gentleman felt "his traditional sources of masculine identity eroded" (19). Gilbert observes, in "Soldier's Heart," that "the gloomily bruised modernist antiheroes churned out by the [First World] War suffer specifically from sexual wounds, as if, having travelled literally or figuratively through No Man's Land, all have become not just No Men, nobodies, but *not* men, *un*men" (198). In a study of a case of WWI war neurosis, Showalter notes that "the anguish of shell shock included . . . general but intense anxieties about masculinity, fears of acting effeminate" (64).

7. On changes in women's roles, see, for example, Ryan, 200–05; Kessler-Harris, 217–49; and Smith-Rosenberg, 245–96. Smith-Rosenberg observes that by "the 1920s, charges of lesbianism had become a common way to discredit women professionals, reformers, and educators—and the feminist political, reform, and education institutions they had founded" (281). That women's increased power and claims for power were perceived as a rejection of heterosexuality and, indeed, a threat to heterosexual marriage indicates that women's removing themselves from positions of submission to, or dependence on, men was perceived as equivalent to women's removing themselves from heterosexuality. That is, the changes in the situations of some women entailed what some men (and some women) found threatening shifts in the coding of gender and sexuality.

8. Friedman's study of the childbirth metaphor observes, "The male comparison of creativity with women's procreativity equates the two as if both were valued equally, whereas they are not. This elevation of procreativity seemingly idealizes woman and thereby obscures woman's real lack of authority to create art as well as babies. As an appropriation of women's (pro)creativity, the male metaphor subtly helps to perpetuate the confinement of women to procreation" (64).

9. Lentricchia notes that "What we know as 'femininity' is internally linked to what we know as 'masculinity' because both designations are highly motivated cultural constructions of biological difference that do powerful social work at the moment when they are lived, when they constitute the barely conscious and barely reflected upon substance of belief" (743). He argues that "modernist poetics in Stevens is a feminization of the literary life motivated by capitalist values, and, at the same time, a struggle to overcome this feminization which is more or less equivalent (in our culture) to the trivialization of literature and the literary impulse" (751). The latter point bears a striking resemblance to Stearns's 1922 argument about intellectual life in America.

In their response to Lentricchia, Gilbert and Gubar point out that they "see modernism, much more broadly than he sees Stevens's poetics, as at least in part constituted out of a painful battle of the sexes that was associated with a crisis of masculinity experienced in particular by a number of literary men" (389). Their response concentrates on the flaws and omissions in Lentricchia's discussions of Stevens's work and of *Madwoman in the Attic*, and points out that Lentricchia himself repeats Stevens's "virilization-as-defense . . . against feminization" (406) without noting that this move and its repetition undermine Lentricchia's argument that because " 'patriarchy' consists also in the oppression of men," "patriarchy against itself dismantles itself from within" (774–75). The defensive response helps preempt any ultimate undoing of inequality.

    10.   The term "lesbian author" is problematic enough, even if one limits it to authors who were or are biologically female. For a good discussion of the problem of defining the territory of a lesbian literary criticism, see O'Brien, 68–71. It is worth noting that Faulkner presents what Adrienne Rich might call "pseudolesbian" images, although not all of these images in *Mosquitoes* are recuperated for heterosexuality (Rich, 146).

    Farwell has argued for the use of lesbian as metaphor for female creativity on the grounds that other metaphors (lover, muse, androgyne, mother) can be arrogated to the male subject, while lesbian is connected to a community that "forges its own identity outside the patriarchy and therefore discovers its own truth" (117). Though Farwell endorses the project of placing the subject " 'outside of the presence/absence and center/margin dichotomies,' " she neglects the implications of the inside/outside dichotomy (115). Farwell demonstrates the ways lesbian-as-metaphor has served women writers, but ignores the possibility that no metaphor is truly "outside," unavailable to appropriation. Certainly there is a distinction between the relatively recent concept of lesbian as woman-identified woman (see Radicalesbians) and the earlier concept of the female invert. But as Newton notes, the shift away "from an exclusive focus on 'inversion' as gender reversal . . . has had only a limited effect on popular ideology" (16, n. 19).

    Faulkner's use of lesbian imagery also owes a debt to the efforts of Gautier, Baudelaire, Swinburne, Louys, and others to *epater le bourgeois* (for a discussion of their works, see Faderman, 254–94), but is distinguished by the nature of his own implication in what he, too, sees as perversity.

    11.   Because of limitations of space, I can do no more than note some of the dizzying complexities of gender surrounding this poem in *Mosquitoes*. The poem is titled "Hermaphroditus," and attributed to a female character with an ambiguously gendered name; the novel's male characters discuss the poem as though it were the work of a man, but see poetry as particularly feminizing. This feminization extends itself to authorship in general, however. By embracing the title of failed poet, Faulkner would have been mastering (and thus masculinizing) a condition felt as enforced failure, inadequacy, powerlessness, femininity. Moreover, his late, broad definition of poetry as "some moving, passionate moment of the human condition distilled to its absolute essence" (*FIU* 202) extends this paradoxical mastery to the prose works as well.

Selected Bibliography

Barthes, Roland. *The Pleasure of the Text*. Translated by Richard Miller. New York: Hill and Wang, 1975.

Chodorow, Nancy. *The Reproduction of Mothering: Psychoanalysis and the Sociology of Gender.* Berkeley: University of California Press, 1978.

Cixous, Hélène. "Castration or Decapitation?" Translated by Annette Kuhn. *Signs: Journal of Women in Culture and Society* 7:11 (1981): 41–55.

de Lauretis, Teresa. "The Technology of Gender." *Technologies of Gender: Essays on Theory, Film, and Fiction.* Bloomington: Indiana University Press, 1987, 1–30.

Ellis, Havelock. *Sexual Inversion.* Vol. 2 of *Studies in the Psychology of Sex.* Philadelphia: Davis Publishing Co. [1901], 1923.

Faderman, Lillian. *Surpassing the Love of Men: Romantic Friendship and Love between Women from the Renaissance to the Present.* New York: William Morrow, 1981.

Fatal Attraction. Directed by Adrian Lyne. 1987.

Farwell, Marilyn R. "Toward a Definition of the Lesbian Literary Imagination." *Signs: Journal of Women in Culture and Society* 14:1 (Autumn 1988): 100–18.

Faulkner, William. *Absalom, Absalom!* 1936. Reprint. New York: Vintage-Random House, 1972.

———. *Faulkner in the University: Class Conferences at the University of Virginia, 1957–1958.* Edited by Frederick L. Gwynn and Joseph L. Blotner. Charlottesville: University Press of Virginia, 1959.

———. "An Introduction to *The Sound and the Fury.*" *Mississippi Quarterly* 26 (Winter 1973): 410–15.

———. "Joseph Hergesheimer." *William Faulkner: Early Prose and Poetry.* Edited by Carvell Collins. Boston: Little Brown and Company, 1962.

———. *Lion in the Garden: Interviews with William Faulkner 1926–1962.* Edited by James B. Meriwether and Michael Millgate. Lincoln: University of Nebraska Press, 1968.

———. *Mosquitoes.* Boni & Liveright, 1927. Reprint. New York: Washington Square Press, 1985.

———. *Selected Letters of William Faulkner.* Edited by Joseph Blotner. New York: Vintage-Random House, 1978.

———. *The Sound and the Fury.* 1929. New York: Vintage-Random House, 1954.

———. *William Faulkner Manuscripts Four: Mosquitoes: the Ribbon Typescript and Miscellaneous Typescript Pages.* Arranged, with Introduction by Joseph Blotner. New York: Garland, 1987.

———. *William Faulkner Manuscripts One: Elmer and "A Portrait of Elmer": the Typescripts, Manuscripts, and Miscellaneous Pages.* Arranged, with Introduction by Thomas L. McHaney. New York: Garland, 1987.

Friedman, Susan Stanford. "Creativity and the Childbirth Metaphor." *Feminist Studies* 13:1 (Spring 1987): 49–82.

Freud, Sigmund. "Femininity." 1933. In *Women and Analysis: Dialogues on Psychoanalytic Views of Femininity.* Edited by Jean Strouse. Boston: G. K. Hall, 1985. 73–94.

Fuller, Margaret. *Woman in the Nineteenth Century.* 1855. New York: Norton, 1971.

Gilbert, Sandra M. "Soldier's Heart: Literary Men, Literary Women, and the Great War." *Behind the Lines: Gender and the Two World Wars.* Edited by Margaret Randolph Higonnet. Jane Jenson, Sonya Michel, Margaret Collins Weitz. New Haven: Yale University Press, 1987. 197–226.

Gilbert, Sandra M. and Susan Gubar. "The Man on the Dump versus the United Dames of America; or, What Does Frank Lentricchia Want?" *Critical Inquiry* 14:2 (Winter 1988): 386–406.

————. *No Man's Land: The Place of the Woman Writer in the Twentieth Century. Volume 1: The War of the Words*. New Haven: Yale University Press, 1988.

Gilman, Sander L. "Black Bodies, White Bodies: Toward an Iconography of Female Sexuality in Late–Nineteenth Century Art, Medicine, and Literature." *Critical Inquiry* 12:1 (Autumn 1985): 204–42.

Hergesheimer, Joseph. "The Feminine Nuisance in American Literature." *Yale Review* 10 (1921): 716–25.

Hite, Shere. *The Hite Report: Women and Love: A Cultural Revolution in Progress*. New York: Knopf, 1987.

Irwin, John. *Doubling and Incest/Repetition and Revenge: A Speculative Reading of Faulkner*. Baltimore: Johns Hopkins University Press, 1975.

Jones, Anne Goodwyn. *Tomorrow is Another Day: The Woman Writer in the South, 1859–1936*. Baton Rouge: Louisiana State University Press, 1981.

Kessler-Harris, Alice. *Out to Work: A History of Wage-Earning Women in the United States*. New York: Oxford University Press, 1982.

Lauter, Paul. "Race and Gender in the Shaping of the American Literary Canon: a Case Study from the Twenties." In *Feminist Criticism and Social Change*. Edited by Judith Newton and Deborah Rosenfelt. New York: Methuen, 1985. 19–44.

Lentricchia, Frank. "Patriarchy Against Itself—The Young Manhood of Wallace Stevens." *Critical Inquiry* 13:4 (Summer 1987): 742–86.

Newton, Esther. "The Mythic Mannish Lesbian: Radclyffe Hall and the New Woman." *The Lesbian Issue: Essays From Signs*. Edited by Estelle B. Freedman, Barbara C. Gelpi, Susan L. Johnson, Kathleen M. Weston. Chicago: University of Chicago Press, 1985. 7–26.

O'Brien, Sharon. " 'The Thing Not Named': Willa Cather as a Lesbian Writer." *The Lesbian Issue: Essays From Signs* ed. Estelle B. Freedman, Barbara C. Gelpi, Susan L. Johnson, Kathleen M. Weston. Chicago: University of Chicago Press, 1985. 67–90.

Radicalesbians. "The Woman Identified Woman." *Notes From the Third Year: Woman's Liberation*. (1971): 81–84.

Rich, Adrienne. "Compulsory Heterosexuality and Lesbian Existence" *The Signs Reader: Women, Gender and Scholarship*. Edited by Elizabeth Abel and Emily K. Abel. Chicago: University of Chicago Press, 1983. 139–68.

Ryan, Mary P. *Womanhood in America: From Colonial Times to the Present*. New York: Franklin Watts, 1983.

Sedgwick, Eve Kosofsky. *Between Men: English Literature and Male Homosocial Desire*. New York: Columbia University Press, 1985.

Showalter, Elaine. "Rivers and Sassoon: The Inscription of Male Gender Anxieties." *Behind the Lines: Gender and the Two World Wars*. Edited by Margaret Randolph Higonnet, Jane Jenson, Sonya Michel, Margaret Collins Weitz. New Haven: Yale University Press, 1987. 61–69.

Smith-Rosenberg, Carroll. *Disorderly Conduct: Visions of Gender in Victorian America*. New York: Oxford University Press, 1986.

Stearns, Harold E. "The Intellectual Life." *Civilization in the United States: An Inquiry by Thirty Americans*. Edited by Harold Stearns. New York: Harcourt Brace, 1922. 135–50.

Stoller, Robert J. "Facts and Fancies: An Examination of Freud's Concept of Bisexuality." *Women and Analysis*. Edited by Jean Strouse. Boston: G. K. Hall, 1985. 343–64.

Winnicott, D. W. *Playing and Reality*. London: Tavistock Publications, 1971.

Part II

Postmodern Theories: Beyond Gender?

> *What are the places in [this discourse] where there is room for possible subjects?*
>
> —Michel Foucault, "What Is an Author?"

> *. . . beyond the limits of "sexual difference" . . .*
>
> —Teresa de Lauretis, "The Technologies of Gender"

Objects of the Postmodern "Masters": Subject-in-Simulation/Woman-in-Effect

Martina Sciolino

> *Love, among these men, once past the simple*
> *feel and orgasming of it, had to do with*
> *masculine technologies, with contracts, with*
> *winning and losing. . . . Beyond simple steel*
> *erection, the Rocket was an entire system* won,
> *away from the feminine darkness, held against*
> *the entropies of lovable but scatterbrained*
> *Mother Nature.*

—Thomas Pynchon, *Gravity's Rainbow*

> *There's no woman who's not, deep inside her,*
> *theoretical. That's why we love, in men. . . .*
> *not them, but their love, we love—our idea*
> *and transubstantiating notion of them. That's*
> *my theory.*

William Gass, *Willie Masters'*
Lonesome Wife

I

Thomas Pynchon, Donald Barthelme, John Barth, and Gilbert Sorrentino deconstruct the conventional novelistic protagonist by writing through the feminine, or, more accurately, by writing male characters who gaze at, long for, and speak about the eroticized female body from a position that is not authoritative but desiring. Despite the prevalence of irony in postmodern fiction, this desire is both anxious and ambivalent.

What determines this lack of authority? From the 1960s to the present, critics did not respond to the sorts of psycho-social dynamics that inform feminism, but to mutations in literary form and varieties of epistemological crisis. Yet, in the unique narrative poetics of Pynchon's *V.*, Barthelme's *The Dead Father*, Barth's *Letters* and Sorrentino's *Mulligan Stew*, such issues are inextricably bound to sexual politics. Perhaps it is the binding of narrative poetics to sexual politics that problematizes authority within these novels in the first place. Perhaps these novels measure resistance to this limit: that authorial androgyny is the single fantasy that cannot be inculcated in narrative prose.

Because a feminist critique of postmodern, male-authored fiction may be hindered if the reader underestimates the literature's problematic departures from realism, the sexual politics I will engage in this essay develop from rhetorical experiment, which, for all of its innovations, cannot speak beyond a symbolic order that differentiates "man" and "woman."

I am indebted to Alice Jardine's *Gynesis*, which studies the problems of representation in postmodern fiction alongside the epistemological concerns of poststructuralist theory. Jardine sees the common denominator between these text obsessed discourses as the female *corpus*. Moreover, she reintroduces the major issues of academic postmodernism in the light of specific social contexts, specifically those created by visionary feminist protest in France and America throughout the 1960s and 70s. *Gynesis* maps a subtle rhetorical trajectory within both fiction and theory by following the "woman-in-effect." My essay will follow the "woman," linking her "effects" to a brief history of the novelistic protagonist as told in America by male-authored postmodern fiction.[1] In my essay's last section, the sequence of effects will lead this "woman" to her rhetorical other, namely the "subject-in-simulation." The purpose of this critical marriage plot should become clear in the following readings.

The structural romance identifiable in these readings indexes a specific curriculum where humanism is constructed through the mouth of "man." In the 1960s and 70s, his voice is troubled, his laughter a little hysterical as if he *expected* trouble—soon—and in apocalyptic proportions. Indeed, according to the canonical history of the novel as well as the expectations readers bring to traditional narrative, the protagonists I consider here are "feminized men," that is, antiheroes twice removed from the privileged position of the humanist self. They have no access to the unified authorial voice, no way to speak a world view from its center without lapsing into paranoia. These are simulations of simulated subjects, characters without character, operatives of fantasy.

In this sense, the postmodern writers discussed here write through the feminine without having to construct a female protagonist and speak through her (as Pynchon does in *The Crying of Lot 49*, where he employs the image of a muted horn to lure Oedipa along the trail of a dead father, a trail that leads back through literary history and forward to a future beyond, while the book closes upon her, the unwilling executrix, who awaits the reading of his will). To consider woman's dubious relationship to verbal representation in these male-authored novels, one need not follow the convoluted shape of femininity in poststructural theory. In its own post-Joycean manner, each fiction sufficiently demonstrates how woman under patriarchy is a precondition of the subject under erasure.

II

Malta became fully independent in 1964—three years after Thomas Pynchon published his first novel, *V.* In it, that ravished, resilient land is treated in archetypal terms, as the body of Mara, Maltese for "woman." Mara is "a spirit, constrained to live in . . . [t]he inhabited plain," from where she teaches "love to every invader from Phoenician to French" even while suffering their violations (434).

Valleta is one of a dozen apparitions that plague protagonist Herbert Stencil. Mara might be an incarnation of Astarte, the very Mother God herself who "shows up as a number of goddesses, minor deities. Disguise is one of her attributes" (435). In Pynchon's novel, the Mother God is manifested in disguises, so finally inchoate in sum, that the reader wonders whether she exists at all (as some transcendental totality), or if these alleged appearances are projections of anxiety and guilt, "symptoms" of a patriarchal psyche that has rediscovered its violent capabilities through two world wars (445).

This is Herbert Stencil's fundamental problem, an identity crisis that he has inherited from his father and that the reader inherits from the author. To finally prove or disprove an absolute presence behind all the novel's V.s would deliver father, son, and reader from the vicissitudes of paranoia, as several Pynchon critics observe.[2] Of course, the problem of paranoia is a psychoanalytic iteration of an ontological problem, a metaphysics whose disintegration disables all Pynchon protagonists and complicates reading.[3] For instance, Herbert Stencil speaks in the third person so that he may "appear as only one among a repertoire of identities" (51). Paradoxically, his very name indicates problematic identity: a stencil is an *empty form* within which one may draw variations *ad infinitum*.

Therefore, Pynchon's Stencil performs a poststructural critique of the humanist subject, illustrating identity not as an essential presence, but in the process of serial reduplication without paradigm. Stencil's character is as plural in its fragmentations as V. is in her infinite disguises. One might even say that, in Pynchon's extremely postmodern version of the quest, the traditional subject and object positions remain intact.[4] The difference is that the "hero" has become as overtly displaced within his role as his "lady" has almost always been in hers. The old priest who councils Herbert Stencil during his trip to Malta at the end of the novel draws an implicit comparison between Stencil's journey and the Crusades: "One cannot come to Valleta without knowing about the Knights" (422). Even in Crusade narratives, the object of the quest was split into at least two levels—the grail is a symbolic object, existing only to call attention to a meaning beyond itself. And despite the fact that the material form of the grail is suggestively yonic, as if depicting maternity, its possession would signal a spiritual union between a knight and a heavenly father. In the late twentieth century, the search for V. symbolically unites Herbert Stencil with his father, Sidney, much in the same way that a virgin bride "insures" a genealogical passage.

The relationship between the postmodern protagonist and his fragmented, multiplied object suggests that, even in the contemporary novel, the poststructural subject is still in the subject position, a position traditionally gendered male. His condition is tentative but nonetheless formed and expressed in a patriarchal way: through a love object gendered female. Is she Valleta, Veronica, Vheissu or Venus? No matter who or what V. signifies, the V. position is always feminine.

Thus, while Pynchon's fiction contains a rich and complex critique of the deep structure of Western patriarchy, it must exploit that very structure in generation. From a feminist perspective, this is what postmodern fiction has in common with poststructural theory (specifically, the work of Derrida and Lacan). The novelists I consider here, who have been included in various lists of "postmodern masters," create texts that are profoundly ambivalent towards inherited, literary structures.[5] These experimental fictions deconstruct inherited tropes, calling their literary patrimony into question, yet remain dependent on them.

For instance, Alan Wilde applauds Donald Barthelme's work for moving beyond the impasses of modernist irony, which, in its disjunction, remained paralyzed by negating its own, desired resolutions. On the other hand, Barthelme's fiction exemplifies suspensive irony, a working-through of modernist problematics, toward affirmation, despite contradiction.

The passage from *The Dead Father* that Wilde cites (46) to demonstrate a "typically Barthelmean" strategy has immediate relevance to the use of the quest structure in postmodern fiction. In it, to quote the critic, "the Dead Father learns that the Golden Fleece he has all along been seeking . . . does not exist—or not in the shape or place he had imagined":

> *No Fleece? asked the Dead Father.*
> *Thomas looked at Julie.*
> *She has it?*
> *Julie lifted her skirt.*
> *Quite golden, said the Dead Father. Quite ample. That's it?*
> *All there is, Julie said. Unfortunately. But this much.*
> *This is where life lives.*

Barthelme makes a maneuver here that is typical of male-authored postmodern fiction in America. By equating textuality (in this instance, by using the quest as a basic narrative unit) and sexuality (fully secularizing the object of the quest—anatomizing the grail), male-authored postmodern fiction attempts to demystify an inherited belief system by foregrounding its constructed and conditional "nature." Robert Coover describes the project in his *"Dedicatoria y Prologo a don Miguel de Cervantes Saavedra"*: "The novelist uses familiar mythic or historical forms to combat the content of these forms and to conduct the reader . . . to the real" (*Pricksongs and Descants* 79).

The organizational strategies in male-authored postmodern fiction are epic in urge but picaresque in execution. Barthelme's desublimation of the quest is carried out by a rhetorical striptease that deflates the metaphorical significance of the object, making object and objective one and the same. Such literalization of an extended metaphor reveals the object of the quest to be what she already was—a vehicle, an aperture that would complete a metaphoric development toward a metaphysical unity currently beyond belief (for "the lady" used to stand for an escape from the mutable body). The "lady" of *The Dead Father* is Julie, stripped bare, exposing her lack, her alterity. At the same time, it should be noted, Barthelme diffuses the anxiety of metaphysical collapse through comic irony. Because Barthelme's writing celebrates the end of the traditions that inform it, *The Dead Father* raises a postmodern problem par excellence: how does a writer speak beyond the very structures that constitute his cultural repertoire?

When Alice Jardine explores such problems in *Gynesis*, she finds that critiques of master narratives expose their "non-knowledge" by revealing an elusive Other. This Other is usually represented structurally as a "space" over which narrative has no control, "and this space has been coded as *feminine*, as *woman*" (25). As the status of a male protagonist is reduced from being to becoming, from transcendence to immanence, his love object still provides an objective, luring him on a quest through a fallen world, a quest whose end is deferred.

"Such major conceptual changes as the breakdown of the sign, the questioning of the Subject and his quest for the Object," Jardine writes, "could only come about in a culture once again radically changing its conception of conceptualization: the loss of *the* Quest, the disappearance of *the* Object" (97). The relationship between the beset postmodern protagonist and his often fractured, multiplied object suggests that, in the contemporary innovative novel, the poststructural subject still occupies the subject position of narrative, a position insistently marked off as male in the historical discourse of humanism. His condition, however problematic, is formed and expressed in a deeply patriarchal way: through a feminine object of pursuit. Again, no matter what V. stands for, the V. *position* is always feminized. In the writing of the postmodern masters (writers whose works are referred to almost exclusively by critics theorizing postmodern American fiction), we see the process of such a disappearance rather than the creation of new tropes that could bring us beyond patriarchal subject and object positioning. As Linda Hutcheon puts it, "postmodernism is always a critical reworking [of the past], never a nostalgic 'return.' . . . It has never replaced liberal humanism, even if it has seriously challenged it. It may mark, however, the site of the struggle" where something new can emerge (4).

This is the writerly struggle that Jardine calls "gynesis." The project not only affects canon formation, it threatens to reinscribe in postmodernity a patriarchal dynamic, wherein difference is feminine and identity, masculine. More importantly, as Jardine notes: "If everyone and everything becomes Woman as a culture obsessively turns itself inside out—where does that leave woman?" (34–35).[6]

III

In quest narrative, the subject is bound to his object by search or adventure. In the narrative structure of the sonnet sequence, the speaker binds himself to his love object through writing. While the stability of both subject and object positions is put into play in the Renaissance form, the basic, transitive structure of the subject taking an object remains intact, tracing the relations of mastery, the conditions of humanist *virtu* (upon which the subject of modern art is founded). According to Susanne Kappeler, the same grammatical/communitive paradigm structures pornographic representation.[7]

John Barth's *Letters* may be viewed as a production of texts without writer or receiver, for in the process of writing letters to all of the protagonists that he has created, Barth fictionalizes the author-position. And yet, this elaborate and lengthy metafiction is also constituted by the oldest courtly dynamics in the West. These are particularly apparent when the character Barth invites Lady Amherst to take the same place vis-à-vis himself that Laura took for Petrarch (52–53). While Barth's novel transports the dynamics of courtly romance and blends the narrative structure of the sonnet sequence with the epistolary traditions of the early novel to innovate a post-realist fiction, he does give his Lady Amherst a "voice" (and a non-courtly name, Germaine Pitt) as well as a contemporary point of view that exposes the author's game for what it is—a male, and, therefore, conditional, fantasy: "No!," she writes. "I am not Literature. I am *not* the Great Tradition! I am *not* the aging Muse of the Realistic Novel!" (57).

Despite such interruptions, *Letters* remains fairly traditional, and seems only to complicate rather than to surrender its inheritance of the Pygmalion paradigm in which an artist (male) makes a "living" creature (female) in a male dream that reverses the actuality wherein women birth living beings.[8] In fact, Cynthia Davis sees Barth's self-reflexive fiction as a search for self-identity played out through the male-female relationship. According to Davis, Barth uses the traditional heterosexual archetype as "a metaphor for the condition of the artist/perceiver." She concludes "that the 'new' myth contains more than the dangers of the old male-female dichotomy; it is a fascinating example of the ways that contemporary subjective relativism can support a myth even more deadening to women" (309).

While Davis is attuned to Barth's textual strategies, "images of woman" criticism is generally too crude a model for feminist critique of postmodern narrative (for instance, it is not "subjective relativism" that is the problem in Barth's rendition of Germaine Pitt). Postmodern narrative does not confirm the conventions of traditional representation. It prohibits suspension of disbelief at every rhetorical turn. But, images of women criticism—whose development coincides with the acceptance of writers like Barth into mainstream literary studies—maintains staple qualities of representational art. Representations of women that are not at issue here, but the figuration of woman is. Tracing such figuration allows us to see that, in fiction's post-Joycean shift from mimesis to poesis, something is left over: An insidious, patriarchal trace still operates in the poetics of reproduction.

When postmodern fiction deconstructs authority, the author becomes a function of a text rather than its originator. Moreover, reproduction becomes mechanical.[9] Sorrentino registers these shifts in *Mulligan Stew*, and, by doing so, he resembles a *bricoleur*, assembling a collage of material from sites of cultural production as different as literary criticism and popular magazines.[10] The text's basic organizational unit is the list, where cataloguing reproduces the process of objectification in consumer capitalism. In Sorrentino's parody of literary postmodernism in the 1970s, a metafiction to end all metafiction, the author character Anthony Lamont loses control of his evolving manuscript and becomes increasingly Pynchonesque, increasingly paranoid, believing that the women in his life have schemed with his male nemesis to ruin his career. Lamont's disintegration from author to paranoid is plotted out in his work-in-progress through the characters of Ned Beaumont and Martin Halpin. Meanwhile, Halpin narrates Beaumont's story of seduction by Corrie Corriendo and Berthe Delamode, two devices who reduce the protagonist device into a desiring machine.

The process begins when the two anonymously send lingerie catalogues to an interested but naive Beaumont. Sorrentino's parody of autotelic metafiction demands his inscription of late-capitalist dynamics that are inseparable from the characters of Corrie Corriendo and Berthe Delamode. They appear in Lamont's work-in-progress as consumer products, barely disguising their plans to merchandise their own bodies rather than the lingerie they model. An excerpt from one of their comically sub-literate catalogues demonstrates that a woman's name and image are (in an economy that is both patriarchal and capitalistic) on the same ontological level as her underwear:

> Nudes in Satine MARLENE . . . a Satine Doll with Undies to match . . . See her divest her street clothes and get ready for action! . . . PAT . . . Neat and Petite, this dark haired lady believes in the Best in Bras, corsets, and Pantys. . . . Watch her disrobe them off as she prepares a bath . . . PHYLLIS . . . this Dusky Beauty is sensational in brown satine and lace corsets and swirling cape to match. . . . See her French maid ANNETT, lace her cruely up garbed in her own outfit of black satine undergarments and black mesh hose. (*Mulligan Stew* 110)

Of course, when he receives this catalogue, Beaumont does not yet know that women have produced it. It is by hiding their authority in various guises that Corrie and Berthe snare Beaumont through his own desire.

Mulligan Stew is a satire of contemporary values that employs the list, or the catalogue, without any more subtle organizing principle in attendance. Because no apparent hierarchy of value operates in this fiction, it seems that subjective relativism eclipses authority. Every element in *Mulligan Stew*, including its characters, are bits in a collage. While no single element has more value than any other, woman is still figured as invariably inscribed by commodity culture (the very condition resisted by the laughably high modernist author manqué, Anthony Lamont).

Her objectifications have less to do with the absence of ultimate standards in *Mulligan Stew* than with the history of the subject in Western art. The precursor for the protagonist under erasure, for the poststructural subject commodified by desire, for the author without authority, is woman in patriarchy. Long before the industrial revolution turned men into machines, woman's status had been predominantly functional. She was valued as an object of exchange between the terms of patriarchal economic, psychological, and social registers.[11] Through female love objects, the various male protagonists of *Mulligan Stew* realize that they are not privileged, sovereign subjects, capable of unlimited self-fashioning, but objectifiable, too. Corrie and Berthe gain the upper hand because they not only recognize their inhuman social status—they exploit it to further their own ends. The little boy in Freud's Oedipus narrative confronts the female anatomy and sees the threat of castration carried out in reality. No matter what extended metaphor or story one uses to describe the situation, it is always one of a male subject who sees his own subjugation prefigured in woman.

IV

The possibility that V. might signify a thing marks the anxiety around which Pynchon draws the character of Benny Profane. Throughout the novel, Profane is called the human yo-yo. He vacillates between two of his author's novelistic inheritances: will he be made in the image of the transcendent, humanist hero, or will he be a naturalistic character, the fallen protagonist whose experiences will be marked by a world of machines that turn him into a device? This fear marks the first chapter devoted to Benny in the novel, where his experiences (especially a love affair with Rachel Owlglass, who has an erotic attraction to her sports car) suggest a completely horizontal, materialistic world in which everything is objectifiable: "love for an object, this was new to him" (14).

V.'s slippage from person to thing is a Profane symptom, reduplicated in the novel's many references to automata. His employment at Anthroresearch Associates is foreshadowed with the defrocking of the False Priest in Malta, who is revealed to be a woman, and, further, to be not fully human—part woman, part machine, an equivalent to Anthroresearch's experimental being. "SHOCK— synthetic human object," created by a scientist who sees his work as a direct entailment of the eighteenth century's *l'homme machina* (265). And, from beginning to end, Profane's fear of objectification is fully entwined with his attraction to and repulsion for Rachel Owlglass, who represents the submission of his will to desire, an abjection that this yo-yo both welcomes and resists.

In fact, it is Rachel Owlglass, an employment agent, who connects Profane to Anthroresearch Associates. Seeing her nameplate on the desk, Profane immediately envisages them in bed where "he could see nothing but a new extemporized daydream in which no other face but this sad one with its brimming slash-slash of eyes tightened slowly in his own shadow, pale under him. God, she had him. . . . Any sovereign or broken yo-yo must feel like this after a short time of lying inert, rolling, falling: suddenly to have its own umbilical string reconnected, and know the other end is in hands it cannot escape" (200). Or, cannot control?

Actually, Profane seems to be an object in a *fort/da* game. In *Beyond the Pleasure Principle*, Freud speculates that the game his nephew played in his mother's absence, one of throwing a reel out of sight and rolling it back again, was a coping mechanism that enabled the child to bear separation from the mother. *V.* is replete with allusions to a matriarchy buried by Western history. It is almost as if the yo-yo Profane is Pynchon's reel, a device that the author employs to cope with a cultural separation that seems as primal as it is literary.

It is appropriate to remember that Freud described the *fort/da* game during his formulation of the death drive. In *Beyond the Pleasure Principle*, Freud demonstrates how the drive toward death is indistinguishable from erotic desire. The conservative drive to homogeneity (eros) is performed in Herbert Stencil's obsession with V. Unpleasure, or heterogeneity, is demonstrated by Stencil's many impersonations of male protagonists in search of a specific thing whose name begins with V., each of whom quests after "a rather sinuous, effeminate Death" (243).

Stencil fears Malta because that was where his father died (51). When he finally travels there, he is accompanied by Benny Profane, "the human yo yo." Malta draws Profane as well, "a clenched fist around a yo yo string" (418). This quest is thanatonic, as Stencil implies: "Stencil went out of his way to bring Profane here. He should have been more careful; he wasn't. Is it really his own extermination he's after?" (425). His interlocutor gestures at the ramparts of Valleta. "Ask her. . . . Ask the rock" (425). It seems as if it is not the paternal threat of castration that Benny and Profane confront in Malta, but some long repressed and doubly threatening maternal revenge that would push the speaking subject beyond language at long last. Envisaging the end of Western civilization, Herbert's father Sidney Stencil feminizes what is to come and fears it. Pere Stencil imagines the

> Third Person of the Trinity. . . . The Father had come and gone . . . the dynamic

figure whose virtu used to be a determinate of history. This had degenerated to the Son. . . . What next? What Apocalypse? . . . Especially on Malta, a matriarchal island. Would the Paraclete be also a mother? Comforter, true. But what gift of communication could ever come from a woman.   (444)

Pynchon may be a satirist when he makes Herbert Stencil visit a psychodontist, but his novel would lose much of its over arching coherence if we did not read it as documenting the progress of Herbert's therapy. Thus, *V.* shares with Freudian discourse the tendency to view subjectivity as male. Its deconstruction of the subject is carried out through a threat signified in the body of the Other, who is always already lacking. Perhaps what worries Herbert Stencil most profoundly is that V. is not a noun at all, but a verb, signifying the state of identity under siege through the process of gynesis that Jardine defines as tracing "the transformation of woman and the feminine into verbs at the interior of those narratives that are today experiencing a crisis of legitimation" (25).

This would adequately describe postmodernity as post-history if all readers could share in the description put forth by Pynchon's Maijstral: "We are western men" (424). But some readers may sense closer affinities to Botticelli's *Venus*: Already represented by patriarchal fantasy, framed, an object of exchange long before consumer capitalism, "she hangs on the western wall" (Pynchon, 138). Jardine observes that the roots of representation are "inseparable from the imperial speaking subject . . . [and have] been denounced as complicitous with a violence as old as Western history itself" (118–19). It is the imperial speaking subject whose death is enacted in *V.*, a position that no woman reader would ever have had even mythic access to anyway.

History has prepared an inheritance for Herbert Stencil and subplot protagonist Benny Profane. This inheritance is an entropic humanism whose empowerment, indeed, whose virtu, required the negation of the other. The condition of stable, absolutely positioned consciousness is not even available for the impersonated precursor Godolphin, whose colonialist experiences demonstrate how such a conception of the subject depends upon the violent, despicable mastery of others as surely as Hegelian self-consciousness demands the submission of slave to master.

Significantly, Godolphin describes this hegemony dependent ontology through a heterosexual metaphor. Immediately following an extensive reference to the custom of patrimony, Godolphin considers the expansion of the British Empire and contrasts his explorer's thirst to the colonial imperative: "They want only the skin of a place, the explorer wants its heart. It is perhaps a little like being in love" (188). Godolphin is an explorer; his *raison d'être* is consummation with a frontier.

Godolphin's confession, told to Victoria Wren, illustrates how the female body figures—or ceases to figure—in the crisis of the natural sign, and, therefore, inscribes a problem crucial issue to postmodern representation and poststructural theory. Early in his quest, Godolphin was something of a Platonist, obsessed by an invisible ideal lying beneath or beyond Vheissu: "I wondered about the soul of that place. If it had a soul. . . . [The inhabitants of Vheissu] are skin too. Like the skin of a tattooed savage . . . as if the place were . . . a woman you had found somewhere out there, a dark woman tattooed from head to toes." Forced to be alone with her, one would fall in love

> At first. But soon that skin, the gaudy godawful riot of pattern and color, would begin to get between you and whatever it was in her that you thought you loved. And soon, in perhaps only a matter of days, it would get so bad that you would begin praying to whatever god you know of to send some leprosy to her. To flay that tattooing to a heap of red, purple and green debris, leave the veins and ligaments raw and quivering and open at last to your eyes and your touch. (155–56)

Finally, Godolphin describes his last expedition, where he "saw what was beneath [Vheissu's] skin": " 'Nothing,' Godolphin whispered. 'It was Nothing I saw' " (188).

Like Godolphin, it seems that postmodern fiction gazes upon and incorporates woman to discover what, in the end, is human—is there something left over, an essence after all? The infidelity of woman—a classical theme in Western literature—is also linked to the schism in the natural sign: She figures a site of vibrant vacillation between the seen and the unseen (as in Alain Robbe-Grillet's fiction of male paranoia, *Jealousy*). The concern for a faithful copy within male desire is most succinctly expressed by Hamlet when he asks of Ophelia, "Are you honest? Are you fair?"—other ways for the soliloquist to say "what am I?"

V

Every "V.-symptom" in Pynchon's novel can be described as Jardine's woman-in-effect, whose plurality of repeated presences lures Herbert Stencil into an entropic cycle *of melancholy as well as paranoia*. He is dispersed by the multiplicity of substitutional objects that "exist" as material signifiers in crisis as each object lures him, first, into dispersal, and, then, towards the place of death, Malta. Herbert's impersonations, including his recreation of his father's story, place both the questing figure and his object in neither an allegorical nor a mimetic space, but within a hyperreal space. Herbert is a subject-in-simulation, baited by the false promise of the natural sign to discover that all is manufactured, especially himself.

Thus, Jardine's woman-in-effect operates the subject-in-simulation. I am using that term as an alternative to "a subject in pulsation" detailed in Regis Durand's reading of *The Dead Father*. By applying Lacan's dialectic of desire to Barthelme's fiction, Durand sees the text, rather than any character, as the subject of pulses: "A text exists in and as the pulsation (*battement*) of different systems whose operations constitute, in effect, its real subject" (157). Accordingly, *The Dead Father* questions conventional paternity and authorship by not placing the father as "a point of origin or of reference in a story of identities, but rather by constructing him as a kind of artifact, half giant, half mechanical device" (161). As both an ancient totem and industrial machine, Barthelme's dead father keeps the reader (and the writer) going back and forth in between an artificial polarity which, like Freud's reel in the game of *fort/da*, has been patterned on an originary, unspeakable displacement—that of the maternal body, which is known by its not-there-ness. Could this body be the deep structure of patriarchy, dismembered like Pynchon's cross-dressed False Priest, buried like Astarte, and dispersed into various disguises? Barthelme's father, however dead, is manifested as a material totality through a plenitude of symbolic systems organized to integrate and preserve his form.

Moreover, turning the text into a Lacanian subject (operated by desire) does little to remedy the problem of the humanist subject (in art, a function of virtu). Both belong to a genealogy best illustrated in Hegel's *Phenomenology of Spirit*, which allows for the existence of only one consciousness in any human relation that would realize self-conscious spirit (or artistic achievement). It is precisely this sort of positioning that Pynchon obsesses over in all of his novels, a conception of selfhood that, it seems, he would exhaust altogether in *Gravity's Rainbow*. (Indeed, his recent *Vineland* makes only light reference to such pressing topics of continental philosophy where it meets American literary theory.)

The Dead Father is an excellent illustration of the impasses of postmodernity as seen from a feminist perspective. As Durand asserts, the fiction attempts a deconstruction of both authority and its traditional reinforcer, patriarchal paternity. But another sort of application of Lacanian desire would produce a reading sensitive to gynesis and the feminization of the male protagonist in postmodern fiction. The following passage from "A Manual for Sons" provides an excellent gloss of Lacan's impossible subject, the unattainable ideal, the subject, capital S:

> The death of fathers: When a father dies, his fatherhood is returned to the All-Father, who is the sum of all dead fathers taken together. (This is not a definition of the All-Father, only an aspect of his being.) The fatherhood is returned to the All-Father, first because that is where it belongs and second in order that it may be denied to you. (178)

The son is denied supreme being because a transfer of power between the dead father and the All-Father is a closed circuit that leaves him out. In this case, Barthelme's son resembles Lacan's woman-not-all and, most importantly, illustrates exactly how the poststructural subject resembles woman in patriarchy.

It is because the son is not actually a woman but resembles one in his uneasy relationship with humanism that I would call such a postmodern character a subject-in-simulation. As I have already noted, that simulation is operated by the woman-in-effect.

Each quest under discussion here is an attempt at what Raymond Olderman calls "transcendent resolution," which occurs at the expense of the other: "The bare, necessary and simple affirmation of life over death . . . is achieved time and again by transcending all questions of morality and social action, and transcending by means of some extreme experience which forces the protagonist to seize upon the very surface texture of life and affirm its value" (7). While Olderman hoped to sound a positive note in this 1972 study of postwar American fiction, his own text was deaf to feminism. The critic's need to theorize conditions for humanist mastery led to a definition of "transcendent resolution" that is remarkably similar to Georges Bataille's "feeling of life"—a desperate affirmation that Bataille articulates in an erotic, pseudo-anthropological fantasy, wherein woman is the sacrificial object and her lover, the sacrificing priest (13–14). As in the fiction considered here, Bataille's speculation and Olderman's criticism project the issues of male sexuality upon the screen of high culture.

In male-authored postmodern fiction, the Other is revealed as a symptom of one's own desire, while mastery is thrown back upon itself. Self-reflexive fiction is, like the poststructural subject, obsessed by what it is not, what it wants to be but cannot see or name, for the process of fixing the object of desire renders nothing: no *other* subject. As in *Mulligan Stew's* consumer catalogues, the subject becomes like the object that his desire creates—differentially reduplicable *ad infinitum*. The relativistic subject interacts with his fractured mirror image and becomes like a slew of figures in a pornograpic pictorial: not a subject whose body in its ontological imperfection obscures the soul within it, but rather one in a "replicative series of underived simulacra" (Bersani, 114).

Notes

1. It would be a mistake to conclude, as Jardine does, that all male-authored postmodern fiction in American only thematises gynesis while the French attain (or submit to) *écriture*, thereby achieving greater formal innovation (257). Such an evaluation only applies to some of this fiction some of the time. In fact, French critic Regis Durand believes that the postmodernism of Pynchon and Barthelme (as well as William Gaddis) shifts the subject toward a mode of operation and that "metafiction is no more than the recognition of such a shift, perhaps *the point at which it slides into formalism*" (158; emphasis mine). Jardine's generalization that American postmodern fiction is overly thematic and, therefore, not constituted by gynesis may result from her task as a translator—to savor the ambiguities between French and English. *Gynesis* does not translate English into French.

2. Examples include Leo Bersani's "Pynchon, Paranoia and Literature" and Neil Schmitz, "Describing the Demon: The Appeal of Thomas Pynchon."

3. See Bersani, 105.

4. Studies of the quest in Pynchon have been carried out by Raymond Olderman and Alfred MacAdam, among many others.

5. Earl Shorris writes: "At the core of [Pynchon's] work is the notion of a layered culture—the palimpsest is his metaphor—in which each new variation is written over the last. . . . The palimpsest is fluid, no erasure is complete; the myths of Western civilization

evolve, for we are the society of history and accumulation, an idea that Mr. Pynchon has caught exactly" (3254).

6. The most recent criticism on experimental fiction compensates for the general absence of female-authored works within the theorization of both modernism and postmodernism in America. Some examples are books by Waugh, Friedman and Fuchs, and special issues of *Tulsa Studies* (Spring 1989) and *College English* (April 1990).

7. In *The Pornography of Representation*, Susanne Kappeler applies the grammatical structures of transitive-intransitive predications to a communications model and sees pornographic representation as a paradigmatic example of a transitive process. Kappeler asserts that *écriture* is also transitive: "By turning social practices into transitive processes, the social partners in the practice are represented as objects and the practice is predicated on a single subject" (214).

8. See Janet A. Kaplan's "Creativity and the Childbirth Metaphor: Gender Difference in Literary Discourse."

9. See Walter Benjamin's "The Work of Art in the Age of Mechanical Reproduction."

10. See Walter Benjamin's "The Author as Producer" and Brian McHale's *Postmodernist Fiction* (112–32).

11. I have described these transactions in "Woman as Object of Exchange in Dickens' *Great Expectations* and Faulkner's *The Sound and the Fury*."

Works Cited

Bataille, Georges. *Death and Sensuality: A Study of Eroticism and the Taboo*. New York: Walker, 1977.

Barth, John. *Letters*. New York: Random House, 1979.

Barthelme, Donald. *The Dead Father*. New York: Farrar, Straus, Giroux, 1975.

Benjamin, Walter. "Author as Producer." 1937. Translated by Edmund Jepheott. In *The Essential Frankfurt School Reader*. Edited by Andrew Arato and Eike Gebhardt. New York: Orizen, 1978. 254–69.

———. "The Work of Art in the Age of Mechanical Reproduction." 1968. Translated by Harry Zohn. *Illuminations*. Edited by Hannah Arendt. New York: Schocken, 1968. 217–51.

Bersani, Leo. "Pynchon, Paranoia and Literature." *Representations* 25 (Winter 1989): 99–118.

Coover, Robert. "The Last Quixote: Marginal Notes on the Gospel According to Samuel Beckett." *In Praise of What Persists*. Edited by Stephen Berg. New York: Harper and Row, 1983. 56–68.

Davis, Cynthia. "Heroes, Earth Mothers and Muses: Gender Identity in Barth's Fiction." *The Centennial Review*. 24 (1980): 309–21.

Durand, Regis. "On the Pertinaciousness of the Father, the Son, and the Subject: The Case of Donald Barthelme." *Les americanistes*. Edited by Ira D. Johnson and Christiane Johnson. Port Washington: Kennikat, 1973. 153–63.

Friedman, Ellen and Miriam Fuchs, eds. *Breaking the Sequence: Women's Experimental Fiction*. New Jersey: Princeton University Press, 1989.

Freud, Sigmund. *Beyond the Pleasure Principle*. 1920. Translated by James Strachey. New York: Norton, 1975.

————. "The Psychological Consequences of the Anatomical Distinction Between the Sexes." 1925. Translated by James Strachey. *Sexuality and the Psychology of Love.* Edited by Philip Rieff. New York: Macmillan, 1963. 183–93.

Gass, William. *Willie Masters' Lonesome Wife.* Evanston: Northwestern University Press, 1968. Reprint. Normal: Illinois State University, Dalckey Archive Press, 1989.

Hegel, G. W. F. *Phenomenology of Spirit.* Edited by J. N. Findlay. Translated by A. V. Miller. Oxford: Clarendon Press, 1977.

Hutcheon, Linda. *A Poetics of Postmodernism: History, Theory, Fiction.* New York: Routledge, 1988.

Jardine, Alice. *Gynesis: Configurations of Woman and Modernity.* Ithaca: Cornell University Press, 1985.

Kaplan, Janet A. "Creativity and the Childbirth Metaphor: Gender Difference in Literary Discourse." *Feminist Studies* 13:1 (Spring 1987): 49–82.

Kappeler, Susanne. *The Pornography of Representation.* Minneapolis: University of Minnesota Press, 1986.

Laird, Holly, ed. "Toward a Gendered Modernity." *Tulsa Studies in Women's Literature* 8:1 (Spring 1989).

MacAdam, Alfred. "Pynchon as Satirist: To Write, To Mean." *Yale Review* (June 1978): 555–66. Reprinted in *Twentieth-Century American Literature.* Edited by Harold Bloom. New York: Chelsea House, 1985. 3260–61.

McHale, Brian. *Postmodernist Fiction.* New York: Methuen, 1987.

Meese, Elizabeth, ed. "Women and Writing." *College English* 52:4 (April 1990).

Olderman, Raymond. *Beyond the Wasteland: A Study of the American Novel in the Nineteen-Sixties.* New Haven: Yale University Press, 1972.

Pynchon, Thomas. *V.* New York: Viking, 1961.

————. *Gravity's Rainbow.* New York: Viking, 1973.

Robbe-Grillet, Alain. *Jealousy.* Translated by Richard Howard. New York: Grove Press, 1978.

Schmitz, Neil. "Describing the Demon: The Appeal of Thomas Pynchon." *Partison Review* (1975): 112–25. Reprinted in Bloom, 3255–60.

Sciolino, Martina. "Woman as Object of Exchange in Dickens' *Great Expectations* and Faulkner's *The Sound and the Fury. Mississippi Review* 49–50 (1989): 97–128.

Shorris, Earl. "The Worldly Palimpsest of Thomas Pynchon." *Harper's* (June 1973): 78–83. Reprinted in Bloom, 3252–55.

Waugh, Patricia. *Feminine Fictions: Revisiting the Postmodern.* New York: Routledge, 1989.

Wilde, Alan. *Horizons of Assent: Modernism, Postmodernism and the Ironic Imagination.* Philadelphia: University of Pennsylvania Press, 1987.

The Politics of Aversion in Theory

Charles Bernheimer

"Theory," writes Teresa de Lauretis, "is a technology of gender."[1] What she means by this, in her words, is that theoretical discourses construct their objects of knowledge in fields of meaning that produce and promote, in however disguised a manner, representations of gender. These representations are ideological, she argues, insofar as they correlate sex to cultural contents according to dominant social, economic, and political values and hierarchies. Since these values regularly organize sexual differences into social inequalities, theory can be seen as subscribing to the patriarchal contract that engenders difference by privileging male sexuality and subjectivity. The task of feminist theory thus becomes doubly critical, for it must denounce its own inevitable collusion with the gender system inherent in theoretical discourses while it also attempts to open a new discursive space outside the ideology of gender. The creation of this new space "elsewhere" is, de Lauretis admits, a goal she has yet to fulfill.

I find this analysis relevant to my work in three ways, which I will explore in this essay. First, it sustains my conclusion in *Figures of Ill Repute: Representing Prostitution in Nineteenth-Century France* (Cambridge: Harvard University Press, 1989), that the treatment of gender as a purely rhetorical signifier of differential relations is most often a misogynist strategy to gain power in fantasy over women's bodies. Second, it points to the importance of critiquing the politics of gender precisely in the discourse that seems most eager to demystify the construction of sexual difference—psychoanalysis, my own privileged theoretical method. Third, it poses in compelling terms the problem of complicity: How can one write from a position elsewhere than inside a technology of gender? In particular, how can I as a male theorist disengage myself from the position of hegemonic authority granted me by the dominant ideology?

Let me begin, then, with the notion that gender has only rhetorical significance, that it is a construction of tropes. The idea appeals by offering a release from a reductive essentialism. It produces the female subject independent of her physiology and of her socio-economic relations in the historical world, treating her as a function of linguistic figures and metaphoric substitutions. Advocates of this view insist that the distinction between the anatomical and the rhetorical must be scrupulously maintained. Any conflation of the two, they argue, represents a retreat to a naïve materialization of sexual difference. Since the body has no presence in a text, any reference to bodily experience can only be in the displaced mode of figural representation. Once this mode is assumed, the difference between male and female bodies falls away, each being able to serve as a figure for the other. "The body is fake, a trope," writes critic Jefferson Humphries, "and within the text of which it is a part, gender difference is merely another trope. Male and female are tropes which may be freely substituted, one for the other" (25).

I quote Humphries not only because he articulates the rhetorical argument in bold terms, but also because he does so in specific reference to my work. The context is a review entitled "Troping the Body: Literature and Feminism" (*Diacritics* 18:1 [Spring 1988]: 25) in which Humphries accuses me and Naomi Schor of betraying what he considers the true project of feminist criticism, "a recognition that gender difference functions as a trope, subject to reversal and substitution" (26). Schor and I are guilty, Humphries claims, of fetishizing gender difference rather than deconstructing it, of insisting on a link between bodies and figures instead of letting them float free from one another. In Humphries's opinion, literature, when correctly understood, "already contains the antidote to phallocentrism" (27) and that antidote is the denial of gender. A good reader, Humphries concludes, is both man and woman.

Alluding to this mode of theoretical argument, Teresa de Lauretis remarks: "This kind of deconstruction of the subject is effectively a way to recontain women in femininity and to reposition female subjectivity *in* the male subject, however that will be defined" (24). This is precisely the lesson taught by my study of representations of female sexuality in nineteenth-century France. The idea that the body, to quote deconstructive critic Rodolphe Gasché (cited approvingly by Humphries), "is nothing other than a sum of names, which are fictive, fictional, circulating, continually being exchanged"[2] would be entirely congenial to Balzac's misogynist criminal hero, Vautrin, for whom the body is a polymorphic fiction through which signs and names, including those of gender, circulate and are exchanged. The condition of Vautrin's troping of the body, as Balzac makes quite clear in *Splendeurs et misères des courtisanes* (*A Harlot High and Low*), is the elimination of the sexually active, loving woman who, exemplifying the author's concept of true femininity, sacrifices herself for her man. Only after she has committed suicide can sexual difference become a function of male invention and the signs of gender be negotiated in the marketplace for semiotic currencies. Balzac's message is clear: Only men have the privilege to deny gender any historical, social reality; only men have the creative power to conceive gender as a trope.

When Baudelaire writes, "Woman is the contrary of the dandy; therefore she must elicit horror,"[3] his conception of the dandy involves an idea of gender as figural instability that foreshadows deconstructive theorizing. The dandy, who can only be male, meticulously constructs his appearance and behavior as representations that display their artificiality. These representations borrow from both masculinity and femininity, for the dandy is a flâneur who, "like those wandering souls in search of a body, enters whenever he wants into anyone's character. For him alone everything is vacant."[4] What Gasché says of the text-body holds for the dandy: His self-creation is "fictive, fictional, circulating." Baudelaire's friend Barbey d'Aurevilly declared, in his little book on the subject, that dandies have "double and multiple natures, of an undecidable intellectual gender (*d'un sexe intellectuel indécis"*—*"sexe,"* in French, covers both sex and gender).[5] The dandy's gender is, like a trope, subject to reversal and substitution. A creature of intelligence working in a field of vacancy, the dandy foregrounds figurality over nature, the undecidable over the referential. Always gallant, he maintains a safe distance from his horrifying opposite, the "abominable" female driven by her instincts.[6] I need not stress that nothing could be less feminist than this dandy strategy for recuperating the feminine as artifice while denegrating female sexuality as a purely animal function. Yet deconstruction pursues its critique of phallocentrism while ascribing to what is, viewed historically, a dandy technology of gender.

This analysis explains why it is not surprising that Derrida should have chosen to address the subject of woman through the texts of Nietzsche, which echo Baudelaire's decadent misogyny. On their basis, Derrida, in *La Question du style* (translated as *Spurs*), theorizes woman as the force of the undecidable that suspends the opposition between truth and falsehood and produces writing's specifically textual style. Or I should say that this is the reading of woman that emerges from Derrida's complex and highly nuanced essay as the one to which he lends his own rhetorical approval, reinforcing it with complementary terms from the deconstruction arsenal (displacement, hymen, and so forth). Granted, he nowhere claims that this is Nietzsche's final word on the woman question, and, indeed, he insists on the irreducible plurality and heterogeneity of Nietzsche's pronouncements on women. Nietzsche was, he says, "a little lost" in this matter of women, unable to organize his thoughts coherently.[7]

Yet Derrida does manage to produce three fundamental propositions that, in his view, summarize, albeit untruthfully because too systematically, Nietzsche's valuations of woman. In the first, woman is condemned in the name of phallogocentric truth as a castrated figure embodying deceit and deception. In the second, woman is condemned for being a femme fatale, who plays with the male fear that she is castrated while knowing that she is not. In the third, woman is recognized as "an affirmative power, dissimulating, artistic, dionysiac. She is not affirmed by man, but affirms herself herself, in herself and within man. No castration occurs" (265–66). Although he numbers these propositions successively, Derrida denies any particular logic to their order since he would have us think of Nietzsche as lost in his text "like a spider unequal to what has been produced through it" (267). But one need not locate some specious system in Nietzsche's plural, disjunctive style in order to see that the operations Derrida describes perform a *process* that replicates *as a whole* a familiar strategy of nineteenth-century misogyny: A threatening image of a castrated and castrating woman is evoked only to be condemned, so that the feminine can be reinvented as an affirmative, integral figure of male creativity.

The third proposition Derrida attributes to Nietzsche is the one he uses to develop his own positive description of the female principle. His analysis is based on a passage in *The Gay Science,* where Nietzsche imagines an artist's flight away from the noise and tumult of his everyday existence to the heights of fantasy. Nietzsche describes this male artist in typically decadent terms as a "dissimulator of naturalness" (*Verhehler der Naturlichkeit;* 123),[8] a phrase reminiscent of Baudelaire's formula for the goal of art, "a sublime deformation of nature." In Nietzsche's fantasy scenario, the artist is disturbed in his exalted flight away from nature by insistent noises that reach him even at his lofty height. It is then that Nietzsche evokes, as an antidote to these noises, the magical effect of the women the visionary artist sees gliding past him, an effect that Derrida analyzes as revealing the truth of woman. To quote Nietzsche: "The magic and the most powerful effect of women, [is] an effect at a distance and, to speak in the language of philosophers, *actio in distans*: but this requires, first of all and above all,—*distance!*" (124). In his commentary on this passage, Derrida plays down the initial negation of nature necessary for the woman effect to become operative. In fact, he simply leaves out of consideration the Baudelairean opening of fragment 59 in *The Gay Science,* which makes quite clear the motivation for flight away from this world: "When we love a woman, we easily conceive a hatred for nature on account of all the repulsive natural functions to which every woman is subject. We prefer not to think of all this" (122).

This observation reflects on Derrida's own omission. It is only after the artist has left the world behind—with its avid women of whom Nietzsche says elsewhere in *The Gay Science* that it is natural for them to want to be physically possessed, body and soul (319)—that women can become magical by effecting still another degree of beneficial distance from the world. "The artist," writes Nietzsche, "likes to think that his better self could live there among women, that in those tranquil regions the most violent tumult would be quieted into a deathly silence, and life would become a dream about life" (124). This suggests that the magical operation of women is to make death liveable for the artist, to allow him to "glide over existence" (123). Put in somewhat different terms, one could say that woman's power, in Nietzsche's view, is her disappearing act: "Enchanting and silent" (123), she passes before the hallucinating eyes of the artist, reminding him of the value of keeping life, and "the repulsive natural functions" of real women, at a safe distance. Nietzsche's reference to the language of philosophy may not be as parodic as Derrida assumes: As a distancing effect, women figures philosophy's retreat from nature into exalted flights of rhetoric. Woman as dissolving figure cancels out woman as animal nature.

Rising to the occasion, Derrida's rhetoric exalts the woman effect while strategically ignoring its production through defensive aversion and denial, *aversion* meant in both senses of the word. Woman as a distancing from distance becomes "non-identity, non-figure, simulacrum, the abyss of distance. . . . There is no essence of woman," declares Derrida, "because woman averts (*écarte*) and averts herself from herself (*s'écarte d'elle-même*). She engulfs, sends to the bottom, without end, without bottom, all essentiality, all identity, all property. Blinded here, philosophical discourse founders—and rushes toward its ruin. There is no truth of woman, but this is because this abyssal gap (*écart*), this non-truth, is the "truth." Woman is the name of this non-truth of the truth" (242, 243). Derrida here seems to be repeating Nietzsche's gesture of averting woman from her animality, of instituting an *écart,* a gap, within woman that allows her to become worthy of a philosopher's love. Woman merits deconstructive praise insofar as she actively distances herself from her natural functions and her social history.

Just as Nietzsche fantasizes that his better self would be restfully at home among women, life having become its own dream, so Derrida imagines a feminization of philosophy whose condition, as has been well analyzed by Gayatri Spivak, is a double displacement of the female body.[9] The dandy notion of the non-truth of truth allows the philosopher to glide over existence, playing with gender as a mere simulacrum ("As soon as you have reached the first stage of deconstruction, then the opposition between women and men stops being pertinent," Derrida declared at a seminar in 1984).[10] He affirms distance as the style of woman, and creatively genders himself in this style ("I would also like to write like [a] woman," he said in response to a question at the Cérisy Nietzsche colloquium).[11] Although Derrida would never espouse Nietzsche's misogynist disparagements of women, his failure to acknowledge any logical connection between that misogyny and the magical work of the woman effect suggests, at the very least, a blindness to the patriarchal gender ideology implicit in his identifying woman with the (non)truth of male theory.[12]

Which, of course, brings us up against the extremely difficult issue of how to speak of sexual difference and of gender from outside such an ideology, of whether this is even possible. I have been suggesting that what is left behind in the dandy play of deconstructive rhetoric are women's bodies, women's history, women's subjective experience. As a male feminist, I consider it important to analyze this distancing *écart*, this aversion, but it would be presumptuous, and foolish, of me to believe that I can speak for or from the corporeal reality of female experience. I can, at best, agree with Naomi Schor, Rosi Braidotti, and other female feminists who have attacked the notion, promoted by deconstructive theory, that any specificity attributed to sexual difference is naïvely essentialist and should give way to a notion of sexual indifferentiation.[13] Schor is no doubt right that "no feminist theoretician *who is not also a woman* has ever fully espoused the claims to female specificity, an irreducible difference."[14] The claim here, as I understand it, is not for an essential feminine difference stable throughout eternity but for a specificity that is culturally constituted in particular historical contexts. The problem of how to articulate such specificity without thereby adhering to patriarchally coded positions and oppositions is perhaps the major challenge being addressed by female feminist theoreticians at the present time. Male feminists, it seems to me, can best aid in this constructive effort by helping to clear the ground of its colonizing technologies and, perhaps, as I shall suggest at the end of this article, by constructing on similarly cleared adjacent ground a materialist theory of their own embodied sexuality.

No modern technology of gender has been more successful in defining and delimiting the ground of female sexuality than psychoanalysis. Although feminist analysts and critics have done a great deal to critique and revise Freudian theory, pernicious tools of the Freudian gender technology continue to be endorsed and used, largely because of their logical efficacy. But the rational power of Freud's arguments sometimes obscures what are, in fact, ideologically driven distortions of logic. Such a distortion is at the basis of Freud's fundamental conceptual tool for explaining sexual difference, castration. I will briefly outline here an analysis that I perform in greater detail elsewhere.[15]

It will be remembered that Freud hypothesizes that all children, male and female, develop the theory that every human has a penis. Faced with the visual evidence that this theory is false, that girls do not have this organ, the little boy—to consider him first, following Freud—does not abandon his monosexual theory. He does not conclude that there is an anatomical difference but rather that a mutilation has occurred. His strategy is to invent "castration" to safeguard his narcissistically flattering theory of universal masculinity. Thus he has twice distanced himself from—put himself at an *écart* from—the female body. He has first furnished that body with an imaginary penis, then he has fantasized that this fantasized organ has been cut off. The young speculator (Freud compares his primary authority for all this, Little Hans, to a misguided philosopher[16]) seems to eagerly espouse, at a distance, the principle of *actio in distans*.

Now, this scenario may well seem plausible historically, given the difficulty Victorian prudery offered to the child's empirical investigations. Childish theory could flourish when visual evidence was so hard to come by. But what is one to make of Freud's conversion of Little Hans's narcissistic fantasy into the universal truth of female sexuality, into what he calls, in both the German and the English versions of his texts, the "fact" of woman's castration? Following Little Hans's lead, Freud strategically, or perhaps unconsciously, forgets that anatomical differ-ence alone is factual and proposes the fantastic result of distancing theoretical speculation as the uncovering of epistemological truth. He promotes castration as factual evidence of woman's lack, whereas it is actually a theoretical veil obscuring her difference.

The psychic function of the theory of castration can thus be seen as fetishistic in terms of Freud's own theory of the fetish. The purpose of the fetish, he argues, is to preserve the fantasy that all humans have a penis and simultaneously to represent a recognition that women lack this organ. Such recognition, however, does not correspond, as Freud would have it, to an acknowledgment of the fact of female castration. Freud is wrong in claiming that the fetishist is eager to deny castration. The contrary is the case: However repulsive the fetishist may find the notion of women's mutilation, he nevertheless embraces castration as a defense against what he finds still more "uncanny and intolerable" (SE 11:95), that is, woman's otherness, her specific difference. The fetishist is not characterized by his incapacity to accept woman's lack but rather by his incapacity not to see women as lacking. This means that the normal man in Freudian theory, including Freud himself, is a fetishist, for Freud claims that it is a normal rite of passage for men to learn to accept what he calls "the unwelcome fact of women's castration" (SE 21:156), and to master what he takes to be the typical accompanying reactions, "horror of the mutilated creature or triumphant contempt for her" (SE 19:252).

Freudian female normality is theorized as the perfect object of male fetishism. One glance at the penis and the little girl "knows that she is without it and wants to have it" (SE 19:252). She is incapable of understanding her sexual organs as autonomous and valuable in themselves. Her discovery of the anatomical distinction between the sexes produces an instantaneous flight to the explanatory power of theory, which, in Freud's view, has only one possible message, "the fact of her castration." Unlike her male counterpart, the girl is no philosophical speculator. Freud does not recreate her intellectual process as she tries to figure out how, when, and by whom her penis, which she cannot conceivably remember ever having, was cut off. Nor does he clarify just what the girl's narcissistic gain might be in her swift assumption of her own inferiority. Castration reinforces the boy's theory of phallic universality. What's in it for the girl?

The answer, I think, has a good deal more to do with the ideological distortion of Freud's technology of gender than it does with psychological cogency. What the little girl gains is what Freud, a theoretical fetishist, wants her to want—that is, male theory. By accepting her own castration, the girl averts herself from her body, displaces it, and enters a field of interpretation whose (non)truth is based on a phallocentric fiction. For a girl to understand her sexuality, she must adopt as the very basis of that understanding her status in male theory. Not to do so, Freud suggests, would be to risk a loss of reality that "in an adult would mean the beginning of psychosis," manifested as a compulsion "to behave as though she were a man" (SE 19:253). Acknowledge your castration or become a mad mannish monster—this is Freud's message, repeated by Lacan. Yet it is evident that to call castration a fact is itself a disturbing symptom of the loss of reality. That loss is woman's gain in Freudian theory: The loss of the real affords access to the truth of lack.

But the real is not entirely lost. Freud's theory of the fetish, which can, I believe, be salvaged as long as castration is displaced from the place of truth, allows for a recognition of difference, albeit veiled. As the fetish object of psychoanalysis, "the castrated woman" not only obscures anatomical difference, it also invites, through its blatantly symbolic status, its own condemnation for fraud.

Exhibiting its double fictionality, its function as a negative version of what never existed in the first place (the phallic woman), "castration" invites the dismantlement of its imposture and a return to the perception of sexual difference that preceded the defensive recourse to theory. But, true to its constitutional duplicity, the fetish simultaneously cancels this invitation and presents the excessive melodrama of castration as the revelation of the truth of gender.

Now it is evident that the perception of sexual difference that I am supposing to be veiled by theoretical aversion cannot be assumed to afford unproblematic epistemological insight. Perception does not occur in an ideological vacuum nor does it function independently of defensive and wish-fulfilling impulses.[17] It may even be, as Laplanche and Pontalis suggest, that disavowal founds human reality.[18] Consequently, there may be no clear viewing without a simultaneous averting of the glance. My intention is not to condemn all modes of aversion but only those which adopt dandy strategies and fetishistic *écarts* to control a horror of woman's sexual difference.

The critical difficulty in analyzing such strategies is to distinguish their motivating force from that of less harmful forms of denial. Since this problem confronted me throughout the writing of *Figures of Ill Repute*, it may be useful to consider my critical dilemma there as, to a certain extent, exemplary. In that book I study the gender politics informing representations of the typical figure of female sexuality in nineteenth-century art and literature, the prostitute. I argue that there is a link between male fantasies of female sexuality as castrated, degenerate, and diseased and the production, in reactive defense, of modernist artistic strategies to contain and master the threatening power of these mutilated bodies. Since I was committed to the thesis that the virulence of these misogynist fantasies provides motivation for modernist technical innovation, I ran the risk of seeming to be complicitous with the disgusted aversion whose forms and energies my criticism retraced. Addressing this issue in my introduction, I wrote:

> My emphasis on the fantasmatic origins of both literary and historical representations of prostitution privileges the image over the real, the word over its referent, symbol over event. . . . If, for example, I claim that what is "beneath" Flaubert's love of his prostitutional idea is his dread of castration, this interpretation remains within the domain of male fantasy and neglects the realities of female exploitation, commodification, poverty, and suffering that constitute the experiential dimension "beneath" any imaginary appropriation of prostitution. I have tried as much as possible to register this neglect in describing the function of fantasy. But since that function is my primary object of analysis, the reader will find that "the real" is rapidly left behind and, with it, any attempt to describe the lived experience of the individual prostitute. (3)

This passage expresses a kind of uneasiness about the facility with which the symbolizing, abstracting qualities of literature serve as a vehicle for misogynist fantasies. One of my primary themes in the book is the analysis and denunciation of those artistic strategies whereby reference to the corporeal and historical realities of prostitution is suspended through an assertion of literature's figural self-reflexivity. But, according to one generally sympathetic reviewer, Jann Matlock, my denunciation of "the aesthetic modernism that divorced these bodies from their histories" still involves a certain collusion with the modernist dandies insofar as I fail to "return to bodies," to "what was happening on a daily basis in the streets of Paris."[19]

Such a "return" is not unlike the one I propose here as a cure to theoretical fetishism and is fraught with many of the same difficulties. Matlock's critique constructs a polarization of history and literature. The representational textuality of history tends to be neglected as the critic yearns for an unmediated knowledge of actual bodies. "Must we give up hope of getting beyond the language and texture of fantasy to the sources of these representations," Matlock asks rhetorically (85). The answer she would like to give is no: If one works hard enough in the archives, she suggests, one can discover the ground of fantasy in legal, economic, political, and social practices. But she is too sophisticated not to recognize that such practices are available to us only insofar as they are discursive, mediated, and, I would add, permeated by fantasies of gender and power that replicate those motivating the production of literary fictions. History is not outside of literature anymore than women's bodies are outside their subjectivities.

But this point need not lead one to embrace the deconstructionist critique that implicates inside and outside in a seamless weave. Just as there is something irreducible about sexual difference, so there are undeniable facts and events in history. The degradation and oppression of women is not only a function of misogynist fantasy. However constructed the accounts of individual women's experiences may be, female experience has an historical continuity implanted by women's class, gender, and race. What is tricky in terms of literary criticism is that reference to the realities of this historical positioning may be thought to entail an effort at mimetic realism, a devalued mode in contemporary theory.[20]

Since treating woman as a metaphor is a highly developed tool of patriarchal culture, feminist critics may wish to privilege a referential impulse that attempts to close the *écarts* of misogynist aversion. To do so is to critique the entire modern theorization of literature's constitutional specificity, with its stress on the distancing operations of self-reflexivity, rhetoricity, and structurality. The theoretical work of the feminine may well involve a revaluation of the notion of reference so that the body's presence to consciousness can be recuperated in literature's discursive register. *L'écriture féminine* represents one version of such a revaluation. Its practice shows that there is no necessary contradiction between mimesis and metaphor and that the female body can make its presence felt in literature through techniques of symbolization, repetition, and figurality most often used for misogynist ends. However, the memory of such uses still contaminates this effort in the minds of many feminists, making *l'écriture féminine* seem like a simple reversal of male modernism rather than its subversion. So the effort continues, an effort that the male feminist can support but in which he cannot participate.

What he can do, and what numbers of female feminists writing in *Men in Feminism* encourage him to do, is respond to Hélène Cixous's challenge: "Men still have everything to say about their own sexuality." One way to address this challenge is to critique male-identified theoretical concepts by testing them out against one's personal somatic experience. By way of conclusion, I will suggest, very briefly, how such a critique might be undertaken of Lacan's concept of the Phallus (which I capitalize for reasons that will become evident shortly).[21]

For some time now, feminist critics have pointed out that the Phallus, which Lacan defines as a pure signifier without anatomical reference, a genderless symbol of discursive power, cannot be divorced from the bodily image it inevitably conjures up.[22] Having torn the veil off the Phallus, revealing, as Jane Gallop puts it, its fallacy,[23] these critics seem to feel that little more need be said. Having denounced the reference to the banal penis in the transcendental Phallus and thereby exposed Lacan's deplorable phallocentrism, they do not explore the theoretical implications of finding a penile image embedded in the high-flying Phallus. Without questioning the validity of this denunciation, I want to suggest that the penis as Phallic referent has a more complex function than has been acknowledged to date. Whereas feminist critics have tended to treat Lacan's anatomical reference as an essentializing gesture that reinscribes patriarchal domination, I believe that reference to the male sexual body may be seen as performing the contrary function, that is, as subverting the hegemonic pretensions of the Phallic signifier.

A moment's thought about the penis should suffice to convince us of its unsuitability as a vehicle of symbolic attribution. Its appearance, for instance, is extremely variable, from limp flaccidity to phallic extension. To distinguish between these states, I will follow the etymological derivation of the world "phallus" from a root suggesting tumescence and use this term, uncapitalized, for the erect penis. Now, it is clear that the changes from penis to phallus, and vice versa, are rarely deliberate acts of will. I can want my phallus and it will not respond to my desire. At other times, I may not be conscious of wanting my phallus and it will present itself, perhaps to my embarrassment. The phallus is capricious. For one thing, it is not always fully itself. Sexologists speak of the "quality" of an erection. Some are better than others, more impressively phallic. Some are more durable than others—just why is often a mystery to the presumed master. Some last longer than I may wish—there are times when I want to lose my phallus but it refuses to come to its explosive climax. And then, of course, there are times when I may lose it despite (to spite) myself.

Thus, reference to the penis does not produce a univocal meaning. The phallic referent is not single, whole, self-identical, unchanging. It does not qualify to symbolize the cultural centrality of the unified male subject. My body contains an otherness to itself that makes the phallus always precarious and provisional. The phallus is latent in the penis, the penis is latent in the phallus, but neither latency has a necessary logic to its manifestation. The temporality of the phallus is erratic, its appearance sporadic, its duration uncertain. To center my attention on the penis/phallus is to experience a loss of the center. In short, the penile referent is far less phallocentric than is the Phallic signifier, which, as Derrida has shown, is an ideal entity not itself subject to semantic mutilation.[24]

If the phallus is temporal, it is also contextual. Theory offers us a phallus always already functioning in a particular manner, whether it be as a signifier of lack (Lacan) or as a lack in the signifier (Derrida). This phallus may circulate, as it does, famously, in Lacan's reading of "The Purloined Letter," but its meaning is never determined or limited by the context in which it finds itself. On the contrary, the context becomes readable in terms of who is provisionally in possession of the Phallus. The positioning of the Phallus creates the psychic choreography of the scene.

In contrast, the phallus as erection has to be produced from its latency in the penis. My phallus is not always already operative; it is brought into being in particular social, historical, sexual, and fantasmatic circumstances. My penis needs the stimulation of an exciting context in order to erect itself into the phallus. Although such contexts vary widely, from the imaginary stimuli of an erotic dream to the physical stimuli of frictional contact, my phallus is entirely dependent on them and vulnerable to their changes. When I have my phallus, I do not want displacement, I want the cohesion and endurance of the stimulating context on which its erection depends. This context may involve erotic displacements and substitutions, but only within a framework that sustains arousal.

In the rhetorical terms that Lacan finds analogous to unconscious process, this dependence on context, whether internal and imaginary or external and real, points to the metonymic quality of the phallus. Whereas Lacan associates the symbolic Phallus with the free substitutions and displacements of metaphoric structure, the phallic referent is far more limited in scope, given that it can function only in metonymic relation to a contiguous presence. This limitation is not to be deplored, however, since it offers access to factors that Lacan leaves out of consideration in his account of the construction of the subject, such as material conditions, personal history, class and racial hierarchies. The nature of this access may have something in common with the Freudian notion of anaclisis, which describes the early dependence of the sexual instincts on the self-preservative ones.[25] Just as sexuality becomes autonomous by repeating autoerotically satisfactions that were first attached to the fulfillment of physical needs, so the Phallic signifier cannot achieve its independent status without leaning up against (the etymological meaning of *anaclisis*) the bodily referent and its sustaining contexts.

Reference to the penis need not, however, be theorized as exclusively metonymic. It also has qualities that can be associated with metaphor. Thinking dialectically, one could say that what the phallus signifies is its loss—not in the place of the female other, as psychoanalytic theory insists, but in its own place, its deflation to become the penis again. Insofar as the desire it embodies is metonymic, my phallus wishes to coincide with its meaning, that is to lose itself, but only by intensifying pleasure to the point of ejaculation. This intensification, which focuses sensual feeling in the organ, is analogous to the poetic function of metaphor as Roman Jakobson defines it: "the superposition of similarity upon contiguity."[26] For Jakobson, the consequence of this superposition is that the semantic content of words becomes secondary to their resemblance in sound and/or rhythm. Similarities in the purely sensuous, material qualities of verbal units are projected from the vertical, metaphoric axis onto the metonymic axis of language, thereby obscuring the function of contextual reference. Analogously, desire obscures contextual specificity by projecting a similarity of aim on all aspects of physical experience. In its metaphoric function the phallus effaces differences in order to arrive at a sensation of sameness. Insofar as this orgasmic goal entails the loss of its erection, the metaphoric phallus can be seen as related to an instinctual desire to return to an earlier state of things. As Freud says, "the pleasure principle seems actually to serve the death instincts."[27] Metaphorically, the phallus inscribes its own death within it. Repetition of this death is assured by the insistence of the drive for pleasure.

The above suggests, however sketchily, that the phallic referent can be understood as imprinted rhetorically in the unconscious. Body language inscribes history into the play of unconscious signification. Although this inscription may appear essentialist in that its basis is anatomy, my point is that the foundational strategy of male essentialism is aversion from the body, defined as inertly female, and identification with transcendence. For men to think through their bodies is for them to acknowledge the common quality of fleshly embodiment shared by both sexes and to read in that embodiment a common, if not equal, subjection to such material factors as biology, history, race, and power. To expose the pernicious effects of a cultural order centered around a Phallus that never returns to its penile form, denying its precarious temporal condition, is to demonstrate the vulnerable artifice of patriarchy's ideological construction. The whole notion of the Phallus as signifier of differential effects should be rethought in terms of those effects being internal to the male subject's somatic awareness. Problematizing the male body as the site of theoretical differences, this, I think, can be a fruitful task for male theoreticians informed by feminism.

Notes

1. Teresa de Lauretis, *Technologies of Gender: Essays on Theory, Film and Fiction* (Bloomington: Indiana University Press, 1987), 19.

2. Rodolphe Gashé, "*Ecce Homo* or the Written Body," *Oxford Literary Review* 7: 1–2 (1985): 23. Cited in Humphries "Troping the Body" 27.

3. Charles Baudelaire, "*Mon coeur mis à nu*," *Oeuvres complètes* (Paris: Pléiade, 1966), 122. All translations from the French in this article are my own.

4. Baudelaire, *Le Spleen de Paris*, in *Oeuvres complètes*, 244.

5. Jules Barbey d'Aurevilly, *Du dandyisme et de George Brummell* (Paris: Balland, 1986), 105.

6. "Woman is *natural*, that is to say, abominable," Baudelaire remarks in "*Mon coeur mis à nu*," *Oeuvres complètes*, 1272.

7. Jacques Derrida, "*La Question du style*," in *Nietzsche aujourd'hui?* Vol. 1. *Intensités* (Paris 10/18, 1973), 267.

8. When necessary, I have revised Walter Kaufman's translation, *The Gay Science* (New York: Vintage, 1974), to which the page numbers in parentheses refer.

9. See Gayatri Chakravorty Spivak, "Displacement and the Discourse of Woman" in *Displacement: Derrida and After*, edited by Mark Krupnick (Bloomington: Indiana University Press, 1983).

10. "Women in the Beehive: A Seminar with Jaques Derrida" in *Men in Feminism*, edited by Alice Jardine and Paul Smith (New York: Methuen, 1987), 194.

11. This is the last remark registered in the discussion after Derrida's presentation of his paper (*Nietzsche aujourd'hui* 299).

12. This blindness is inherited by some of the most astute critics working in Derrida's wake. For instance, Shoshana Felman offers as the theoretical core of her essay "Rereading Femininity" a Derridean description of the woman-effect that assumes its value for feminism: "The signifier 'femininity',", she writes, "is precisely constituted in *ambiguity*, it signifies itself in the uncanny space *between two signs, between* the institutions of masculinity and femininity" (*Yale French Studies* 62 [1981]: 32).

13. See Naomi Schor, "Dreaming Dissymmetry: Barthes, Foucault, and Sexual Difference," and Rosi Braidotti, "Envy: or With My Brains and Your Looks" in *Men in Feminism*.

14. Schor, 109.

15. See Charles Bernheimer, " 'Castration' as Fetish," *Paragraph* 14:1 (1991): 1–9.

16. See the *Standard Edition* of Freud's works, 24 vols., abbreviated hereafter SE (London: Hogarth Press, 1953–1973), 10:12.

17. I owe this point to a spirited discussion with Dr. Humphrey Morris.

18. J. Laplanche and J.-B. Pontalis, *The Language of Psycho-Analysis* (New York: Norton, 1973), 120.

19. Jann Matlock, " 'Modernist Obsessions: New Interdisciplinary Perspectives," *French Politics and Society* 8:2 (Spring 1990): 83.

20. Sandy Petrey's recent book, *Realism and Revolution: Balzac, Stendhal, Zola, and the Performances of History* (Ithaca: Cornell University Press, 1988), uses Austin's theory of speech acts to show that mimesis is always a performative effect whose basis is an initial liberation of language from the referential illusion. Petrey's Marxist reading of mimesis preserves the poststructuralist analysis of the sign's arbitrary character while showing the historical efficacy of speech acts that construct realist reference as a convention collectively agreed to. His stimulating analysis may be useful for feminist thinking about the referent.

21. What follows is a condensed version of an argument I make at greater length in "Penile Reference in Phallic Theory," *Differences* 4:1 (Spring 1992).

22.   See for instance Jane Gallop, *Thinking Through the Body* (New York: Columbia University Press, 1988): 124–33; Mary Ann Doane, "Woman's Stake: Filming the Female Body," *October* 17 (1981): 27–28; Diana Fuss, *Essentially Speaking* (New York: Routledge, 1989): 8–9.

23.   Gallop, *Thinking Through the Body*, 129.

24.   See Jacques Derrida, "The Purveyor of Truth" in *Yale French Studies* 52 (1975).

25.   For an excellent discussion of anaclisis, see Jean Laplanche, *Life and Death in Psychoanalysis* (Baltimore: Johns Hopkins University Press, 1976). I connect anaclisis and metonymy in the theoretical introduction to *Flaubert and Kafka* (New Haven: Yale University Press, 1982).

26.   Roman Jakobson, "Linguistics and Poetics," in *The Structuralists from Marx to Lévi-Strauss* (New York: Anchor Books, 1972): 114.

27.   Sigmund Freud, *Beyond the Pleasure Principle* (New York: Liveright, 1961): 57.

Five Propositions on the Future of Men in Feminism

Jonathan Culler

We have been asked to reflect on the future of men in feminism: how should men and women conceive of this relation and how might they most productively pursue it? Let me offer five propositions for discussion.

1. These days one might say that men are in feminism as they are in language or in history: A man necessarily positions himself in relation to feminist thinking and writing of one sort or another, whether he quotes it, argues with it, ignores it, or seeks to carry it further. In literary studies at least, it seems to me that men cannot choose whether to be in feminism or to keep out. If this is so, then the proper attitude is to take feminist arguments and issues seriously, to engage with them, to try to learn from them, to ally oneself with them or argue with them, and, above all, not to allow oneself to act as if there were *a* feminist view or position on any issue.

2. Although it seems to me that there are not feminist theoretical or interpretive utterances that could not in principle be produced by male critics or theorists, the male subject position, and, thus, position of enunciation, will not be that of a woman producing the same utterance, so that for a man to call what he does "feminism" or "a feminist reading" is to obscure an important tension between *énoncé* and *énonciation*. For any particular feminist position or reading, one can admit that it could have been produced by a man, but it would seem to me tendentious and appropriative for a man to call what he is doing feminism.

3. The counterview, which has some merit, would be that for a man to situate himself in feminism, by saying that he is doing feminist theory or a feminist reading of *Madame Bovary*, say, is to adopt an instructive position of discipleship in relation to women critics and scholars, inscribing himself as apprentice in an enterprise whose leaders are obviously women. However, the tradition of male hegemony is sufficiently strong that any man doing this may be suspected of trying to show women how to do feminism, so that the alleged justification may evaporate

---

These remarks were a contribution to a panel discussion on "Men in Feminism" at the 1988 Convention of the Modern Language Association.

without taking effect. It seems to me preferable, then, for men not to claim to be doing feminist readings, leaving it to others to describe his criticism as they think fit.

4.   Indeed, if men want to do feminist work their most productive strategy might be, as Alice Jardine has suggested, to investigate not feminine sexuality but masculine sexuality and associated issues, such as technology, sports, and the construction of the male subject, or narcissism, voyeurism, fetishism, and pornography. There is, as Jardine says, interesting and productive work to be done here that could contribute to feminist thinking.

5.   But, finally, to urge that men put themselves in the position of learning, from feminist writings, how to correct their biases, assumptions, limitations of perspectives, opens a paradox which may well prove intractable. Feminism shows white males that they are not universal subjects, and when limitations of one's vision or understanding are pointed out, rather than resist the lesson, one should attempt to correct these limitations. In my *Flaubert: The Uses of Uncertainty* (written fifteen years ago), while claiming to question traditional conceptions of the novel, I accepted without question the critical commonplace that *Madame Bovary* is a portrait of a foolish woman, without considering whether what is identified as her foolishness is not a product of a male vantage point and oppressive circumstances. Feminist criticism, such as Naomi Schor's writing on Flaubert, enabled me, in an afterword for a new edition, to attempt to reflect on this blindness and on the complicity between the hypostatization of Emma's essential foolishness and the claim that this is the novel of all novels that the criticism of fiction cannot overlook (it is as though Flaubert's genius were to have made something magnificent out of a subject [a female subject] so quintessentially trivial; for Madame Bovary to be seen as *un livre sur rien*, Emma must be seen as *rien*).

To think about such questions now seems to me essential to anyone working on Flaubert, and I thus conclude that feminist readings should provoke male critics to investigate and to seek to correct their own sexist assumptions and those of the critical tradition. But insofar as this is an attempt to avoid the biases of a limited point of view and an attempt to make oneself a more universal subject, it unavoidably partakes of the initial problem that feminism seeks to counter: the white Western male's inclination to consider himself a universal subject. To try to make oneself the universal subject that men have blithely assumed themselves to be seems a perverse result of learning from feminism, but the problematical character of this result should not serve as excuse for a failure to take account of what feminism shows men. To try to become a more universal subject is not to cease to be male but to try to make that role into less of an agent of oppression and disregard. And if the paradox of universality, of *correcting* bias, prevents men from finding a comfortable position either in feminism or outside it, that seems to me neither surprising nor particularly regrettable.

Two Conversations on
Literature, Theory, and the Question
of Genders

Robert Con Davis and Thaïs E. Morgan

Conversation One: Women's, Gay & Lesbian, and Gender Studies

THAÏS MORGAN: One of the main goals of *Men Writing the Feminine* is to encourage further discussion of the directions feminism—both as a methodology for interpreting literary texts and as a socio-political ground for acting in the world—may be moving during the 1990s. I am especially interested in recent changes in the ways in which feminism appeals across what Sandra Gilbert and Susan Gubar have called the "no man's land" of sexual battle lines drawn between women and men. During the 1980s, there was widespread integration of women's studies across the curriculum in the humanities and social sciences. At the same time, the full range of contemporary critical theories—from Derridean deconstruction to Althusserian Marxism, from Lyotardian postmodernism to Lacanian psychoanalysis—has been explored by feminists, resulting in diverse feminisms. Most recently, these theoretically informed feminisms have been deployed by gays and lesbians to contest long-established boundaries, drawn not only between men and women but between men and men, women and women.

ROBERT CON DAVIS: I, too, am struck by the new directions that women's studies has taken and by the plurality of feminisms that have emerged today. In particular, I'd like to discuss the appropriateness of some of the issues Jonathan Culler raises in "Five Propositions on the Future of Men in Feminism" (originally part of a panel at the Modern Language Association meeting in 1988). He clearly indicates the unavoidability of male literary scholars' and cultural critics' participation in feminism, implying that there is an historical necessity for this encounter. Feminists have been arguing for such an encounter at least since Simone de Beauvoir's *The Second Sex,* but Culler's frankness about men's role is helpful and may well encourage men to take more risks in engaging in feminist work.

However, I also notice that several of the pieces in *Men Writing the Feminine* explicitly work against many of the limitations Culler proposes for men's participation in feminism. Charles Bernheimer, for example, adopts a critical perspective in relation to the male body. His thinking about his own body and his own penis in terms of both identity and otherness creates a sort of hyper-real body that parallels the traditional patriarchal construction of the female body as the object of the gaze. This critique of man's social and sexual presence seems to me to indicate a direction for men in feminism that is not the same as Culler's call for men to balance respectful distance with supportiveness in working with feminist criticism. Instead, Bernheimer is pushing on the limits of what it means to be a "man" in the first place, and, thus is questioning what a feminist intervention by a "man" could signify. This testing of theoretical presuppositions about gender is important, even if the way forward is not always clear.

THAÏS MORGAN: Yet what strikes me most is precisely how the notion of "appropriateness" itself has tended to inform male theoretical discourse of feminism. On one hand, I think that you and I would both agree with Culler that "[t]hese days . . . men are in feminism as they are in language or in history." On the other hand, the idea that men should strive to attain an "appropriate"—which I interpret to mean both self-regulated and regulatory—relation to feminism makes me suspicious about your ultimate intentions with regard to feminism.

ROBERT CON DAVIS: I see what you mean. Your comment reminds me of some of the issues Elaine Showalter has brought up in "Critical Cross-Dressing: Male Feminists and the Woman of the Year." Showalter worries about the "illegitimacy" of men in feminism and points out what she considers to be the "unsettling"spectacle of men's attempt to speak in women's voices and languages. This kind of condemnation, as far as I am concerned, is dead-ended.

Nonetheless, I am aware that several problems arise when men appropriate feminist criticism and theory for their own interests. In academic discourse, men too often opportunistically support feminist positions, only to abandon these stands when they are no longer convenient or useful. As a result, many readers of *Men Writing the Feminine* may be suspicious, at least initially, when they see Peter Murphy talking about "the woman writer" in a male novelist's work, or Christopher Benfey analyzing "the woman in the mirror" as the identity of a male poet, or even me discussing feminism in this conversation with you. What are Murphy's motives, or Benfey's, or mine? Such suspicion needs to be there on historical and perhaps personal grounds, but somehow there also needs to be some good-faith experimentation with the ways in which men can understand and participate in feminism. I think that this is the most effective way in which feminism can move out of the sphere of women's studies and into the wider domain of cultural studies, as it is in the process of doing now.

THAÏS MORGAN: Admittedly, some approaches to the question of men's participation in feminism lead to an essentialist impasse: "me Woman, you Man." Consider, for example, the debates in Alice Jardine and Paul Smith's *Men in Feminism,* circling as they do around the apparently insuperable barrier of sexual difference. Their difficulties with negotiating between assertions of separate sexual identities by women and by men, by straights and by gays, have yet to be resolved and remain as a challenge in the 1990s.

ROBERT CON DAVIS: I agree: those barriers must be challenged, and I see no other way to do it except by trying, even if there are always some experiments that don't succeed.

THAÏS MORGAN: Speaking of experiments, I am reminded of the spectrum of positions taken up during a 1988 MLA panel called "The Future of Men *with* Feminism, The Future of Feminism *with* Men," which attempted to mediate some of the anxieties over sexual difference which had emerged in previous dialogues over "men *in* feminism." What interested me most about this panel was the way in which concern for "appropriateness" (perhaps equivalent to what we are nowadays calling "political correctness") in one's stance vis-à-vis feminism burdened both women's and men's statements, for instance, not only Culler's talk (printed here) but also, even if to a lesser extent, Alice Jardine's. At the same time, I remember being surprised at the importance that inhabiting a female *versus* a male body was accorded, for example, in both Robert Scholes's and Leslie Rabine's talks on this panel. Are the 1990s going to see the rise of a New Essentialism in women's and gay & lesbian studies?

ROBERT CON DAVIS: Not necessarily. This is where I think that gender studies comes into the discussion. What is the relation of gender studies to feminism, especially to feminism as practiced through women's studies?

For my part, I have noticed that many of the essays in this collection use the same approaches that organize feminist scholarship. There are thematic explorations of "woman," by which I mean consideration of how male authors deal with issues thought to be natural to or revealing about female characters, as in Susan Wolfson's reconsideration of William Wordsworth's portrayal of the feminine. There are also semiotic analyses of gender construction that attempt to identify underlying assumptions and specific techniques that male writers employ to achieve an illusion of femininity, as in Béatrice Durand's essay on Diderot's ventriloquism of a nun.

THAÏS MORGAN: Yes, both "gynocriticism" and "feminist critique," as Showalter has termed the feminist study of authors and the feminist practice of reading, respectively (in "Feminist Criticism in Wilderness"), inform many of the essays in *Men Writing the Feminine.* However, I don't think that these two familiar models constrain any of the contributors here; rather, each line of argument is going elsewhere—to places that might best be embraced under the heading of gender studies. Still, I want to make clear that I see a crucial historical tie between feminism, which is often institutionally equated with "women's studies," and the relatively new field called "gender studies," even though their premises and methods are not identical. I'd like to see *Men Writing the Feminine* used by scholars, teachers, students, and administrators in order to develop a dialogue between women's and gender studies.

ROBERT CON DAVIS: This kind of dialogue is in fact happening: look at the feminist classicist scholarship by, for instance, Page duBois (*Sowing the Body*), and feminist theoretical works such as Joan Cocks's *The Oppositional Imagination*.

THAÏS MORGAN: Another important dialogue between women's and gender studies can be found in the collection *Engendering Men: The Question of Male Feminist Criticism*. Do you know that book? In their Introduction, Joseph Boone and Michael Cadden emphasize the debt owed by scholarship on the construction of masculinities to feminism, which, as they say, "has engineered us, even as we strive to engender a practice that might not always be *the same* as feminist practice, but that remains in contiguity with its politics" (their emphasis). This is an interesting example of Culler's notion of the "discipleship" of male-feminist to female-feminist critics—one that sets an optimistic precedent for future exchange, and one that is conciliatory in contrast to Showalter's agonistic model (although, ironically, Showalter is singled out by Boone and Cadden as the mother of their text). Still, Boone and Cadden admit that men's "efforts at engendered self-clarification cannot help but be complicated by [their] access to male privilege" (2).

ROBERT CON DAVIS: Discipleship is an important option, and a male critic should not hesitate to take this kind of position in relation to feminism. But, in addition, male critics must be willing to take chances and work on literary and other cultural texts in ways that leave them open to critique from a variety of other viewpoints. For instance, I might be a disciple of Luce Irigaray, but she can't grant me diplomatic immunity in regard to the feminist criticism I write. For a man, then, it may not be possible to avoid the appearance—and even the reality—of opportunism, for men do engage in feminist criticism within the context of their "access to male privilege." We will learn a lot more about what is possible when more men start working with the full range of feminisms.

Speaking optimistically, I do think that there is a certain degree of tolerance in the academy not only for crossing the lines of sexual difference but also for the inevitably mixed results that will come out of such practices. We should also remember that our jobs as teachers and scholars *include* taking risks, so we shouldn't fail to take the ones we can. It is important to realize that our work can make a real contribution to cultural change in the 1990s. The encounter of literary and cultural theory with gender studies is an especially promising site for men and women to shape the future of feminism.

Conversation Two: Postmodern Theories of Gender

THAÏS MORGAN: In discussing the title of this collection—*Men Writing the Feminine*—with its contributors, I have found that everyone, no matter what her or his style of feminism, concurs on one point: When men write the feminine, they engage in gender construction and, moreover, what is under construction is never only femininity but always also masculinity.

ROBERT CON DAVIS: Yes, I find that the essays in *Men Writing the Feminine* point away from arguments about sexual difference toward the notion of a gendered continuum. For example, look at Frann Michel's essay on William Faulkner. Michel constructs "lesbian author" not as a substantial category but as a posture in relation to texts, one, which in Faulkner's fiction, expresses the male writer's response to "gender anxiety associated with male authorship." I find this approach fascinating and likely to generate many new insights into Faulkner. Unlike Showalter, then, I myself see nothing "unsettling" about Faulkner's textual cross-dressing, or the "critical cross-dressing" of any male writer or theorist who takes up a position within feminist discourse (see Conversation One).

THAÏS MORGAN: My feelings about men writing the feminine, whether it be George Herbert's doing so in *Memoriae Matris Sacrum,* or Paul Verlaine's in *The Women-Friends,* or even Jonathan Culler's in "Reading As a Woman" (in *On Deconstruction*), are decidedly more mixed than yours. In the first place, I regard female impersonation in any context as suspect *for women*—potentially misogynist because it too often turns out, upon closer analysis, to be a mockery and expulsion of the feminine in men by men: here I would agree with Showalter's reading of Dustin Hoffman's masquerade of femininity in the film *Tootsie.* At the same time, I see female impersonation as liberating *for men*—potentially disruptive of normative heterosexual masculinity. Finally, though, I do not think that gender crossing—such as Denis Diderot's "transvestism" in *The Nun* or John Hawkes's multiple (and multiply pornographic) female impersonation in *Virginie: Her Two Lives*—either transcends or erases the historical effects of the sex-gender system, which often operates not despite but through gender crossing.

ROBERT CON DAVIS: You are describing a potential betrayal of women's concerns through men's practices of cross-dressing and cross-voicing that is a real danger. To that degree, I share your skepticism about men writing the feminine, whether in literary characters or in critical theories. I take your argument, however, to lead not to a condemnation of men for writing feminism but to a call for continuous critical vigilance, especially for the kind of critical vigilance possible to a (male or female) feminist who is a cultural theorist.

THAÏS MORGAN: What, then, do you see as the connection between postmodern theories, gender studies, and feminism today?

ROBERT CON DAVIS: I think that there is a present need to sort through what men and women contribute to the understanding of gender. The critical function is crucial in all kinds of feminism. I'm definitely *not* arguing, though, for political correctness: I'm against that. But I am arguing for the judicious exercise of vigilance among all literary critics and theorists. On that point, I agree with you and with Showalter.

There are other areas of gender politics to be addressed, too. Craig Owens, in "Outlaws: Gay Men in Feminism," argues that women's skepticism about men participating in feminism—or in any activities marked as feminine—may partly result from homophobia. Perhaps homophobia underlies some of the fear of "critical cross-dressing."

THAÏS MORGAN: I see things a bit differently. First of all, I must admit that the way you are applying Derrida's call for "critical vigilance" (issued in the context of the deconstruction of Western metaphysics) to political correctness (as exercised in the context of gender politics) makes me nervous. Won't we be setting up a system of surveillance very like that, say, of compulsory heterosexuality (see Adrienne Rich, "Compulsory Heterosexuality and Lesbian Existence") if we require that feminist cultural critics—women and men alike—act as judges of what will be appropriate and what inappropriate in the new field of gender studies? How would each critic's investments in sexual orientation and gender identity play into this sort of "vigilance"?

Second, I would challenge what Owens says, but not because I am in a hurry to absolve feminists from the charge of homophobia. Teresa de Lauretis's discussion of feminists' "heterosexual fundamentalism" offers a very convincing caution on this point ("The Essence of the Triangle or, Taking the Risk of Essentialism Seriously: Feminist Theory in Italy, the U. S., and Britain" 29). Rather, I want to complicate the discussion of the gender politics of literary criticism and theory by suggesting that female impersonation activates not only heterosexual men's and women's homophobia, but also what might be called an internalized feminophobia on the part of women—one implicit in Freud's theory of why daughters disdain their mothers and prefer to model themselves after their fathers—as well as a misogynistically directed, internalized homophobia on the part of men. (See Showalter's discussion of *Tootsie*, which, significantly, considers the "oppression of women" carried out through female impersonation but not its oppression of men by men).

ROBERT CON DAVIS: I'm not sure anymore that we are disagreeing. Postmodern theorists engaged in rethinking the gendered body in relation to language as well as to cultural representations more generally emphasize the parallel between bodies and discourses than essentialist boundaries.

THAÏS MORGAN: Like you, I am eager to move beyond the boundaries fixed by sexual difference. Indeed, I think that's one of the most productive aspects of combining postmodern—by which I mean poststructuralist—theories with gender studies. I take the purpose of this combined approach to be interrogating long-established ideas of "woman" and "man" with the aim of challenging the absoluteness of sex-gender assignments and the material consequences that follow from them.

Nevertheless, I am not eager to refuse or bracket what Teresa de Lauretis has called "the risk of essentialism." No matter how appealing I find poststructuralist theories and the flexible subjectivity that they foresee for both men and women— for you and me—, I cannot get past the essential difference between us. I mean less a simple (and deconstructible) difference of biological ground, or the female versus the male body, than the more complex (and resistant) difference of our "historical specificity" within discourses, institutions, and practices of the body because we have been culturally encoded as "woman" or as "man."

ROBERT CON DAVIS: I, too, am interested in questioning the origin and status of such encoding by sex and gender. Is there a speaking "I" that is encoded as female or male? Is the unconscious somehow encoded as female or male? However one might answer, I think that female and male already belong to a cultural discourse in which gender categories are not boxes to put things in but constructions that are always in motion and, therefore, probably not as limited as the opposable terms "female" and "male" suggest.

THAÏS MORGAN: I agree with you. In using such theories as semiotics, deconstruction, and Lacanian psychoanalysis to question gender as a major category that defines subjectivity, or who and what we are, the contributors to *Men Writing the Feminine* show themselves to be working within what Lyotard has dubbed "the postmodern condition."

ROBERT CON DAVIS: What you are saying about postmodern theory and gender studies also sheds a new light on a remark made by Culler in his essay, which we've discussed earlier (see Conversation One). Referring to men in feminism, he speaks of "the instructive position of discipleship in relation to women critics and scholars." What bothers me about this, I now realize, is the assumption of fixed categories of gender identity, which imply that we already know who we are as men and as women, and that the men just need to be more open to what the women can *add* to what men already know. All this confident "knowing" strikes me as misguided and dangerous. I am worried about what I would call the gender realism being advanced here. In contrast, I appreciate the several attempts in *Men Writing the Feminine* to think about the construction of gender.

THAÏS MORGAN: The distinction you are making between gender realism and gender construction is very useful. The essays in *Men Writing the Feminine* are postmodernist in the way that they attempt to move away from a mimetically grounded discourse of sexual difference, based on the body or the opposition of male versus female, toward a historicizing and linguistically alert discourse focused on the slippage between "sex" and "gender"—between nature and culture, between fact and construct, and ultimately between the oppositions male/female and masculinity/femininity.

ROBERT CON DAVIS: I would go even further. Several of the essays in *Men Writing the Feminine* take an approach to gender that is not exactly feminist critique and not exactly gender constructionism but more difficult to describe—one that takes a semiotic view of representation in most respects, but at some point projects gender as a positive grounding of all social and cultural discourse. I think that Charles Bernheimer does this in his discussion of the male body and men's positioning vis-à-vis feminism here.

THAÏS MORGAN: I am intrigued by your idea that gender may be taken as a "positive grounding" of discourse. Do you mean that "gender" is silently replacing "sex" as the referential base for postmodern theories?

ROBERT CON DAVIS: I mean that for some postmodern theorists "gender" is like Noam Chomsky's "little black box" for language acquisition, a formally situated and absolute mystery. By way of an example, consider the several essay in *Men Writing the Feminine* that, as Bernheimer suggests, connect gender theory with the "personal and experiential" dimensions of the *male* body.

In particular, Bernheimer's essay aims to "reduce [the] inevitable gap" between feminist critiques of masculinity and men's perceptions of their own bodies, or gender and sex. He challenges men—including himself—to engage more directly in critiquing their own gendered positions in language and social practice. Nonetheless, I am aware that thinking through the physical experience of "having" a penis in relation to the cultural authority of the instituted phallus is not the same as generating a feminist discourse. Bernheimer describes this "male" discourse as what men can do to "be of most use to the feminist project," and that's different from any feminist discourse during the 1980s that I've ever seen.

THAÏS MORGAN: Now you sound as if you are prepared to agree with the position taken by Showalter and Scholes in *Men in Feminism*. They argue that men are finally excluded from the "truth" of feminism because they *are* men, sexually different from women and therefore culturally privileged just because they (you) have a penis/phallus and women (I) don't.

ROBERT CON DAVIS: No; I'm saying the opposite. Initially, Bernheimer grants that gender—for instance, the authority of the phallus—is "brought into being in particular social, historical, sexual and fantasmatic circumstances." This implies that gender is entirely the product of a signifying practice. However, having entertained this possibility, Bernheimer goes on to ask about the "last instance," an ultimate grounding for gender, the final reference that sponsors not only gender but all other cultural institutions. His answer, which is a little surprising given his earlier comments about social and cultural "construction," does not confirm a semiotic view at all. Instead, he argues that "[j]ust as there is something *irreducible* about sexual difference, so there are undeniable facts and events in history. The degradation and oppression of women is not only a function of misogynist fantasy. However constructed accounts of individual women's experiences may be, female experience has an historical continuity implanted by women's class, gender and race" (emphasis added). Now, I do appreciate what Bernheimer is saying about the "real" effects of oppression on women, the epic "hurt" of history. No denial is possible there.

THAÏS MORGAN: What you and Bernheimer are saying resonates with certain aspects of feminist women's positions, including those of de Lauretis and Showalter, in its emphasis on the actual effects of men's social practices on women.

ROBERT CON DAVIS: Let's pursue the idea of the reinscription of the "real" in semiotics as it bears upon gender theory. Note that in positing a material and historical "something irreducible about sexual difference," Bernheimer does not mean Derridean *"différance"* or some version of the "trace." (On deconstruction and genders, see the introductory essay to this book.) Rather, he collapses the discourse of semiotics into an assortment of "real" distinctions and problems reminiscent of Saul Kripke's "essentialist metaphysics"—that is, the epistemological reliance on connections to *nodes* of "real" experiences in an utterly non-semiotic world. I believe that Bernheimer's realism on this point undercuts his earlier comments about the social construction of gender.

THAÏS MORGAN: As a semiotician and a constructionist, I must admit that what you are saying makes sense, which leads me once again to remark upon the potential convergence of male feminist thinking with feminist thinking by women. Although you and Bernheimer are not saying exactly the same thing about the relation of sex and gender, you both are participating in currents of thinking by feminist women on the irreducibility of "sexual difference," however that term is defined in theory, whether psychoanalytically, socio-economically, semiotically, or otherwise.

ROBERT CON DAVIS: But I'm still uncomfortable with the position we are now describing. Bernheimer's argument goes this way: Whether we see the force of gender distinctions as political in some complex way, or just intuitive (as what we *know* to be the case), sexual difference is indisputably there to be reckoned with in our personal experience and in our culture all the same. Moreover, there's no use in ignoring the pervasiveness of sexual difference on the technicality that we cannot account for that difference theoretically. Once again, what bothers me is the assumption here that we *do* already know what gender differences, "men" and "women," are. I maintain that this approach starts the whole discussion about gender at too advanced a point, presupposes too much, and institutes gender realism with too little consideration of the effects of doing so. In other words, this approach concedes that culture is constructed but continues to assume that sexual difference is so fundamental as to slip out of the frame of constructedness because it is constant, natural, and so on.

THAÏS MORGAN: You're talking about a recurrent dilemma for feminisms (essentialist or post-Woman?), gay and lesbian identity politics (in or out of the closet?), and generally for gender studies as a field.

ROBERT CON DAVIS: Quite frankly, I just don't know what a "natural" sexual difference would be. Therefore, I am not prepared to accept it, at least not on any of the terms we have so far considered. I don't know how to go about what I want to describe, but I still want to talk about sexual difference as a cultural construction—not universal and not inevitable in particular forms.

THAÏS MORGAN: At some point in this conversation, the very distinction between "sex" and "gender" that has enabled feminist discourses in humanities and social sciences over the past fifteen years seems to have evaporated. I'm not sure whether I find that a liberating or a paralyzing prospect. In *Making Sex: Body and Gender from the Greeks to Freud*, Thomas Laqueur has problematized exactly this tendency to assume that what we now call "biological sex" has always provided "a solid foundation for the cultural category of gender" (124). From the semiotic, constructivist, and poststructuralist points of view, sexual difference does have the epistemological status of gender: Sex is a construct, too, just as gender is. But then, recalling Martina Sciolino's discussion of gender as a discursive effect in postmodern novels here, I find myself asking: am I just another "woman-in-effect" (female feminist) and you "a subject-in-simulation" (male feminist)?

ROBERT CON DAVIS: I don't mind those categories. I keep thinking of Gilles Deleuze and Félix Guattari's notion not of two, three, or even four gender categories but of "n sexes"—dozens, hundreds, probably thousands of genders for which we as yet have no models and certainly no names (see *Anti-Oedipus: Capitalism and Schizophrenia*). This suggests neither a strictly binary and symmetrical world of men and women, nor a four-fold world of male/female heterosexuals/homosexuals, but a world of many differences: gender configurations that are not just theoretically possible or trivial, but ones that in actual situations are defining and formative for actual people. These genders may finally turn out to be—and this is Deleuze and Guattari's implicit argument—what exceeds the conspiratorial and confining ideology of heterosexual/homosexual relations.

THAÏS MORGAN: Although it is very attractive, I'm not entirely persuaded that Deleuze and Guattari's theory of "n sexes" isn't a utopian vision. Michel's idea that "however firmly the heterosexual [opposition] of masculine/feminine is entrenched . . . it does not constitute the only conceptual dyad available even within the confines of phallogocentric symbolic systems" strikes me as more immediately practicable. I believe that we must acknowledge the historical weight of our ideological situatedness and that, for this reason, the notion that we can suddenly free ourselves from the traditional, hierarchized sex-gender system through revolutionary desire is wishful thinking.

In any case, I think that it's especially interesting that the body has become the focal point not only of woman-centered but also of man-centered theories of gender, just at the time that postmodernist theories are proposing to see the "self" and "identity" as "n" positions in an open field of subjectivities or desiring machines. So, are we now talking about the institution of "n studies" instead of gender studies?

ROERT CON DAVIS: Some day maybe, and perhaps sooner than we think, though not as a vision of utopia but as part of a successful postmodern critique of the formulation and imposition of heterosexual/homosexual relations which constitute our ongoing discourse on Oedipus.

THAÏS MORGAN: I'm starting to wonder about alternative titles for this book, say, "N Writing the N_1. . . ." Thank you for discussing questions concerning critical theory and genders that arise from *Men Writing the Feminine* with me.

ROBERT CON DAVIS: And thank you. I have a feeling that this book will bring us and others together to discuss many of these issues further.

Bibliography

The following articles and books are referred to during the two conversations between Robert Con Davis and Thaïs Morgan.

Boone, Joseph A. and Michael Cadden, eds. *Engendering Men: The Question of Male Feminist Criticism* London: Routledge, 1990.

Cocks, Joan. *The Oppositional Imagination: Feminism, Critique, and Political Theory.* New York: Routledge, 1989.

Culler, Jonathan. "Reading As a Woman" in *On Deconstruction: Theory and Criticism After Structuralism.* Ithaca: Cornell University Press, 1982. 43–64.

de Beauvoir, Simone. *The Second Sex.* 1949. Translated by H. M. Parshley. Harmondsworth: Penguin, 1972.

de Lauretis, Teresa. "The Essence of the Triangle or, Taking the Risk of Essentialism Seriously: Feminist Theory in Italy, the U. S., and Britain." *Differences* 1:2 (1989): 3–37.

Deleuze, Giles and Félix Guattari. *Anti-Oedipus: Capitalism and Schizophrenia* (1983). Translated by Robert Hurley et al. Minneapolis: University of Minnesota Press, 1983.

DuBois, Page. *Sowing the Body: Psychoanalysis and Ancient Representations of Women.* Chicago: University of Chicago Press, 1988.

Gilbert, Sandra and Susan Gubar. *No Man's Land: The Place of the Woman Writer in the Twentieth Century.* 2 vols. New Haven: Yale University Press, 1988, 1989.

Jardine, Alice and Paul Smith, eds. *Men in Feminism.* New York: Methuen, 1987.

Laqueur, Thomas. *Making Sex: Body and Gender from the Greeks to Freud.* Cambridge: Harvard University Press, 1990.

Lyotard, François. *The Post-Modern Condition: A Report on Knowledge.* Translated by Geoff Bennington and Brian Massumi. Minneapolis: University of Minnesota Press, 1983.

Owens, Craig. "Outlaws: Gay Men in Feminism" in *Men in Feminism*, 219–32.

Rich, Adrienne. "Compulsory Heterosexuality and Lesbian Existence." 190; reprinted in *The Signs Reader: Women, Gender, and Scholarship*. Chicago: University of Chicago Press, 1983. 139–68.

Scholes, Robert. "Reading Like a Man" in *Men in Feminism*, 204–18.

Sedgwick, Eve K. Across Gender, Across Sexuality: Willa Cather and Others" in *Displacing Homophobia: Gay Perspectives in Literature and Culture*, edited by Ronald R. Butters et al. Durham: Duke University Press, 1989. 53–72.

Showalter, Elaine. "Critical Cross-Dressing: Male Feminists and the Woman of the Year" in *Men in Feminism*, 116–32.

———"Feminist Criticism in the Wilderness" in *The New Feminist Criticism: Essays on Woman, Literature, and Theory*. New York: Pantheon, 1985. 243–70.

For Further Reading

Barthes, Roland. *S/Z*. New York: Hill and Wang, 1974.

Boone, James A. and Michael Cadden, eds. *Engendering Men: The Question of Male Feminist Criticism*. London: Routledge, 1990.

Butler, Judith. *Gender Trouble: Feminism and the Subversion of Identity*. London: Routledge, 1990.

Claridge, Laura and Elizabeth Langland, eds. *Out of Bounds: Male Writers and Gender(ed) Criticism*. Amherst: University of Massachusetts Press, 1990.

DeJean, Joan. *Fictions of Sappho, 1546–1937*. Chicago: University of Chicago, 1989.

de Lauretis, Teresa. *Technologies of Gender: Essays on Theory, Film, and Fiction*. Bloomington: Indiana University Press, 1987.

Flynn, Elizabeth A. and Patrocino P. Schweickart, eds. *Gender and Reading: Essays on Readers, Texts, and Contexts*. Baltimore: Johns Hopkins University Press, 1986.

Garber, Marjorie. *Vested Interests: Cross-Dressing and Cultural Anxiety*. New York: Routledge, 1991.

Gilbert, Sandra and Susan Gubar. *Sexchanges*, vol. 2 in *No Man's Land*. New Haven: Yale University Press, 1989.

Goldsmith, Elizabeth C., ed. *Writing the Female Voice: Essays on Epistolary Literature*. Boston: Northeastern University Press, 1989.

Jardine, Alice A. *Gynesis: Configurations of Modernity*. Ithaca: Cornell University Press, 1985.

Jardine, Alice and Paul Smith, eds. *Men in Feminism*. New York: Methuen, 1987.

Kahn, Madelaine. *Narrative Transvestism: Rhetoric and Gender in the Eighteenth-Century British Novel*. Ithaca: Cornell University Press, 1991.

Kauffman, Linda. *Discourses of Desire: Gender, Genre, and Epistolary Fictions*. Ithaca: Cornell University Press, 1986.

Kelly, Dorothy. *Fictional Genders: Role and Representation in Nineteenth-Century French Narrative*. Lincoln: University of Nebraska Press, 1989.

Sedgwick, Eve K. *Between Men: English Literature and Male Homosocial Desire*. New York: Columbia University Press, 1985.

Showalter, Elaine. ed. *Speaking of Gender*. London: Routledge, 1989.

List of Contributors

Benfey, Christopher. Mount Holyoke College. Author of *Emily Dickinson and the Problem of Others* (1984) and *The Double Life of Stephen Crane* (1992). Regular contributor to *The New Republic* on modern poetry.

Bernheimer, Charles. University of Pennsylvania. Author of numerous articles on comparative literature and on psychoanalytic theory, including " 'Castration' as Fetish" (*Paragraph* 1991) and "Penile Reference in Phallic Theory" (*Differences* 1992). Author of two books, *Flaubert and Kafka: Studies in Psychopoetic Structure* (1982) and *Figures of Ill Repute: Representing Prostitution in Nineteenth-Century France* (1989).

Con Davis, Robert. University of Oklahoma. Author of numerous articles on literature, psychoanalytic theory, and cultural studies, including "Woman as Oppositional Reader" (1988) and "Freud, Lacan, and the Subject of Cultural Studies" (*College English* 1991). Coauthor of *Criticism and Culture* (1991) and *Culture and Cognition* (1992), and author of a recently published work in Women's Studies, *The Paternal Romance: Reading God the Father in Early Western Culture* (1993).

Culler, Jonathan. Cornell University. Author of numerous articles and books on literary criticism and theory, including *The Pursuit of Signs: Semiotics, Literature, Deconstruction* (1981); *On Deconstruction* (1982); *Roland Barthes* (1983); *Framing the Sign: Criticism and Its Institutions* (1988).

Durand, Béatrice. University of Potsdam (Germany). Author of several articles on eighteenth-century literature and culture, including "Mme. de Staël et la condition post-révolutionnaire" (*Romanic Review* 1991). Editor of *Denis Diderot: Ecrits sur la musique* (1987).

Michel, Frann. Willamette University. Author of articles on American fiction and feminist theory, including "Displacing Castration: Nightwood, Ladies Almanack, and Feminine Writing" (*Contemporary Literature* 1989).

Milech, Barbara. Curtin University (Australia). General co-editor of *Southern*

Review (Australia) and editor of *Gender/Text*. Milech is writing a book on *Constitutive Metaphors of Feminist Thought*.

Morgan, Thaïs E. Arizona State University. Author of numerous articles on literary theory, gender theory, and nineteenth-century studies, including "A Whip of One's Own: Dominatrix Pornography and the Construction of a Postmodern (Female) Subjectivity" (*American Journal of Semiotics* 1989) and "Male Lesbian Bodies: Alternative Masculinities in Courbet, Baudelaire, and Swinburne" (*Genders* 1992). Editor of *Victorian Sages and Cultural Discourse: Renegotiating Gender and Power* (1990).

Murphy, Peter F. Empire State College, SUNY. Author of articles on poststructuralist theory, including "Cultural Studies as Praxis" (1992). Editor of *The Fiction of Masculinity: Literary Constructions of Manhood* (New York University Press, 1994).

Rubin, Deborah. Nassau Community College. Author of forthcoming articles on sixteenth-century English literature and culture and literary theory. Author of *Ovid's Metamorphoses Englished: George Sands as Translator and Mythographer* (1985).

Sciolina, Martina. University of Southern Mississippi. Author of several articles on postmodernism, including "Kathy Acker and the Postmodern Subject of Feminism" (*College English* 1990) and "Confession of a Kleptomaniac" (*Review of Contemporary Fiction* 1989).

Siegel, Carol. Washington State University. Author of several articles on fiction and gender theory, including "Male Masochism and Colonialist Impulse" (*Novel* 1991) and "Postmodern Women Novelists Review Victorian Male Masochism" (*Genders* 1991). Author of *Lawrence Among the Woman: Wavering Boundaries in Women's Literary Traditions* (1991).

Wolfson, Susan J. Princeton University. Author of numerous articles on English Romantic poetry and literary theory, including "'A Problem Few Dare Imitate': Byron's *Sardanapulus* and 'Effeminate Character'" (1991); "Feminizing Keats" (1990); "Individual and Community: Dorothy Wordsworth in Conversation with William" (1988); and "'Their She Condition': Cross-dressing and the Politics of Gender in *Don Juan*" (1987). Author of *Questioning Presence: Wordsworth, Keats, and the Interrogative Mode in Romantic Poetry* (1986).

Index